C0-AMV-277

# CORRECTIONAL ADMINISTRATION

# CORRECTIONAL ADMINISTRATION

The Management
of Probation, Institutions
and Parole

Alan Coffey

*Santa Clara County Probation Department*

Prentice-Hall, Inc., Englewood Cliffs, New Jersey

4-7-83

Library of Congress Cataloging in Publication Data

COFFEY, ALAN.
Correctional administration.
Includes bibliographical references.
1. Corrections—Administration. 2. Corrections.
3. Correctional personnel. I. Title.
HV9275.C57      364.6      74-8755
ISBN   0-13-188284-8

HV 9275 .C57
Coffey, Alan.
Correctional administratio

Prentice-Hall Series in Law Enforcement
James D. Stinchcomb, *Editor*

© 1975 by Prentice-Hall, Inc., Englewood Cliffs, N.J.

All rights reserved. No part of this book may be reproduced in any form or by any means without permission
in writing from the publisher.

Printed in the United States of America

10   9   8   7   6   5   4   3   2   1

Prentice-Hall International, Inc., *London*
Prentice-Hall of Australia, Pty. Ltd., *Sydney*
Prentice-Hall of Canada, Ltd., *Toronto*
Prentice-Hall of Japan, Inc., *Tokyo*
Prentice-Hall of India Private Limited, *New Delhi*

For Margaret, Beverly, Alison,
Annette, Alana and Jenny . . .
my four generations of fine ladies

# Contents

# Preface

Recent years have witnessed what amounts to a mounting tide of criticism of the entire system of American criminal justice. Concern with crime and delinquency has moved far beyond the "safe-street" criticisms of a decade ago, to encompass not only police but courts and corrections as well.

As these concerns relate to corrections, the correctional process and the content of correctional programs bear the brunt. But it remains clear that any concern with correctional effectiveness is concern with management and administration, rather than "process and program content."

This book, then, is about the *administration* and the *management* of corrections, and *not* about the practice of corrections.

In isolating management as opposed to the practice of corrections, the wide variation in organizational approaches from state to state is hopefully minimized in significance. The citing of administrative examples whether from "county agencies," or "state agencies," or "city agencies" does not, then, suggest an organizational advantage, but rather serves to illustrate that managerial excellence can function in virtually any organizational variation that exists in American corrections.

The book is in three parts: (1) the relation of corrections to criminal justice in terms of administering, managing and supervising correctional programs; (2) operating probation, institutions, parole and community programs; and (3) the staffing of corrections.

Although addressed to a complex subject, the philosophy of this book is quite simple; *Make a clear distinction between the practice of corrections and the management of corrections.*

# Acknowledgements

Without exception, *all* of the correctional administrators with whom this author has associated have influenced this book in some manner— some in substance, others in form. In this regard, the profound influence of Richard W. Bothman, Chief of the Santa Clara County (CA) Proba- tion Department has given both substance and form to not only parts of this book but the correctional field in general—profound influence de- serving both gratitude and respect.

Of course the encouragement, support and thoughtful criticism of teaching colleagues gains my sincerest gratitude—with regrets on the limitation of space precluding the inclusion of the many who will recog- nize their influence on these pages.

Finally, for reasons possibly clear only to the families of those who seek to reduce mountains of research to a single volume, my deepest con- tinuing gratitude to my lovely wife Bev and our daughters Annette and Alana, for choosing not to notice on those occasions when the wind-mills would fight back at me.

Alan R. Coffey

# CORRECTIONAL ADMINISTRATION

# ADMINISTERING THE FIELD OF CORRECTIONS

# ONE

# Corrections and Criminal Justice

# Chapter 1

To most of the thousands of men and women devoting their lives and careers to the field of corrections, it came as no surprise when the National Advisory Commission on Criminal Justice Standards and Goals included correctional *planning* in their 1973 report:

> It is an unfortunate reality that most correction agencies do not engage in planning in the fullest sense. While many have a general notion of where they are going and some engage in specific aspects of planning such as facilities construction, few are engaged in the full planning process. This process involves development of integrated long-range, intermediate-range, and short-range plans for the complete spectrum of their administrative and operational functions. . . .[1]

But to those same thousands of correctional practitioners not surprised by this focus upon the need for planning, a kind of cynicism about the prospects for planning lingers in spite of the obvious priority given this

[1] National Advisory Commission on Criminal Justice Standards and Goals, *Corrections*, U. S. Gov't Printing Office, Washington, D.C., 1973, pp. 446–47.

pressing need. Such cynicism is born of many influences, not the least of which is the "reputation" of most bureaucracy:

> Problems in bureaucracy are endless. They range from ritualism and over-conformity to self-perpetuation and self-interest. Following the rules often becomes more important than achieving the goals, and organizations are run for the benefit of staff and administration rather than for clients.[2]

The unfortunate validity of this observation is far too significant to ignore—as is the validity of many similar assertions about bureaucracy's inadequacy. Nevertheless, the final quarter of the twentieth century demands attention to planning in all spheres of government, and corrections is no exception. More specifically, the *management* of corrections is no exception.

The management of corrections, then, is in need of general improvement in planning activities. But with improvements in planning must come improvements in other managerial functions, and ultimately improvements in correctional administration. This text is addressed to such improvements in both the administration and the management of the correctional field—first to improvement in planning, quickly followed by overall improvement in management.

The administration and the management of corrections, like the practice of corrections, occurs within the framework of a system of criminal justice. Before addressing the specific subject of managing and administering corrections, it might be useful to examine the relationship between corrections and the "system of justice"—the relationship of *probation, correctional institutions* and *parole*, to the functions of *law enforcement, courts* and *prosecution-defense*. In this regard:

> The criminal justice system has many segments, all strategically important and interrelated. Police, courts, prosecution-defense, corrections and the law itself interrelate in many crucial ways, and these interrelationships actually form the basis of developing a manageable system of criminal justice . . . criminal justice can function systematically only to the degree that each segment of the system takes into account all other segments.[3]

Later discussion of the administrative, managerial and supervisory functions of every segment of corrections will illustrate many similarities between even widely varied correctional activities. Such managerial similarities also exist between corrections and other segments of criminal

[2] Harold H. Weissman, *Overcoming Mismanagement in the Human Service Professions*, Jossey-Bass Publishers, San Francisco, 1973, p. 1.
[3] Alan R. Coffey, *Administration of Criminal Justice: A Management Systems Approach*, Prentice-Hall, Englewood Cliffs, New Jersey, 1974, p. 6.

justice—particularly when the relationship between mission, goals, objectives and operations are considered *within* each segment of criminal justice.

## MISSION, GOALS, OBJECTIVES AND OPERATIONS

One reason it is difficult to recognize the systematic relationship between segments of criminal justice is the identity of the *operations* of various segments. Police operations, for example, vary from prison operations. And yet the mission of both police and prison (as well as probation and parole) is to control crime. In other words, all segments of criminal justice serve (or should serve) the same mission even though their particular operations vary.

Particular goals and particular objectives may also vary between segments of criminal justice. But this in no way precludes the fundamental and systematic relationship that does (or should) exist between all organized efforts to cope with crime and delinquency. The criminal justice system is one of many varied operations, but all operations form interrelationships.[4]

One way in which to consider these interrelationships is through the flow process of the various functions. Consider the diagram on the next page.

Of course, the diagram assumes a rational and systematic relationship among the various criminal justice functions, when in reality this is not always the case:

> The precise manner in which the criminal justice system suffers fragmentation can vary from one part of the United States to another, or from one jurisdiction to another. Ineffective criminal justice that occurs through fragmentation between segments may be caused by many different things. When police operate without regard to the prosecution or when courts show indifference to corrections . . . the system is clearly not operating in an effective way.[5]

Moreover, the correctional field itself poses a number of questions regarding the rational and systematic relationships depicted in the flow process of the diagram above:

> Corrections have not evolved rationally by devising, evaluating, and modifying its programs according to their relationship to explicitly defined criteria. Rather, the field has developed out of the efforts of humanitarians and on

[4] *Ibid.*
[5] *Ibid.*

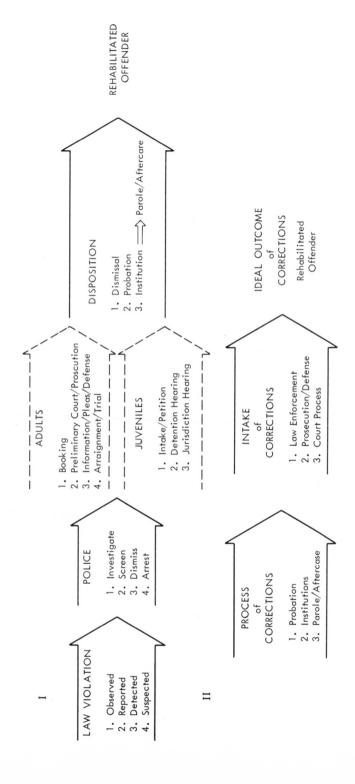

I

LAW VIOLATION

1. Observed
2. Reported
3. Detected
4. Suspected

POLICE

1. Investigate
2. Screen
3. Dismiss
4. Arrest

ADULTS

1. Booking
2. Preliminary Court/Proscution
3. Information/Pleas/Defense
4. Arraignment/Trial

JUVENILES

1. Intake/Petition
2. Detention Hearing
3. Jurisdiction Hearing

DISPOSITION

1. Dismissal
2. Probation
3. Institution ⟹ Parole/Aftercare

REHABILITATED OFFENDER

II

PROCESS of CORRECTIONS

1. Probation
2. Institutions
3. Parole/Aftercase

INTAKE of CORRECTIONS

1. Law Enforcement
2. Prosecution/Defense
3. Court Process

IDEAL OUTCOME of CORRECTIONS

Rehabilitated Offender

the basis of public reaction to inhumane treatment and prison riots. But even more important, the lack of systematic information is due to the fact that corrections was developed on the basis of political expediency. Correctional programs have been devised not on the basis of an overall correctional plan, or on the basis of effectiveness, but rather on the basis of "who has the inside track with this or that legislator." [6]

Even though the problems from which this observation flows are very real, the harshness of the comments can and should be modified before moving on:

Present day corrections have evolved considerably in both thought and practice in attempting to deal with the difficult problems of punishing, deterring, and rehabilitating offenders. None of these thoughts or practices have resolved these problems completely. Most of the changes that have come about in corrections have probably not been the result of scientific investigation; rather, they have been the result of a more humanistic, philosophical approach to mankind.[7]

Fitting such correctional realities into the overall system of criminal justice is the purpose of this chapter. But before proceeding, let us consider some of the influences, beyond those already noted, that tend to impede the rational and systematic relationship between the elements of the American system of criminal justice; that is, influences that tend to fragment criminal justice and generate what has been referred to as a "nonsystem."

## CRIMINAL JUSTICE FRAGMENTATION AND THE NONSYSTEM

In order to conceive of "fragmenting" a system, or of a system being a "nonsystem," we must accept the premise that criminal justice *is* (or at least should be) a system. Garabedian says:

In brief, a modification in one part of the criminal justice system results in changes that take place in other parts of the system, and clearly suggests that law enforcement, the courts, and corrections comprise a *single* system and *not* three separate systems.[8]

[6] P. G. Garabedian, "Challenges for Contemporary Corrections," *Federal Probation*, Vol. 33, No. 1 (March 1969), 6.
[7] W. Hartinger, E. Eldefonso, and A. Coffey, *Corrections: A Component of the Criminal Justice System* (Pacific Palisades, Calif.: Goodyear Publishing Co., Inc., 1973), p. 155.
[8] Garabedian, "Challenges for Contemporary Corrections," p. 7.

*Systems and Their Analysis*

Perhaps some clarification of what is meant by *systems* would be useful in examining the relationships within criminal justice. A great deal of technical literature exists on the subject of systems,[9] but for the purposes of this chapter, consider the following:

> Systems have existed since earliest times, the most notable example being that of resource cultivation, protection and allocation. From the time that man became a cultivator, the idea of resources and resource containers came into being. The most dramatic of such containers is the vessel that is the product of the potter's craft—perhaps the earliest science, and one of the earliest arts. The pot held the corn needed for the next season's planting, but other pots and similar containers also held surpluses that could be stored and allocated. Every such vessel had various levels that gave rise to units of *data*. This data not only adjusted resource levels but also reflected the transactions or events or items that had to precede such resource manipulations.[10]

Of more relevance to the system of criminal justice is the following:

> All living systems are open systems—systems in contact with their environment, with input and output across system boundaries. What then is the use of talking about a closed system? What *is* a closed system? It means that the system is temporarily assumed to have a leak-tight boundary— there is relatively little, if any, commerce across the boundary. We know that no such system can be found in reality, but it is sometimes essential to analyze a system as if it were closed so as to examine the operations of the system as affected "only by the conditions previously established by the environment and not changing at the time of analysis, plus the relationships among the internal elements of the system." [11]

Perhaps further elaboration of the concept of systems is unneeded, particularly since there appears to be some risk of confusion in such elaboration:

> It has often been stated that we are in the "era of systems." There are behavioral systems, communication systems, data processing systems, trans-

---

[9] See, for example, Brian Rothery, ed., *The Art of Systems Analysis* (Englewood Cliffs, N.J.: Prentice-Hall, Inc., 1971); Coffey, *Administration of Criminal Justice;* Richard Neuschel, *Management by System* (New York: McGraw-Hill Book Company, 1960); Peter P. Schoderbek, ed., *Management Systems* (New York: John Wiley & Sons, Inc., 1971); and Prentice-Hall Editorial Staff, *Encyclopedic Dictionary of Systems and Procedures* (Englewood Cliffs, N.J.: Prentice-Hall, Inc., 1966).

[10] Brendan Byrne, Alan Mullally, and Brian Rothery, *The Art of Systems Analysis,* (Englewood Cliffs, N.J.: Prentice-Hall, Inc., 1971), p. 3.

[11] Warren G. Bennis, Kenneth D. Benne, and Robert Chin, "The Utility of System Models and Development Models for Practitioners," in *The Planning of Change* (New York: Holt, Rinehart & Winston, Inc., 1961), pp. 201–14.

portation systems, information systems, records systems, and innumerable others. And to further befuddle the layman utilizing operational systems, these have been categorized as closed, open, structured, unstructured, controlled feedback, uncontrolled feedback, deterministic, oscillating, manmade, real time, reproducible, isomorphic, simple action, and by an ever-growing list of other euphonious labels.[12]

So for purposes of this chapter, a system is simply a series of interrelationships having input and output across its boundaries. A system can best be examined, however, as though it were a "closed system," *without* input or output across its boundaries. In other words, to explore the system of criminal justice for the purpose of establishing a context for correctional administration, it is best to conceive of it as an isolated concept, a closed system, even though criminal justice, and particularly corrections, *could not function on a closed-system basis.* Later chapters will examine the many vital outside influences that prove that the administration of corrections *must* function on the basis of an open system—a system open to the influence not only of police and courts, but of the community as well.

In examining the system of criminal justice as though it were "closed," we can use systems analysis to clarify the interrelationships that can be fragmented to the point of creating a nonsystem. Concerning systems analysis, Howlett and Hurst have stated:

Where traditional approaches simply describe existing agencies and support services, the systems approach provides the means whereby the processes of the system as well as each of its elements may be analyzed. (1) It provides for *formulation of workable definitions of the parameters of the criminal justice system within the particular jurisdiction under study.* "Parameters" refer to the outer limits or observable universe of services, agencies, etc., that tend to impinge upon the operations of the justice system. (2) It provides for *functional examination of the system's major elements.* "Function" is defined as the contribution a particular element of the system makes, or can potentially make, to maintenance of the system of which it is a part, and evaluation of this contribution in terms of the system's attempts to realize its goals. The "major elements" of the system are those units (or agencies) which, taken one at a time, clearly and significantly affect the system's operations or have the potential to do so. Examples of the major elements in the justice system are courts, jails or workhouses, and probation services, as well as the clients of these agencies and supportive services.[13]

As we will see in the next chapter, administrative and managerial application of systems concepts is somewhat more involved. But for our

---

[12] Schoderbek, "Total Management Systems," in *Management Systems*, p. 308.
[13] F. W. Howlett and H. Hurst, "A Systems Approach to Comprehensive Criminal Justice Planning," *Crime and Delinquency*, Vol. 17, No. 4 (October 1971), 347.

purposes, a systems analysis can be thought of simply as examining that combination of "those units (or agencies) which . . . clearly and significantly affect the system's operations." These various units or agencies may then be thought of as subsystems of the overall system of criminal justice.

### Subsystems

The idea of police, of courts, of corrections as subsystems of a main system of criminal justice is useful in several ways. For one thing, it permits fragmentation and nonsystem concepts to be examined in specific relation to the overall system. Of equal importance, the subsystem approach permits further consideration of the parts of *each* subsystem—as "subsystems of subsystems." In other words, the criminal justice subsystem of corrections can be thought of as itself a correctional system, having the subsystems of probation, institutions, and parole—all using the same systems approach, regardless of the level involved.

Still another advantage of the subsystem approach has to do with perceiving how a system depends upon each part to function properly in achieving a desirable goal—as with the analogy of an airplane "system" depending upon the "engine subsystem" and the "wings subsystem" to remain aloft.

From this reference point, fragmentation can be dealt with totally in terms of relevance to the main system of American criminal justice.

### Subsystem Fragmentation

Consider the following commentary:

> Despite the improvements, however, a vacuum continuously appeared between the various parts of the system, each of which was functioning independently. For example, judges just do not know what the problems of the prisons are, nor does the police officer understand the role of the probation and parole office. Survey data collected on a statewide group of criminal law and justice system personnel showed that of the seventeen separate components of the system, the only people who had realistic information about each part as well as the whole were those who had had experience in each—the criminals. And as could be expected, the lack of information and understanding among the various parts of the system bred distrust.[14]

---

[14] M. L. Pettit and B. K. Holmberg, "Let's Put It All Together, An Integrated Approach to Criminal Law and Justice," *Journal of Police Science and Administration*, Vol. 1, No. 1 (March 1973), 113.

The "informational" implications of these comments are different from those that will be dealt with shortly in terms of nonsystem—a nonsystem such as that suggested in the following:

There is a fundamental fallacy in assuming that any one system, even if it were not split down the middle between conflicting motives of punishment and rehabilitation, can overcome both the prior life circumstances and the situation into which the released prisoner or parolee is returned. It is not the better part of wisdom to make this claim, consciously or unwittingly, and then simply demand additional means and manpower to implement it.[15]

The fragmentation of criminal justice subsystems referred to for purposes of the present discussion has more to do with major variations in procedures *between* the criminal justice subsystems than with the variations within the subsystems themselves. Arrest practices on the part of law enforcement that do not recognize the realities of either the courts or prosecution, for example, tend to fragment the subsystems of criminal justice. Similarly, court practices in sentencing that do not reflect the reality of the resources of corrections tend to fragment criminal justice subsystems:

Even superficial analysis of court and probation operations reveals wide discrepancies in policies relating to who is detained, who is charged or who is committed. Commitment rates to State institutions vary widely, even from areas of apparent similar socio-economic composition.[16]

Subsystem fragmentation also relates to variations in outcome that result from variations in practices. These variations could scarcely be called surprising in view of the numerous paradoxical procedures within criminal justice, some of which have been strongly criticized:

The principal reason for the Courts' general failure is the outworn system of legal and correctional fictions. Under the fiction of "treatment," for example, juveniles receive sentences that exceed those given adults for the same crime. Without a single exception, the cases continue to uphold juvenile commitments that are longer than adult commitments for the same offense on the grounds that since the special purpose of the juvenile's incarceration is treatment, who knows how long it will take to cure his delinquency? Similarly, under the guise of "individualization," abuses in parole are condoned.[17]

[15] J. Otis, "Correctional Manpower Utilization," *Crime and Delinquency*, Vol. 12, No. 3 (July 1966), 267.
[16] H. Ohmart, "The Challenge of Crime in a Free Society," *California Youth Authority Quarterly*, Vol. 21, No. 3 (Fall 1968), 2–11.
[17] Sol Rubin, "Developments in Correctional Law," *Crime and Delinquency*, Vol. 18, No. 2 (April 1972), 213.

Such contradiction, even if later established as absolutely necessary for successful corrections, cannot be ignored if the criminal justice system is to provide consistent reduction in the crime problem—regardless of whether or not there is justification for the harshness of the critical comments just quoted.

In other words, fragmented subsystems cannot be allowed to produce a criminal justice nonsystem.

### Criminal Justice Nonsystem

*The term "nonsystem" refers to what happens when the practices of the various subsystems differ so radically that a systematic reduction of crime cannot occur.*

To specifically isolate the correctional subsystem within a context of potential nonsystem, consider the following: "The legal structure controls the use of community treatment, suspended sentence, probation, and fines; specifies the length and place of confinement; and limits or facilitates a parole board's operation." [18] When the *law* controls (or tries to control) corrections, its frame of reference is often the crime committed, instead of the correction of the offender.

In contrast to this legal influence on corrections, there is the influence of criminology:

> In recent years criminology has moved from an exclusive emphasis on the genesis of criminal behavior to a concern with other factors involved in the crime problem. Some have stressed the role of authorities in attaching the label of criminal to certain individuals. Others have examined the role of the contribution of the victim to a crime and the loss suffered by the victim of a criminal act.[19]

With such contrasting—even contradicting—influences, corrections is a subsystem easily influenced toward a vacillation between "conflicting motives of punishment and rehabilitation," [20] a vacillation seriously conducive to a nonsystem outcome. Compounding the correctional problems related to these conflicting motives is the unpredictability of the legal structure's control of corrections—contradictory laws and new laws that generate nonsystems among criminal justice subsystems.

Even more significant are Supreme Court decisions that impinge directly on the correctional field's ability to function systematically in rela-

---

[18] Council of Judges, NCCD, "Model Sentencing Act," *Crime and Delinquency*, Vol. 18, No. 4 (October 1972), 344.
[19] J. E. Conklin, "Dimensions of Community Response to the Crime Problem," *Social Problems*, Vol. 18, No. 3 (Winter 1971), 373–74.
[20] Otis, "Correctional Manpower Utilization."

tion to other criminal justice elements. The profound impact of Supreme Court decisions is readily discernible in such cases as Miranda, Escabedo, Gault, and several others.[21]

Less discernible, but of equal significance, is the shifting pattern of the Supreme Court:

> The Burger Court, in its criminal law decisions of the October 1971 Term, on occasion confounded both its critics and protagonists. This is equally true of its decisions in other areas. Thus, by way of example, in the criminal law area it struck down the Administration's domestic wiretapping program. In dealing with the First Amendment's safeguard of the free exercise of religion, the Court held that the Amish need not comply with Wisconsin's compulsory formal education requirement after the eighth grade; compliance, in the Court's view, was inconsistent with the free exercise of their religious beliefs. In both cases the decisions were written by President Nixon's appointees—Justice Powell in the wiretapping case, and Chief Justice Burger in the Amish case.[22]

To the degree that avoiding fragmentation and nonsystem depends upon *predictable* goals and objectives for criminal justice, to that same degree are the changes in law and shifting patterns of Supreme Court decisions a major concern for the system of criminal justice.

The clarity with which the function and role of the criminal court are explicitly defined determines the clarity of the other two major justice functions—enforcement and corrections. The Supreme Court decisions that either clarify or obscure the function and role of the criminal court are then far more significant than simply influencing procedure. The significance of Supreme Court decisions includes indirect influence on the very definition of the correctional function.

Against this brief, somewhat cursory background of some of the considerations involved in creating and sustaining systematic relationships between the various subsystems, attention is now turned to corrections as a part of the system of criminal justice.


## CORRECTIONS AND LAW ENFORCEMENT

As noted early in this chapter, the administration and management of the correctional field occur within a system of criminal justice—a system made up of various subsystems. Law enforcement is, for a number of rea-

---

[21] For an in-depth exploration of these cases, see, for example, E. Eldefonso, A. Coffey, and J. Sullivan, *Police and the Criminal Law* (Pacific Palisades, Calif.: Goodyear Publishing Co., Inc., 1972).

[22] A. J. Goldberg, "Supreme Court Review, 1972," *The Journal of Criminal Law, Criminology and Police Science*, Vol. 63, No. 4 (December 1972), 463.

sons, the first of these subsystems. For one thing, police "select" the offenders with whom the other subsystems of criminal justice must deal:

> The administrative practices of the police subsystem virtually determine the management of the entire system of criminal justice. The input of the criminal justice system is "selected law violation." Although police do not *make* the laws, they are forced to be "selective" regarding which laws are enforced . . . determine which offender, and how many offenders the other subsystems of criminal justice will process. And because administrative practice depends on the nature and volume of offenders involved, the administrative practices of the police subsystem determine the administrative practices of American criminal justice in general—local and isolated exceptions . . . notwithstanding.[23]

This no doubt accounts for the increasingly strong recommendation that "every police agency should immediately act to ensure understanding and cooperation between itself and all other elements of the criminal justice system." [24]

Such cooperation with police is of singular advantage in terms of managing the correctional field. For example, police can divert many of the time- and resource-consuming correctional cases away from the correctional system, thereby permitting corrections to concentrate on cases more in need of its available services.

Fortunately, a trend toward such diversion by police appears to be developing: "Every police agency should, where permitted by law, immediately provide that individuals who come to the attention of police and for whom the purpose of the criminal or juvenile justice process would be inappropriate or in whose case other resources would be more effective be diverted from the criminal and juvenile justice system." [25]

The correctional advantage of good working relations with police goes far beyond case diversion. Sad is the correctional administrator in whose jurisdiction police do not understand the goals, objectives, or methods of the correctional process. Correctionally disruptive arrest patterns, arrest dispositions, and negative publicity are only a part of such problems where they exist; there can emerge from them what amounts to a virtual interruption in the system of criminal justice—the emergence of a nonsystem:

> Unfortunately, there is a great gap between the rights afforded the criminal defendant and the reality of unlawful police practices. Only when the defendant is protected by court processes do these rights become a reality.

---

[23] Coffey, *Administration of Criminal Justice*, p. 198.
[24] *Working Papers for the National Conference on Criminal Justice*, LEAA (Jan. 23–26, 1973), Washington, D.C., p. 100.
[25] *Ibid.*, p. 105.

The need to study and understand basic constitutional limitations imposed on police officials cannot be overestimated.[26]

Fortunately, however, the overwhelming majority of correctional subsystems in America enjoy excellent working relations with all other criminal justice subsystems, including the courts, as well as the police.

## CORRECTIONS AND THE COURTS

The correctional process begins formally with adults when the criminal court finds a defendant guilty of violating a criminal law. It begins less formally with children when the juvenile court receives a complaint or a referral alleging delinquency, but becomes formal when an adjudication of delinquency is made.[27]

Like the police, then, the court subsystem also serves as the "intake" of corrections—at least the formal intake—although probation deals with many cases prior to court, especially in juvenile matters. These prior exceptions notwithstanding, courts function as a significant part of the intake of the correctional field in most instances—of correctional institutions and parole totally, probation partially.

It should not then be surprising that a trend appears to be developing in which the court subsystem becomes related to other criminal justice subsystems in an operational manner:

The standards in the corrections field regarding sentencing are very closely related to the call for elimination of plea negotiation. The Courts Task Force adopted the position of the Corrections Task Force on sentencing to set forth that the trial judge shall impose a maximum sentence limitation while other agencies shall have the authority to determine the actual length of any detention or the total time period for supervision within the system. . . . All elements interface on an operational level and work together toward the common goal of reducing crime in every jurisdiction.[28]

It is within this operational context that the relationship of the courts and corrections can best be examined with greatest clarity—particularly when the examination occurs within the closed-system concept:

On a mechanical level, sentencing determines whether correctional agencies will receive an individual as well as the conditions under which these agencies will receive him. Thus a defendant may be sentenced to im-

[26] Eldefonso, Coffey, and Sullivan, *Police and the Criminal Law*, p. 218.
[27] V. Fox, *Introduction to Corrections* (Englewood Cliffs, N.J.: Prentice-Hall, Inc., 1972), p. 23.
[28] *Working Papers for the NCCJ*, p. Ct-5.

prisonment or to probation; in the latter situation, correctional authorities do not have the power to use full-time institutionalization as a means of treating the offender. Sentencing also affects the correctional process on a more subtle level. The extent to which a defendant regards his sentence as fair may influence his willingness to participate in correctional programs. Moreover, certain sentencing practices give correctional officials authority to detain an offender until his chances of successful integration into the community are at a maximum; other sentencing practices may require earlier release or detention beyond that point.

Sentencing is related to community security insofar as it affects the ability of correctional agencies to change the behavior of convicted offenders. It also may help curtail crimes by persons other than the offender being sentenced. This may occur through deterrence—the creation of conscious fear of swift and certain punishment—or through more complex means, such as reinforcing social norms by the imposition of severe penalties.[29]

From such a perspective, the significance of the relationship between courts and corrections is magnified manyfold. Even removing the artificial concept of the closed system fails to reduce the significance of the relationship of court and corrections.

And, as will be noted in later chapters, the administrative significance of the courts' relationship to probation and to correctional institutions can be of great concern in many areas independent of the sentencing impact upon the correctional field. Among the more powerful of these areas of concern is the great potential for judicial influence upon administrative programming. Indeed, the judicial function, when poorly defined in relation to the enforcement and correctional functions, may well account for what amounts to the virtual fragmentation of justice as a concept in many jurisdictions—an administrative consideration that will be explored in Chapter 5.

## CORRECTIONS AND THE PROSECUTION–DEFENSE

The relationship between correctional subsystems and the process of prosecution–defense is, for the most part, indirect. More often than not in adult matters, the relationship has to do with disposition of court cases: a prosecutor seeking commitment to a correctional institution while the defense attorney seeks probation, as a typical example. Juvenile cases, in many jurisdictions, may involve a substantially more direct relationship, because of the probation officers' role in the juvenile court—a unique role, which will be explored in depth in later chapters.

But for the most part, two generalizations can be made about prosecu-

---

[29] *Ibid.*, p. Ct-83.

tion–defense as this process relates to the correctional subsystem: (1) The relationship is significant, and (2) the relationship is mostly indirect.

Put another way, examining the relationship of corrections to a system of criminal justice requires that prosecution–defense be acknowledged even though its impact upon corrections is neither as immediate nor as direct as the arrest practices of police or the sentencing practices of courts. The decision to prosecute and the effort to provide criminal defense form a process that in many ways affects corrections just as significantly as the actual arrest and sentencing—particularly since sentencing virtually depends upon the outcome of prosecution–defense in most cases.

In the next chapter, the process of administering corrections will be presented within the context of a system that includes law enforcement, courts, and the process of prosecution–defense.


## SUMMARY

This chapter introduces the administration and management of the correctional field in terms of interrelationships among all elements of criminal justice.

The "flow process" of criminal justice was presented as police activities, the activities that make up the court process, and correctional activities—the last defined as probation, correctional institutions, and parole.

The concept of systems was presented in terms of interrelationships among criminal justice elements. Analysis of systems was considered in terms of "closed systems"—emphasizing that the concept serves the purpose of analysis only, since no functional system is actually closed from related systems. The fragmentation of subsystems and the problem of "nonsystem" were examined within this context of systems analysis.

Potentially disruptive influences from changes in law and patterns of Supreme Court decisions were considered briefly.

The particular relationship between corrections and other criminal justice subsystems was examined. Police activities were presented as the "intake" of the overall system of criminal justice. From the correctional viewpoint, the courts were presented as the "formal intake" of correctional institutions and parole, and partially of probation—with exceptions within the probation element deferred to subsequent chapters for elaboration.

The prosecution–defense process was dealt with as a significant although indirect influence upon corrections, owing to its major influence upon the court's sentencing practices.

## Discussion Topics

1. Relate corrections to criminal justice as a system.
2. Relate corrections to police.
3. Discuss the relationship of corrections to the courts.
4. Elaborate on the significance of prosecution–defense to corrections.
5. Discuss the "flow process" of criminal justice.
6. Discuss any reason for relating corrections and criminal justice to the administration and management of the correctional field.
7. Elaborate on system fragmentation and "nonsystem."

## Annotated References

BYRNE, B., A. MULLALLY, and B. ROTHERY, *The Art of Systems Analysis.* Englewood Cliffs, N.J.: Prentice-Hall, Inc., 1971. An excellent introductory text for the reader interested in exploring what this chapter presented as analysis of systems.

COFFEY, A., *Administration of Criminal Justice: A Management Systems Approach.* Englewood Cliffs, N.J.: Prentice-Hall, Inc., 1974. A comprehensive text covering systems theory, management theory, and administrative models for managing the entire system of criminal justice.

HOWLETT, F. W., and H. HURST, "A Systems Approach to Comprehensive Criminal Justice Planning," *Crime and Delinquency*, Vol. 17, No. 4 (October 1971), pp. 347–57. An outstanding elaboration of what this chapter discussed as "nonsystem."

*Working Papers for the National Conference on Criminal Justice*, LEAA (January 23–26, 1973). An excellent compilation of significant variables affecting what this chapter presented as the relationships between criminal justice subsystems.

# Elements of
# Administrative
# Process

# Chapter 2

Having considered the relationship of corrections to the overall system of criminal justice, attention is now turned specifically to administering the field of corrections—to some of the key elements of a process hopefully geared to reducing the potential fragmentation discussed in the preceding chapter.

In dealing with the selected elements of correctional administration, this chapter will examine the scope of corrections as well as the process by which the correctional field is administered. Of course, no single chapter could cover the entire process of administering a correctional organization. For this reason, the overall administration of corrections will be divided into three parts: administrative process involving correctional administrators to be discussed in this chapter; the management of the correctional organization to be presented in the following chapter; and supervision as part of the administrative process to be presented in the ensuing chapter. These distinctions may be clarified somewhat by the technical considerations of this and the next two chapters. The main clarification that needs to occur, however, has to do with the context in which distinctions between correctional administration, management and supervision are to be made. The National Advisory Commission on Criminal Justice Standards and Goals sums up a great deal of this context:

> Managing a human resource organization is probably even more difficult than managing other public agencies because many traditional management tools are not directly applicable. Data describing effects of the correctional process relate to behavior or attitudes and are subject to subjective, frequently conflicting interpretations. The feedback loops necessary for judging the consequences of policies are difficult to create and suffer from incomplete and inaccurate information. There has not been in corrections an organized and consistent relation between evaluative research and management action.
>
> The management of corrections as a human resource organization must be viewed broadly in terms of how offenders, employees, and various organization processes (communications, decisionmaking, and others) are combined into what is called 'the corrections process'. [1]

Regardless of the particular state, federal, city or county models used as examples, and regardless of the technical factors in modern management, correctional administration occurs in a particularly unique (and at times difficult) context. Bearing this context in mind, this chapter will deal with certain elements.

As a background for exploring these elements, we shall consider certain influences that tend to actually *define* correctional administration. For just as there are influences that impinge upon criminal justice in terms of fragmenting elements, so also are there influences impinging upon the very process intended to reduce such fragmentation—the process of administrators' administering the field of corrections, as opposed to managing and supervising it, which will be discussed in the two chapters that follow.

## DEFINING ADMINISTRATIVE PROCESS

Even after the sometimes difficult task of distinguishing between the practice and the management of corrections, a clear definition of *what administration is* may not be easy. The reason for this is that administration is a process rather than a specific activity. Moreover, this process requires a particular perspective to function properly—an "administrative perspective" that is different from that of the *practice* of corrections, and in many ways different from the "management perspective" we shall

[1] National Advisory Commission on Criminal Justice Standards and Goals, *Corrections*, U. S. Gov't Printing Office, Washington, D.C., 1973, p. 442.

examine in the next chapter. A definition of this administrative process is clearly called for.

There are many approaches to defining the process of administration, even when consideration is narrowed to that part of it involving administrators. Some believe that administration is as old as man himself:

> Some years ago an author wrote a book on prostitution entitled *The World's Oldest Profession*. While the title was catchy, it was also erroneous. The world's oldest profession is administration.
>
> The practice of administration is of such ancient vintage that it predates the advent of man himself. The ants, who achieved their current level of evolutionary development some 20 million years ago, provide a compelling picture of administration in action. Their systematic way of dividing and coordinating their efforts could fill a modern-day buraucrat with awe and wonder.[2]

This viewpoint, although intriguing, suggests a definitional scope as wide as history itself. It might be useful to narrow the definition through consideration of what is meant by *administrative process:*

> Administration refers to the organization and management of the delivery system that brings goods and services to the consumer. Correctional administration refers to the organization and management of a system that brings the basic necessities and the treatment programs of the correctional institutions or agencies to the correctional clients. In all types of administration, the administrator is a facilitator who expedites action. There are systematic approaches to each phase of administration, such as budgeting, program supervision, planning, and many other facets, that are basic to an ongoing successful program.[3]

"Systematic approaches to each phase of administration" does *not* mean the simple adoption of systems concepts as shown in the introductory chapter. Nevertheless, the use of "system thinking" can prove useful in understanding administrative process:

> It would be misleading to offer a definition of the systems approach with any pretense that it would be universally understood. First of all, it is not useful to use the term to describe what may be produced by a small team. Second, for the term to serve any useful purpose, it must not encompass all management of complex and large-scale activity, but must serve to distinguish some types from some others.[4]

[2] G. E. Berkley, *The Administrative Revolution: Notes on the Passing of Organization Man* (Englewood Cliffs, N.J.: Prentice-Hall, Inc., 1971), p. 3.
[3] V. Fox, *Introduction to Corrections* (Englewood Cliffs, N.J.: Prentice-Hall, Inc., 1972), p. 345.
[4] G. Black, "Systems Analysis in Government," *Management Science*, October 1967, pp. 41–58.

By thinking of a system as "closed" for purposes of analysis and understanding, we can use the system of administration "to distinguish some types [of management] from some others," while at the same time avoiding the system definition that "encompasses all management," or all history.

(This concept of distinguishing between types of management is "new," in the sense that as late as the 1950s, virtually *all* management— and administration and supervision—was simply a matter of *planning, organizing, staffing, directing, coordinating, research,* and *budgeting*— "POSDCORB," as it was known for many years. Then the technology of systems analysis and a wide range of other variables evolved in such a manner that POSDCORB, as well as many other traditional management concepts of the twentieth century, became either modified or discarded entirely.) [5]

Indeed, understanding the influences that impinge on the definition of administrative process may require this distinction between types, and therefore we shall focus our attention directly upon it. First, however, consider what administration "does":

> The administrative process begins when the chief executive of an organization, fully aware that he is ultimately responsible for achieving the objectives of the organization, realizes that he cannot fulfill his responsibilities by himself.
>
> He needs help because he lacks the physical and mental capacities to do so. This is where the organization process begins. Essentially, it is a subdivision of the work of the chief executive into workable areas and the commensurate delegation of authority and responsibility to perform such work. The subdivision of the work must encompass compatible duties and the delegation must be clearcut and there can be no overlapping. For instance, a typical organization can be broken down into these divisions: Operations, Personnel, Planning and Research, Budget and Accounting. A Bureau Chief who is directly responsible to the chief executive is appointed to head each bureau, and because he, too, lacks the physical and mental capacity to perform all of the work he is responsible for, must engage in the organizational process within his bureau, subdividing the work and delegating appropriate authority and responsibility. This process is carried on right through the organization to the first line supervisors and their subordinates. We might therefore say that organization is essentially a subdivision of the work with a granting of appropriate authority and responsibility to perform work which has been delegated.[6]

In a general way, this statement sums up much of what administration in *total* "does": administrators, managers, and supervisors—"distinctions between types of management."

[5] A. R. Coffey, *Administration of Criminal Justice: A Management Systems Approach* (Englewood Cliffs, N.J.: Prentice-Hall, Inc., 1974), Chap. 2.
[6] *Principles of Civil Service Administration and Management* (Santa Cruz, Calif.: Davis Publishing Co., 1972), p. 2.

In relating these distinctions to influences upon the definition of administrative process, we must keep in mind what administration does *not* do as well as what it does. It has been stated that "much of what is thought of as criminal justice administration and even management is sometimes little more than mere supervision." [7] This statement suggests that although supervision is a part of overall administration, the administrative process and the management process are not "supervision"—at least, not if a distinction is made between administrators, managers, and supervisors within the administration of the correctional organization.

### Administration; Management; Supervision

Virtually all large correctional organizations are staffed with four distinct levels of management functions—supervisory, middle, executive, and administrative. Although this book is geared to the administrative function, it is important to recognize each managerial level in order to understand administration. The two chapters that follow will deal with management at the executive planning level, the middle-management level, and the supervisory level. For purposes of the present discussion, the four levels will be reduced to three—administrative, managerial, and supervisory.

Understanding the distinctions between the functions of supervision, management, and administration goes far beyond the mere identification of influences upon the definition of administrative process. The reason these distinctions are more important is that administrators depend upon managers and supervisors for separate functions. Similarly, managers and supervisors depend upon administrators to perform a separate function. The various managerial functions involved in a successful correctional organization relate to one another in many ways, as we shall see.

As the discussion of administration moves into the subject of organization, it will be noted that the management of "conflicting goals" (as noted on the diagram) not only cuts across all levels of managerial function, but tends to establish the basis of the relationship between managerial functions. The success of each function depends upon the success of the other two—achieving administratively defined goals depends upon the success of the managerial functions in reducing or managing goal conflict, just as the managerial functions depend upon clearly defined goals to reduce goal conflict. This, in effect, establishes a virtual interdependence between the managerial functions of administration, management, and supervision.

In addition, the correctional organization itself creates a great deal of interdependence. Perhaps all organizations create such interdependence in one way or another:

[7] Coffey, *Administration of Criminal Justice*, p. 106.

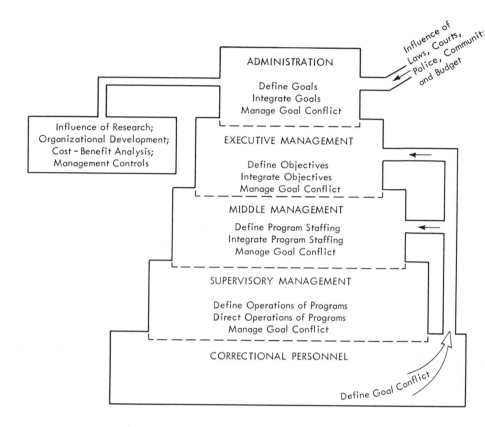

**SELECTED MANAGERIAL FUNCTIONS**

The proper function of an organization is to orchestrate the application of its members' skills and energies to the solution of larger problems than any of them could handle separately. "Orchestration" in this sense implies that the total contribution of all the individuals in the organization is made greater than its mere sum. If an organization does not multiply, at least to some extent, what its members could achieve severally, there is no reason for it to exist. But to orchestrate implies more than just producing more. It also means that skills are blended and optimized. An organization justifies itself by applying its skills deftly, not just massively.[8]

Organization, then, like the distinction between administration, management, and supervision, is extremely useful in defining that part of correctional administration involving the administrator.

[8] S. W. Gellerman, *Management By Motivation* (St. Louis, Mo.: Vail-Ballou Press, 1968), p. 251.

## Organization

Exploring organization for the purpose of clarifying influences upon the definition of administrative process suggests consideration of the "intent" of organization—at least its general goals:

> Organization has three goals which may be either intermeshed or independent ends in themselves. They are growth, stability, and interaction. The last goal refers to organizations which exist primarily to provide a medium for association of its members with others. Interestingly enough, these goals seem to apply to different forms of organization at varying levels of complexity, ranging from simple clockwork mechanisms to social systems.[9]

The idea that organizations have "general goals" offers several distinct advantages, particularly with reference to the correctional organization:

> A stress on goals shifts the focus away from an exclusive concern with the offender and his characteristics toward a view that places him within a correctional system continuously accommodating itself to a larger social order; it calls special attention to the manner in which a correctional system organizes to achieve its goals, establishes relationships with offenders, and defines its priorities through the allocation of power and resources. The major premise underlying this line of inquiry is that one can understand a correctional system and the behavior of the persons within it only by understanding the processes for attaining the system's goals and for managing the competition among them.[10]

Administrative process, then, can be related to the system's goals and managing the competition among them. Reconsidering the diagram of the selected managerial functions, note that all functions include managing conflicts in goals. Of course, it must be remembered that this competition between various goals within the system at times poses major problems, not only for the administration but for management and supervision as well, since competition between goals is by no means isolated to that part of the correctional administration involving administrators. For example, some correctional personnel may emphasize *rehabilitation* to the point of excluding the goal of what others consider *protection of the community*. When and if these two goals are not integrated, major difficulties may emerge for administrators, managers, and supervisors alike.

[9] W. G. Scott, "Organization Theory: An Overview and an Appraisal," *Journal of the Academy of Management*, Vol. 4, No. 1 (April 1961), 7–26.
[10] V. O'Leary and D. Duffee, "Correctional Policy, A Classification of Goals Designed for Change," *Crime and Delinquency*, Vol. 17, No. 4 (October 1971), 374.

But in terms of what will be discussed later as the administrative responsibility to define organizational goals, the administrative process of "managing conflict between goals" is singularly important.

In managing competition between organizational goals, the administrative process far more than management and supervision must cope with the reality that . . .

> . . . an organization is not a mechanical system in which one part can be changed without a concomitant effect on the other parts. Rather, an organizational system shares with biological systems the property of an intense interdependence of parts such that a change in one part has an impact on the others. . . .[11]

Managing competition between goals within a context of "a change in one part has impact on the others" is anything but easy. Goal oriented administrative process, however, retains a powerful advantage in coping with some of the major administrative problems that emerge through conflict between goals.

Retention of such a powerful advantage, of course, depends in large measure on the administrative ability to examine whether or not administrative process is moving the organization toward its goals. Consider the following diagram.

### Sensor Matrix

A correctional administrator concerned with whether or not administrative process moves the organization toward goals has only to establish a reliable system of community and organizational sensors to detect variation. Just as the heat-gauge on an automobile dashboard warns of pending trouble requiring corrective action, so also does a matrix of sensors warn that certain administrative or managerial corrections may be necessary to achieve goals.

Discussions presented in the next two chapters suggest many alternatives in using management functions for such a "sensor matrix" within the organization. Literally *any* community-based program function can systematically provide such corrective information from outside the organization—from the community.

Such information, of course, differs significantly from what will be discussed in the context of *management information*. The main difference has to do with decision aiding information within administrative

---

[11] P. R. Lawrence and J. W. Lorsch, *Developing Organizations: Diagnosis and Action* (Reading, Mass.: Addison-Wesley Publishing Co., 1969), pp. 9–10.

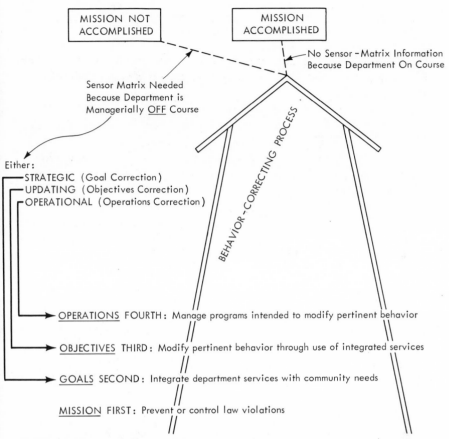

| MISSION NOT ACCOMPLISHED | MISSION ACCOMPLISHED |

No Sensor – Matrix Information Because Department On Course

Sensor Matrix Needed Because Department is Managerially OFF Course

Either:
- STRATEGIC (Goal Correction)
- UPDATING (Objectives Correction)
- OPERATIONAL (Operations Correction)

BEHAVIOR-CORRECTING PROCESS

OPERATIONS FOURTH: Manage programs intended to modify pertinent behavior

OBJECTIVES THIRD: Modify pertinent behavior through use of integrated services

GOALS SECOND: Integrate department services with community needs

MISSION FIRST: Prevent or control law violations

SENSOR-MATRIX IN MISSION DIRECTED AND GOAL ORIENTED CORRECTIONAL ADMINISTRATION

process being management information as opposed to information from outside administrative process being sensor matrix. In terms of administrative process, however, the justification for the effort required to establish a sensor matrix is retention of the powerful advantage of goal oriented administration. Retention of this advantage is, in large measure, the goal orientation itself—the emphasis upon "accommodation to a larger social order" already noted, combined with the cohesive influence of establishing goals—retention of goals being a vital characteristic of effective organization:

Organizations—companies, groups of parts in a machine, the functional elements of the human body—operate together in a communication network, but they also exhibit another characteristic: the elements of an organization operate together to reach or maintain an external goal (or its goal image within the organization). . . .[12]

That is, goal-oriented administration tends to develop what we have discussed as a system whose input and output cross system boundaries—an "open system."

### Administrative Process Defined

Now that we have considered several influences on the definition of administrative process, it is possible to suggest a definition that can be used for still further exploration of that process:

> *Successful administrative process can be defined as administrators creating a results-achieving system out of a correctional organization*—and creating such a system in the presence of many influences.

## ADMINISTRATIVE RESPONSIBILITIES

Reviewing some of the many influences on administration permits an exploration of certain dimensions of the actual process of administering a correctional organization. For example, from our discussion of these influences we can compile a partial but adequate list of the major administrative responsibilities, regardless of whether or not administrators do the actual work involved:

| | | |
|---|---|---|
| Operations | Programming | Goal definition |
| Personnel | Budgeting | Policy |
| Planning | Accounting | Leadership |
| Research | Training | Organization |

It should be emphasized that this list by no means exhausts the scope of administrative responsibility. Indeed, *every* facet of organizational activity is the responsibility of the administration; a clear distinction between the management and the practice of corrections notwithstanding, even the "casework" of line–staff is the administration's responsibility. But to understand administrative process, it is necessary to understand how these responsibilities are met.

Selection of a few samples from our listing may be particularly useful

---

[12] C. W. Churchman, R. L. Ackoff, and E. L. Arnoff, "Analysis of the Organization," in *Introduction to Operations Research* (New York: John Wiley & Sons, Inc., 1957), pp. 69–88.

in understanding the nature of administrative involvement in the actual administration of a correctional organization.

## Goal Definitions

Clarifying the administrative process through goal definitions, of course, requires some consideration of correctional goals in general, and this in turn suggests at least a brief examination of the *total* correctional process —which may or may not be capable of achieving certain goals that might be defined administratively.

Concerning this process, a study authorized by the federal government had this to say:

For purposes of this analysis, the total correctional process will be divided into three parts:

1. *The pre-trial period.* The pre-trial period is a port-of-entry into the correctional system. It is a crucial period because there is increasing evidence that the mere insertion of a person into the system, especially through detention or jail while waiting adjudication of guilt or innocence, may increase rather than lessen the likelihood that he will remain in the system and be a continuing problem to the state. . . .

2. *The post-trial period.* If the offender is found guilty, judges and correctional personnel are confronted with a basic choice of whether to imprison him or to choose among a variety of other alternatives. Ordinarily, probation or a fine may be used for the juvenile, the first offender, and the person who commits a nonserious crime. But what if there is serious concern over the use of fines or probation for some offenders? What other alternatives, other than incarceration, are available? What are the implications of these alternatives? What modifications in the correctional system might be needed if they are to be used?

The choices that are made here are no less important than those made in the pre-trial period. The post-trial period is a second port-of-entry, one which leads either into a supervised yet continuing participation in ordinary community life, or into a complex time of incarceration in which the process of labeling by society or the process of labeling one's self by the individual is solidified. If the choice is incarceration then, more than ever, the status of "criminal," "lawbreaker," "outsider," is likely to be assigned to the offender. . . .

3. *The post-incarceration period.* Assuming that all correctional decisions have led to incarceration for the offender, there is still the possibility that the period of incarceration might be shortened or supplemented by other alternatives. In addition to traditional parole, there might be other ways to deal with the offender so that his return to the community will be aided or speeded up. What are these alternatives? What is the rationale for using them, their possible strengths and weaknesses? What dates them? Theoretically, they are of crucial importance because incarceration enhances the

problem of reintegration, the adjustment of the individual to his community. He is not the same person who left it; he has problems which he did not possess before he was imprisoned, especially if his confinement was for an extended period in a maximum security setting. . . .[13]

As can be seen in this brief analysis, the correctional process covers a fairly wide range: pre-trial, post-trial, and post-incarceration—probation, institutions, and parole. Broadening the threshold further are the distinctions between adult and juvenile process, along with a growing list of prevention and diversion functions.

Administrative goal definitions are of necessity influenced by this process, and by its complexity, if for no other reason than that the process may be *unable* to achieve some goals. Administratively, this poses a major problem, since much if not most of the correctional process is rigidly controlled by law and what amounts to inflexible court control. The problem can be negotiated in many instances, however, through consideration of organizational structure.

ORGANIZATIONAL STRUCTURE. The influence of the law and the courts is somewhat difficult to modify in order to make changes in correctional process that might achieve certain goals; the organizational structure of corrections is in most cases substantially easier to modify for this purpose. And in addition, organizational structure is much easier to relate to goals—to the desired outcome of the correctional process. In this regard, it is noteworthy that administratively defining desired correctional goals is one thing, but having the organizational capability of achieving such goals may be another. And unlike the case with law and judicial structure, modifying organizations to increase their capability is constantly within the realm of realistic possibility in many if not most jurisdictions.

An example of possibilities in modifying correctional organizations is shown in the accompanying diagram.

In terms of the goals that might be defined based on our discussion of the overall correctional process, note that the example organizational diagram has at least the structural capability to achieve virtually *all* reasonable correctional goals—conceivably, even within the framework of rigid legal and judicial restrictions. Note also the possible structural distinctions between administration, management, and supervision:

ADMINISTRATION: Directors IV and III
MANAGEMENT:     Executive—Director II
                Middle—Director I and Manager III
SUPERVISOR:     Managers I and II (not shown)

[13] L. T. Empey, "Alternatives to Incarceration," *Studies in Delinquency*, U. S. Department of Health, Education and Welfare, Office of Juvenile Delinquency and Youth Development, 1967, pp. 9–11.

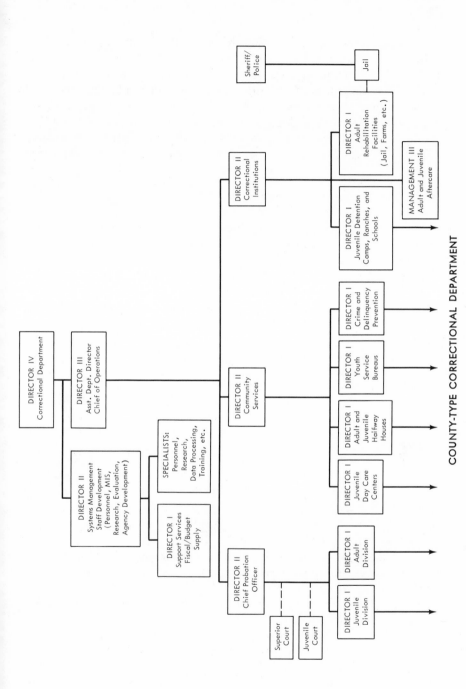

COUNTY-TYPE CORRECTIONAL DEPARTMENT

DIRECTOR IV
Correctional Department

DIRECTOR III
Asst. Dept. Director
Chief of Operations

DIRECTOR II
Systems Management
Staff Development
(Personnel, MIS,
Research, Evaluation,
Agency Development)

SPECIALISTS:
Personnel,
Research,
Data Processing,
Training, etc.

DIRECTOR I
Suppor Services
Fiscal/Budget
Supply

DIRECTOR II
Chief Probation
Officer

Superior
Court

Juvenile
Court

DIRECTOR I
Juvenile
Division

DIRECTOR I
Adult
Division

DIRECTOR II
Community
Services

DIRECTOR I
Juvenile
Day Care
Centers

DIRECTOR I
Adult and
Juvenile
Halfway
Houses

DIRECTOR I
Youth
Service
Bureaus

DIRECTOR I
Crime and
Delinquency
Prevention

DIRECTOR II
Correctional
Institutions

DIRECTOR I
Juvenile Detention
Camps, Ranches, and
Schools

DIRECTOR I
Adult
Rehabilitation
Facilities
(Jail, Farms, etc.)

MANAGEMENT III
Adult and Juvenile
Aftercare

Sheriff/
Police

Jail

Although the titles differ somewhat from the traditional "supervising probation officer" approach to identifying managerial role, there is nonetheless an advantage in their suggesting the management function involved. But regardless of the title, the point is that administrative goal setting is probably no more restricted than the potential afforded by organizational structure, legal and judicial restrictions notwithstanding. Nevertheless, there are other significant influences or possible settings, one of which is the distinction between *responsibility* and *accountability*.

RESPONSIBILITY VERSUS ACCOUNTABILITY. Implicit in the overused saying, "The buck stops here," is that the chief executive of an organization is 100 percent responsible for the organization's welfare. This does not, of course, prevent successful delegation of enough authority to hold management and supervisors accountable for certain measurable functions. Such accountability, however, never relieves top administration of the entire responsibility for the organization.

In an administrative model suggested for criminal justice organizations in general, the managerial functions involved in the distinctions between *responsibility* and *accountability* have been described as: [14]

1. Define *results* (Function of Administrative Role)
2. Define *what* is needed to achieve results (Function of Executive-Management Role)
3. Define *who* is needed to achieve results (Function of Middle-Management Role)
4. Define *how* results are to be achieved (Function of Supervisory Management)

From this somewhat oversimplified version of certain managerial functions, it can be seen that the administrative role, while remaining 100 percent *responsible* for the entire organization, can nonetheless systematically distribute *accountability* for key managerial functions, via delegation of the authority required.

To the role of administrator, already responsible for 100 percent of the overall organization, there is assigned 100 percent *accountability* for defining *results* to be achieved.

To the role of executive management there is assigned 100 percent *accountability* for defining *what* is needed to achieve results—to define objectives for the goals, to plan.

To the role of middle manager there is assigned 100 percent *ac-*

[14] There has been elaborated a complete systems management model including organizational synergetics, role–function interfacing, cybernated planning and decision procedures, cost–benefit, information systems, and sensor matrix in Coffey, *Administration of Criminal Justice*, Chaps. 4–8.

*countability* for defining *who* is needed to achieve results—to be accountable for personnel assignments in terms of the organizational objectives.

To the role of supervisor there is assigned 100 percent *accountability* for *how* results are achieved—the techniques and the methods of "applied corrections."

In effect, administratively defined results *are* definitions of goals. But by distinguishing between *responsibility* and *accountability*, it is possible to go beyond organizational "goal setting" to systematic goal achievement.

Beyond the influences of organizational structure, responsibility versus accountability, and managerial functions by role, there is a vast array of influences impinging upon the process of defining goals, many of which are also significant. Among these are the influences of the employees within the organization, which in many ways are as significant as those of the community.

## Correctional Employees and Administrative Goals

Employee organizations are already a reality in criminal justice. What remains to be seen is whether or not the labor union movement and managerial programming are to move in the same direction.[15]

The number of correctional administrators who are concerned with the implications of employee organizations is large and growing larger, even though labor negotiations with union officials do not customarily involve the correctional administration itself; ". . . but limited though direct labor negotiations may be in criminal justice administration, the significance of labor unions and other employee groups is enormous—even when the participatory function is performed well. . . ." [16]

By "participatory function" is meant "participatory management"—a concept that will be examined in the next chapter, revealing a great number of variables that establish correctional-employee organizations as an increasingly influential consideration. Indeed, beyond goal setting, employee groups are increasingly influential in all areas, as we shall see in chapters that deal with probation, institutions, and parole.

CORRECTIONAL ADMINISTRATORS. Still another consideration that might serve to illustrate the many influences upon the administrative process of goal definitions is the administrators themselves—those who actually lead the correctional field. The subject of *personnel*, as such, will be

---

[15] Coffey, *Administration of Criminal Justice*, p. 140.
[16] *Ibid.*, p. 139.

dealt with later in this volume. However, in terms of administrative responsibility to define goals, the following statistics have come to light:

What are the men and women like who lead the correction field in this country? Who are the leaders who shape its goals and basic policies, interpret them to the opinion-makers and to the public at large, and guide the implementation of policy in day-to-day interaction with offenders in the various correctional settings? What are their backgrounds? What do they perceive as the goals for corrections? How do they envision the force field of relationships in which they work? What do they see as their principal problems? What do they read? To what organizations do they belong? How do they view their jobs and, more significantly, themselves in the work milieu? We sought both the answers to these questions and some of their broader implications in our study. . . .

. . . Women made up slightly less than 19 percent of the administrators in the sample. . . .

. . . Seventy-five percent of the top administrators and 55 percent of the middle-managers were over 45 years of age. . . .

. . . Among the top administrators, the probation and parole heads had the longest correctional service records, with over 80 percent having been in corrections more than 10 years. . . .

. . . The middle administrators had a slightly different pattern. . . . Over 66 percent had been in corrections over 10 years and 66 percent in administration over 10 years. Middle-level probation and parole administrators had spent slightly less time in correctional jobs. . . .

. . . Juvenile institution administrators had significantly more degrees at the Master's level than did those in any of the other settings. Headquarters executives held the largest percent of higher degrees; nearly one-third of them had an M.D., a Ph.D., or some other advanced degree. . . .[17]

In this regard, administrative goal setting is influenced a great deal by the pattern of the administrator's career—that is, the pattern by which correctional managers advance in their careers. The influence of this pattern has generated sufficient concern to launch a great deal of investigation under the title "mobliography":

Mobliography is the study of the mobility patterns of managers and executives, the distribution and number of mobile managers, and their delays and difficulties en route. This new science can prevent and remedy problems that have been largely beyond the grasp of personnel departments of large business corporations: the talented manager lost in the corporate maze, the mobile executive going too fast up the corporate ladder, the

[17] E. K. Nelson, Jr., and C. H. Lovell, "A Profile of the Correctional Administrator," in Joint Commission on Correctional Manpower Development, *Developing Correctional Administrators* (Lebanon, Pa.: Sowers Printing, November 1969), pp. 23–26.

promising manager who is without proper training and development, or the executive headed for a career crisis.[18]

Although geared currently to the private corporation, mobliography has clear implications for correctional administrators, not only in the responsibility of setting goals but throughout the administrative process.

Of course, organizational structure, role and function, responsibility versus accountability, employee organizations, and the administrators themselves are only examples of administrative process intended to clarify its nature; there are many other influences upon administrative process or defining of goals. These examples do, however, establish the fact that influence upon goal setting does exist. Other influences, such as related criminal justice subsystems and the community itself, will be considered in other contexts in later chapters.

For purposes of further clarifying the nature of administrative process, let us now direct our attention toward the administrative responsibility for planning.

## Planning

There exists in some business and government quarters surprising resistance to developing systematic and comprehensive planning. Naturally there are a great many reasons for such resistance, but failure to grasp the significance of effective planning is more important that it should be.[19]

In correctional organizations where *real* planning efforts have been made, there are few, if any, correctional administrators and managers who would not verify the commentary above. Unfortunately, it is also true that in many situations, the administrator himself resists this extremely significant segment of administrative responsibility.

Assuming, however, that increasing public concern with the effectiveness of criminal justice will gradually reduce resistance regardless of what form it takes, a more positive discussion of this vital segment of administrative process is possible:

Regardless of changes, an effective management is always thinking five years ahead. . . . Though constant updating of plans . . . may appear chaotic in nature, the updating is actually tranquil in comparison to the radical adjustments that are forced to occur when there have been [no plan

---

[18] E. E. Jennings, "Charting the Difficulties to the Top: A Study of Executive Mobility Patterns," *Management Personnel Quarterly*, Vol. 6, No. 2 (Summer 1967), 13.
[19] G. A. Steiner, "The Critical Role of Top Management in Long-Range Planning," *Arizona Review*, Vol. 14, No. 4 (April 1966), 5.

updates]. . . . Few if any probation, parole, or prison administrators have not felt some degree of pressure of this kind. . . .[20]

Planning—updated planning—then, is vitally necessary to the correctional administrator, even though "so severe are some social changes and so accelerated the pace that even the most sophisticated updating process occasionally lags."[21]

Because this is a discussion of the administrator's role in the administrative process, it should be noted that the actual "updating" emphasized here is a function of executive-management roles. For that matter, the plans may well have been originally developed by these same managerial executives, but optimally in relation to organizational goals defined by top administration. The point is that the administrative process includes plans on which decisions can be made—plans instead of policy whenever possible, since updated plans are invariably more useful than dependence upon policy.

Perhaps the administrative responsibility to set policy, then, is another clarifying dimension of the administrative process.

## Policy

One way to clarify *policy* as an administrative responsibility is to think of *decisions*—that is, of decision making on the part of managers. In the effective correctional organization, administration has usually dealt with this through assignment:

> Decision-making responsibility is assigned at the lowest point in the organization where the needed skills and competence, on the one hand, and the needed information, on the other hand, can reasonably be brought together. A great improvement is believed to result in any firm when the creative talents of responsible individuals are encouraged to develop in a climate of individual responsibility, authority, and dignity—a climate that is made possible by the decentralization of decision making.[22]

To many correctional administrators, however, the concept of decentralizing seems to pose problems in terms of "lost control":

> Even without going any further, it is clear that in the control of the typical organization, perfect decentralization is not possible because of the limitations on enforcement rules associated with uncertainty and risk aver-

---

[20] Coffey, *Administration of Criminal Justice*, p. 117.
[21] *Ibid.*
[22] J. F. Burlingame, "Information Technology and Decentralization," *Harvard Business Review*, November–December 1961, p. 121.

sion. The top management of the organization will always have to have some information about the internal workings of the individual activity.[23]

This need for "information about the internal workings of the individual activity" brings many correctional administrators squarely to grips with the role played by administrative policy.

On the one hand, *all* decisions could be made by the administration if *all* information were available—"all information" being a mythological illusion retained by some in the face of overwhelming evidence that no one person can have "all information."

On the other hand, delegating authority to make decisions at the lowest point in the organization carries what seems to many to be great risks of chaotic, uncontrolled operations.

Setting policy between these two extremes is a kind of tacit acknowledgment that an administrator must have assistance in processing the enormous flow of information in virtually all correctional organizations. It is also a tacit effort to "control" the help offered—to "guide" the help to policy.

But policy can play still another more potentially productive role in the administrative process.

FUNCTION ACCOUNTABILITY, THEN POLICY. Recalling the earlier mention in this chapter of *results, what, who* and *how* as managerial functions, consider the possibility that policy is merely a "fail-safe" for situations in which these functions do not produce some *measurable results.* In other words, perhaps all managerial decisions should be made in terms of achieving results rather than of policy—at least until it is measurably demonstrated that results are not forthcoming, and then policy can be used for decision making.

Administrative concern for continuity of program is dealt with simply through administrative definition of results to be achieved and measured—a rather absolute form of control. Administrative concern with control is dealt with by the use of policy as the basis of decisions at the first measurable sign that the desired results are not being achieved.

But insofar as tangible, measurable results *are* being achieved, the use of policy can never be made to compete with responsible, goal-oriented management judgments. This is true if for no other reason than that policy can never be made to fit all the situations that judgment can, even when judgment is restricted to achieving a goal.

Superimposing policy ahead of managerial judgment in such an instance is a genuine waste—wasted managerial judgment that was not used, and wasted incentive frustrated through systematic use of "the

[23] K. J. Arrow, "Control in Large Organizations," *Management Science*, Vol. 10, No. 3 (April 1964), 397–401.

book" instead of managerial initiative. Worst of all, systematically preventing managerial judgment and replacing it with policy interpretation raises the question of whether priority in the field of corrections is actually being given to corrections or to survival—since the interpretation of policy in many instances varies more widely than does goal-oriented management judgment.

Of course, no responsible administrator would be foolhardy enough to simply replace policy; there is a great deal of managerial complexity involved in establishing the clearly defined accountability needed for success through "functional judgment" over policy.[24]

Policy, of course, serves a wide range of administrative interests even when *not* used as a "fail-safe"—even when used as the primary influence on decision making. *Continuity* of programming, *uniformity* of operations, *efficiency* of decisive reaction are but a few of the advantages of clearly stated policy.

But in terms of exploring some of the dimensions of administrative process, policy setting illustrates that again the administrator faces a number of complexities in even this, one of the simpler of his administrative responsibilities.

Goal definitions and policy setting refer to segments of administrative responsibility involving *direct* administrative participation. Other responsibilities that are clearly those of the administrator, however, do not involve direct participation—at least not in many criminal justice organizations.

For example, even though the administration of a correctional organization is usually responsible for research, budget–accounting, and training, actual administrators are rarely involved to anything like the degree to which they directly deal with operations, personnel, planning, programming, policy, and organization.

### Budget and Accounting

Budgets for correctional organizations are customarily managed by the management instead of by the administration. The administrative process incorporates budget primarily in terms of proposing annual fiscal outlays for the correctional organization, and in terms of an administrative accounting system. Such a system, however, does not complete administrative responsibility:

> The mere existence of a good accounting system is not an automatic guarantee that management will have good cost controls. The accounting

---

[24] See, for example, a management model that includes systematic accountability in Chapters 4 through 8 of Coffey, *Administration of Criminal Justice.*

system, as such, is historical—it summarizes what happened several weeks ago on an "after-the-fact" basis.[25]

Administrative failure to recognize the "historical" nature of some accounting systems can in turn generate considerable complexity:

> Managerial processes involving information, decisions, and planning . . . are relatively simple in comparison to the fiscal procedures to which many criminal justice administrators are subjected. . . .[26]

It might be added that the complexity to which these administrators may be subjected is in large measure "optional."

LIMITS ON AUTHORITY DELEGATED. Unlike the delegation of various levels of authority in the operations of corrections, the budget and accounting activities tend to increase in complexity in proportion to how far they are removed from direct administrative involvement.

For example, a chief probation officer who is sophisticated enough to administer the operations of his department through the accountability for managerial functions (as discussed earlier in this chapter) greatly simplifies his programming. Indeed, the less involved he is in managerial functions, the more accountable the assigned manager— blame or credit flowing to the manager assigned rather than to the administrator who intervenes.

Consider the distinctions between adult pre-sentence investigations for the criminal court, the pre-hearing juvenile court investigation, field supervision for adult offenders on probation, and, say, supervision of juvenile foster homes. All these diversified functions are a part of operations, and as such, are administrative responsibilities.

By assigning a director of the adult division to be accountable for planning *what* it will take to achieve the administratively desired results, the administrator has simplified his problem—at least if he has delegated sufficient authority for this director to, in turn, assign accountability to second-line supervisors, who manage the plan and who, in turn, can assign accountability for operation to line supervisors.

Operations, then, need not be a confused mess made up of adult and juvenile specialties, *as long as the administrator actually removes specific management from the administrative process*—that is, if the administrator "stays out" long enough to hold managers accountable for managing. The sophisticated administrator recognizes that he reduces the manager's accountability whenever administrative intervention occurs.

---

[25] T. S. Dudick, *Cost Controls for Industry* (Englewood Cliffs, N.J.: Prentice-Hall, Inc., 1962), p. 106.
[26] Coffey, *Administration of Criminal Justice*, p. 123.

Budget and accounting, however, tend to follow this pattern only in the "mechanics"—the administration freeing itself only of the book-keeping. This is true in part because the administration can hold management of operations accountable for achieving some measurable result only to the degree that the managers of operations have funds available to achieve results. Although the total of these funds is limited, the managerial judgments as to how the funds are utilized must remain with management if it is to be held accountable for results.

This means, in effect, that the operational manager spends virtually as he pleases, as long as the total is not exceeded. It also means that the authority to prevent the manager from spending the funds must not be delegated to the budget analysts and accountants within the criminal justice organization. Administrators must retain sufficient control of the budget and accounting to insure that management can be held accountable.

Of great assistance in simplifying some of the complex segments involved in administrative control of accounting and budget is *cost–benefit analysis*.

BUDGET AND COST–BENEFIT

A frequently ignored budget consideration is cost–benefit. By this is meant how much in the way of planned results the budget will buy—how expensive achieving results is.

Even when cost–benefit is considered, still another factor is often overlooked: the cost of building and maintaining the organization in addition to the cost of operating it.

Although sophisticated cost–benefit analysis is complex and consulting specialists are usually required to assist the administrator, there is a relatively simple way of conceptualizing the task so as to avoid the problem of overlooking major costs such as building and maintaining the organization.[27]

Cost–benefit, then, is administrative effort to compare the total achievement of measurable results to the total cost of corrections. With the focus upon this comparison, the complexities of budget and accounting remain within the administrative process, but in a far simpler conceptual framework.

Perhaps one final example of administrative responsibility may suffice to illustrate the nature of the administrative process. This is another area in which administrators tend not to be *directly* involved—research.

[27] Coffey, *Administration of Criminal Justice*, pp. 123–24.

## Research

Those who have thought and written about management often refer to management "know-how" as an essential ingredient of success. By know-how they apparently mean the ability of the manager to understand what is going on in his environment. It is the chief concern of the management scientist to translate these vague stipulations about management knowledge into precise and verifiable assertions about how decisions are made and how decisions ought to be made.[28]

Research, as a correctional concept, has a substantially different definition from the one implied in this quotation, at least for most administrators. And yet as soon as the research needed by the scientists mentioned above is considered, it becomes immediately clear that both the administrator and the manager can be as directly involved in research as can line–staff and probation, parole, and correctional institutions. In many instances, the differences in research exist only in the specialty of a researching consultant.[29]

As in so much of the administrative process, lines of demarcation between direct administrative involvement and complete administrative absence are not clear. As with budget–accounting, however, the significance of research, particularly applied research, is sufficient justification to retain direct control whether or not the research is geared to management rather than the methods and techniques of corrections.

When used literally, applied research produces major 'decisions about programs, methods, and techniques. Regardless of the validity of the interpretation of research findings, there remains a certain amount of organizational impact whenever these findings are applied—whenever new findings change the rules.

Although the technology surrounding sophisticated research is scarcely a part of administrative process and certainly does not include administrators in the successful criminal justice organization, assessment of the impact of research nevertheless remains a crucial element of any successful administration. The absence of research of any kind is highly detrimental in an area of increasing public concern with the effectiveness of corrections, but the absence of control of research can prove equally unfortunate.

To afford a context for examining this somewhat equivocal element of correctional administration, consider the following:

[28] C. W. Churchman, "Managerial Acceptance of Scientific Recommendations," *California Management Review*, Fall 1964, p. 31.
[29] Coffey, *Administration of Criminal Justice*, Chap. 14.

A review of the whole correctional field reveals a remarkable dearth of experiments in which theory, action, and research are joined together effectively. Both the professions and the social sciences are without the traditions and the experience by which experimentation is facilitated.

In the absence of such traditions, it is difficult to suggest what the necessary elements of an experimental model might be. But, logically, certain elements are implied by their very nature:

1. *Statement of Objectives.* In many correctional settings, consensus on objectives is lacking. Correctional workers disagree as to whether their main concern is with custody, treatment, vocational education, or some other objective. And when there is no consensus on objectives, there is no logical means for choosing one approach over another, one kind of staff over another, one program component over another. It would not make sense to initiate an experimental effort unless objectives were made explicit and a set of priorities chosen.

2. *Theoretical Assumptions.* As mentioned above, the data that are obtained in any problem-identification process do not provide answers for correctional problems; they only isolate crucial issues and areas. Therefore, a second basic element that would be necessary would be a series of theoretical assumptions regarding the nature of the problems that are identified: What are the problems? What causes them? What should be done about them?

3. *Program Strategy.* Once a set of assumptions is chosen from the various logical alternatives, the next step in implementing an experimental program would be making these assumptions operational for action and research purposes; that is, reducing them from abstract to operational terms and translating them into the kinds of functions which a staff and its organization are expected to perform. This is a most difficult task concerned with making clear what factors—attitudes, group variables, organizational characteristics—are to be altered and how they are to be altered.

This step is one in which the collaboration of the scientist, policy maker, and professional is vitally needed. The difficulties inherent in trying to operationalize theory are great, and, in the past, have rarely been overcome successfully. It is virtually impossible to demonstrate that various correctional staff members share any common conceptual framework, even for experimental purposes, by which they organize their efforts and, furthermore, that they actually perform their functions as they say they should perform them.

4. *Research Design.* The fourth major component would be research. Research, ideally, would be tied to the other components of the experimental model in such a way as to contribute most effectively to the derivation of knowledge about the particular correctional approach under question. It would flow, logically, like the action program, from the particular set of theoretical assumptions around which the action program is organized. Research would be of greatest value if it could contribute knowledge in three main areas: about the adequacy of basic assumptions, about the nature and problems of the program itself, and about its outcome.

5. *Research Feedback.* The final element of any experimental model would

be a feedback system by which the findings of any endeavor could be communicated, and their implications assessed, for both action and research people. The importance of this particular element cannot be overestimated because of the tremendous difficulties inherent in maintaining collaboration among administrative, professional, and research people.

Research feedback is vital in two ways; first, as a method of quality control by which to insure that a program operates as closely as possible to theoretical design, and second, as a method of contributing to knowledge and future experimentation. At present, experimental programs tend to be discrete entities with little continuity from one program to another. By contrast, it might be hoped that, with greater dedication to research, one experiment might provide the basis upon which another is based.

The final research resource that would be needed in the development of a comprehensive correctional system would be a central data repository. Such a repository is needed as a method of evaluating the performance of offenders after their release from correctional programs. Until such repositories are available, it will be impossible to conduct followup studies across jurisidictional lines, to evaluate parole performance, for example, on a national basis. Furthermore, depending upon the data collected, a data repository could be used to indicate more precise information on release problems and successes than the singular factor of law violation. It would obviously be a necessary element in the development and evaluation of various alternatives in incarceration.[30]

Perhaps discussion of programming or leadership, or further discussion of operations and personnel, might clarify the nature of the administrative process even more. But the definition of correctional process and the few selected dimensions of that process presented thus far should prove adequate as a context for the two chapters that follow—on the *management* and the *supervision* of the correctional organization. Establishing such a context is desirable because management and supervision not only depend upon administrative process; they are critically important segments of the overall administration of probation, institutions, and parole.

## SUMMARY

This chapter presented certain elements of the process of correctional administration, in terms of that segment involving administrators, as opposed to administrative activities involving managers and supervisors.

Administrative process involving administrators was defined as "administrators creating a results-achieving system out of a correctional organization". Several influences that impinge upon this definition were considered, and in turn used to derive key administrative responsibilities.

[30] Empey, "Alternatives to Incarceration," pp. 80–82.

Certain of these responsibilities were discussed as clarification of the nature of administrative process within the correctional field. The responsibilities selected were goal definitions, planning, budget–accounting, and research—all considered as examples of the many administrative responsibilities within the correctional organization.

The inclusion of supervision and management within the correctional administration was emphasized as a background for the two chapters that follow.

### Discussion Topics

1. Relate fragmentation of criminal justice as presented in Chapter 1 to correctional administration as introduced in this chapter.

2. Relate systems, organization, and operations to the definition given of administrative process.

3. Distinguish between administrative process and the concepts of management and supervision.

4. Discuss relationships among any four of the administrative responsibilities that were derived from the discussion of defining administrative process.

5. Elaborate on the influences upon defining goals.

6. Elaborate on the influences on planning.

7. Compare goals and planning with budget and research in administrative process.

8. Discuss how the presentation of examples such as goals, planning, budget, and research clarify administrative process in general.

### Annotated References

BERKLEY, G. E., *The Administrative Revolution: Notes on the Passing of Organization Man.* Englewood Cliffs, N.J.: Prentice-Hall, Inc., 1971. An excellent context, examining the absolute necessity of recognizing the need for removing administrative process from the control of tradition.

COFFEY, A., *Administration of Criminal Justice: A Management Systems Approach.* Englewood Cliffs, N.J.: Prentice-Hall, Inc., 1974. A comprehensive examination of the functions of administrative role in management; see, in particular, Chapters 4 through 8.

COFFEY, A., E. ELDEFONSO, and W. HARTINGER, *Introduction to the Criminal Justice System and Process.* Englewood Cliffs, N.J.: Prentice-Hall, Inc., 1974. A comprehensive text exploring what this chapter presented as the relationship of correctional administration to criminal justice fragmentation.

Fox, V., *Introduction to Corrections.* Englewood Cliffs, N.J.: Prentice-Hall, Inc., 1972. A good overview of what this chapter dealt with briefly as the "total correctional process." See also: Hartinger, W., E. Eldefonso, and A. Coffey, *Corrections.* Pacific Palisades, Calif.: Goodyear Publishing Co., Inc., 1973.

LAWRENCE, P. R., and J. W. LORSCH, *Developing Organizations: Diagnosis and Action.* Reading, Mass.: Addison-Wesley Publishing Co., Inc., 1969. Good elaboration of what this chapter dealt with as organizational influence upon the administrative responsibility to set organizational goals.

# The Managerial
# Element of
# Correctional
# Administration

# Chapter 3

Now that we have considered that part of corrections involving the administrators of correctional organizations, this chapter presents the actual *management* of the organization—the specific process of achieving goals established by the administrator.

To reiterate the distinction between the administrative elements and the managerial elements of managing a correctional organization, consider the following:

> The basic distinction between administration and management is probably that between setting policy and carrying out the day-to-day activity. Administration is the higher order of activity. Though these distinctions do exist, they often tend to blur, and no attempt will be made here to make careful distinction. The lack of clearcut distinction in the use of the two words is much like the rather interchangeable use of words, such as executive, administrator, and manager. Successive, narrowly divided hierarchical levels now used in organizations may be a root cause. . . .[1]

[1] Joint Commission on Correctional Manpower and Training, *Perspectives on Correctional Manpower and Training* (Lebanon, Pa.: Sowers Printing Co., January 1970), p. 51.

Against this brief suggestion as to what constitutes the managerial process of correctional administration, let us turn to the key considerations of that process—the achieving of goals set by administration.

The managerial process varies tremendously from one organization to the next, from one manager to the next. These variations could be simplified somewhat by exploring the history of criminal justice management from ancient times, as has been done in other writings.[2] More to the point of isolating the specific process of managing correctional organizations, however, is consideration of methods and approaches to this process, and some of the salient managerial styles involved.

While fully acknowledging the historically significant contributions [3] of Taylor, Gantt, Argyris, Maslow, McGregor, Hertzberg and Likert, attention is focused on the styles and methods of managing corrections.

## MANAGERIAL STYLES

Before examining styles of management, it might be well to reestablish the context in which correctional management will exist—"will exist" of course referring to the future. In the preface to their excellent book of readings, Bartlett and Kayser provide an excellent description of what will probably be expected of managers in the future—managers of private industry, or corrections:

> The manager of the future will certainly be called upon to operate within both a technical and a social system that becomes ever more complex, dynamic, interrelated, and synergistic. The probabilities seem high that the structure and governance of organizations will vary considerably from that of the present-day bureaucratic model as we know it.
>
> This manager of the future will need, of course, to be fully cognizant of the total organization as a gestalt—that is, 'an organized, meaningful whole,' in which his subsystem is an integral part rather than a fragmented part. He will need to assimilate, in a real-time framework, the mission and goals of the total organization. Of more importance, however, will be the need—and demand—of his organization that he function as the 'complete manager' of his own component within the total system.
>
> As a complete manager he will have to be much more adept in the planning function so as to elaborate clear, concise, operational goals that are not only attainable but also consistent with those of the total organization. He and his subordinates undoubtedly will be quite facile in utilizing a concept such as management by objectives.

[2] See, for example, Chapter 2 of A. R. Coffey, *Administration of Criminal Justice: A Management Systems Approach* (Englewood Cliffs, N.J.: Prentice-Hall, Inc., 1974).

[3] *Ibid.*

Once these objectives are fixed, however, tomorrow's complete manager will shift to a framework similar to management by results. In this framework he will need to develop and maintain a control system which will: (1) provide him with accurate feedback as to when a deviation occurs; (2) assist him in understanding why there was deviation; and, (3) lend itself to ascertaining how to correct the deviation as well as to ensure that the same deviation will not recur. The emphasis is on problem-solving not blame-fixing. Since normal performance is expected, he will not want to know when the goals are being accomplished; instead, the complete manager will concentrate on dealing with the exceptions.

He will, of course, review the deviations from expected. Of far more importance, though, he will need to be capable both of formulating plans for change which will normalize the system again and of implementing the changes.

In addition, some change programs are either so time consuming or so involved that they may require the assistance of one or more change agents from outside the system. This suggests that the complete manager will have to be sufficiently knowledgeable to know what change agents do as well as how and why they do it.[4]

From this futuristic perspective, then, the styles in which corrections is managed will be examined.

The tremendous variation in styles with which correctional organizations are managed relates to two significant variables: (1) Variations in the personal approach each manager brings to bear on his responsibilities; and (2) Variations in the definition of management. In order to focus directly upon the single variable of personal approaches or managerial style, variations in the definition of management will be eliminated by defining management for purposes of this volume as: *the organizational process of directing and controlling achievement of goals defined by the administration.*

Although this process will be divided into executive management, middle-management and supervisory management, the definition will nevertheless prevail. This, then, allows exploration of personal variations and approaches to the managerial process—variation in style:

It is true that every manager's style is unique, but as a part of our characteristic human tendency to group similar phenomena into categories so that we can simplify reality enough to cope with it, we perceive similarities and ignore differences so that we can apply generalized labels. Accordingly, we speak of different managers as being paternalistic, authoritarian, democratic, permissive, "bull of the woods," soft, hard, firm but fair, scientific, production-centered, employee-centered, etc. Thus we categorize similar, but by no means identical, patterns of behavior into managerial styles. Once

---

4 As appears in "Preface" of Alton C. Bartlett and Thomas A. Kayser (eds.), *Changing Organizational Behavior* (Englewood Cliffs, N.J.: Prentice-Hall, Inc., 1973), pp. xi–xii.

again, it is our *perception* of reality that enables us to attach these labels to groups of managers. No individual is as completely consistent in his own behavior or as similar to others as the label implies.[5]

Perhaps the point that labels do not accurately describe a manager should be emphasized—and reemphasized. But for purposes of clarifying the process by which correctional organizations are managed, the necessity of examining similarities of styles and categorizing them can scarcely be ignored. One of the most useful tools developed for this purpose is the work of Robert Blake and Jane Mouton, creators of the Grid®.

Although the Grid® evolved in the private sector, its potential in correctional management is great. The value of this tool emerges in these comments:

THE MANAGERIAL GRID

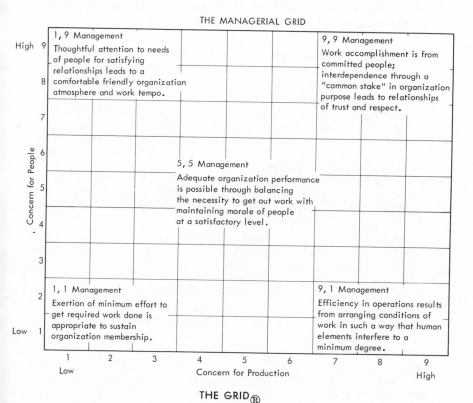

THE GRID®

Source: R. R. Blake and J. S. Mouton, *The Managerial Grid* (Houston: Gulf Publishing Company, 1964), p. 10. Reproduced by permission.

[5] D. McGregor, *The Professional Manager* (New York: McGraw-Hill Book Company, 1967), p. 58.

Whenever he acts as a manager, there are two matters on his mind. One is production—the results of his efforts. How much he thinks about results can be described as his degree of concern for production. It is a nine-point continuum, where 9 shows high concern for production and 1, low concern. A manager is also thinking about those around him, either bosses, colleagues, or those whose work he directs. The vertical axis represents his concern for people. This too is on a nine-point continuum with 9 a high degree and 1 a low degree.[6]

With relative ease, then, it becomes possible to quickly conceptualize not only distinctions between two major areas of emphasis (production and people) but the degree of emphasis as well—both readily discernible.

The relevance to corrections of the Grid® has been increasingly clear since the earliest Probation Management Institutes offered by the National Council on Crime and Delinquency.[7] The further relevance to correctional management is reflected in the following:

This conceptual frame affords virtually endless analytical possibilities, particularly in terms of shades and degrees. Regardless of the nature of the organization structure, the style of management in the organization can be plotted.

Of course, the theoretical ideal is depicted in the upper right corner as 9, 9—full commitment to both people *and* production. Excessive concern for harmony raises certain problems with the 1, 9 (a kind of "country club"), just as excessive concern for production to the exclusion of concern for people poses management problems for the 9, 1 (a kind of "I'm boss"). A sort of "split-the-difference" approach to balancing people and production is the 5, 5—a particularly tempting managerial position in the publicly limelighted administration of most criminal justice organizations. Of course the 1, 1 manager is in effect "pre-retired."

In essence, three of the approaches depicted on the grid rest on the assumption that production concerns and people concerns are incongruent. The 9, 1 depicted in the lower right-hand corner is the type of management Argyris spoke of in evolving incongruence as a concept; the 9, 1 manager relies heavily on formal authority and appointive power.

The upper left-hand corner—1, 9, or "country-club manager"—reflects the opposite extreme referred to by McGregor. Conflict is denied (or stifled) in the managerial activities that focus totally on harmony—to the virtual exclusion of concern for production.

The lower left-hand corner of the grid is impoverished by virtue of the fact that 1, 1 is in reality without concern for production *or* people. The ability of this manager, of course, depends upon his ability to appear

[6] R. R. Blake, and J. S. Mouton, *Building a Dynamic Corporation through Grid Organizational Development* (Reading, Mass.: Addison-Wesley Publishing Co., Inc., 1969), p. 60.
[7] Nationwide "traveling workshops" by Drs. O'Leary and Hall on behalf of NCCD, originated and conducted since the late 1960s.

interested in both while remaining interested in neither. Buck-passing and defensive procedures, along with other nonproductive features, characterize this particular style.

The mixture of the first three approaches occurs with the 5, 5, "middle-of-the-road," manager, operating what is hoped will remain a live-and-let-live organizational climate. This was conceptualized by Blake and Mouton as ineffective in dealing with organizational problems—an inherent weakness in "split-the-difference" management.

The upper right-hand corner, 9, 9 grid position, is the ideal of team management—"ideal" in the sense that optimum production is forthcoming as a result of optimum concern for people. This theoretically perfect mixture has been presented by Blake and Mouton as being dependent on behavioral sciences. Fuller elaboration of the managerial potential of the grid is reflected in the later Blake–Mouton publication, *Building a Dynamic Corporation through Grid Organization Development* (Reading, Mass.: Addison-Wesley Publishing Co., Inc., 1969).[8]

The simplicity of these managerial styles need not diminish even the most complex assessment of "interpersonal" aspects of management. The 9, 1 can be either ingratiating or infuriating, or anything in between, as a personality. The ideal 9, 9 can similarly be popular or disliked as a personality. Few if any can gain years of experience in correctional management without meeting the 1, 1, either as a charming procrastinator or an embittered cynic.

Managerial styles can be clarified yet further by recalling the brief discussion on research in the preceding chapter, in the following context:

> How best to organize the efforts of individuals to achieve desired objectives has long been one of the world's most important, difficult, and controversial problems. Many people have worked hard to find better ways, but progress has been slow. In recent years, a new approach is being made based on advances in research methodology. It is now possible to measure such dimensions of organizational functioning as motivational forces, communication effectiveness, and decision-making processes. Rigorous quantitative research can now be used in place of the cruder methods available previously. The sample-interview survey, controlled field experiments, and refined methods of statistical and mathematical analysis are some of the tools useful in such research.[9]

Bringing research to bear directly upon "such dimensions of organizational functioning as motivational forces, communication effectiveness, and decision-making processes" necessarily improves understanding of the impact of certain managerial styles. And this understanding in

---

[8] Coffey, *Administration of Criminal Justice*, pp. 30–31.
[9] R. Likert, *New Patterns of Management* (New York: McGraw-Hill Book Company, 1961), p. 5.

turn increases the possibility of successfully utilizing many of the managerial methods that will now be presented.

## MANAGERIAL METHODS

The methods involved in managing the correctional organization are significant beyond the immediate and obvious utility of "having methods". The very existence of such methods, regardless of whether they are good or poor, clarifies the key distinction between the practice and the management of corrections.

However, a great deal of what passes for managerial methods in the correctional field can be reduced to little more than "span-of-control" exercises—a term that refers to the number of employees that can be controlled by one manager at any given time. This is unfortunate, because of the limitations such a restricted concept imposes on managerial creativity, and because of the error often found in control-span "rules":

> Span of control has long been a controversial subject. Unfortunately, discussion for the most part has been limited to consideration of Urwick's simple hypothesis: "No superior can supervise directly the work of more than five, or at most six, subordinates whose work interlocks." The controversy, though bitter, has been limited to a few active participants. Among most managers the rule is widely quoted (without the final qualification) as one of the cardinal principles of management.
>
> Rules of thumb are extremely handy, a quality that undoubtedly contributes to their popularity. But such important decisions as those involving organization structure should be guided by more than a simple rule, particularly when the basis for the rule is unknown to most. Only a full awareness of the basic issues involved will result in organization structures truly suited to the fundamental purposes of each enterprise.[10]

Legitimate though concern with control spans may be, the limitations and potential for error that are inherent in conceiving of managerial methods in such a context justify a wider concept, a broader scope.

If we keep in mind the discussion of managerial functions presented in Chapter 2, it becomes possible to introduce managerial methods in a manner that incorporates control-span concepts but also goes on to establish *accountability* for each segment of the management process—since accountability is a critical factor in goal-oriented administration—through consideration of managerial *roles* and managerial *functions*, which are the main segment of managerial *methods*.

[10] R. E. Thompson, "Span of Control Conceptions and Misconceptions," *Business Horizons*, Vol. 7, No. 2 (Summer 1964), 49.

## Methods, Roles, and Functions

The rationale for relating roles and functions to managerial methods is, simply stated, that *any method of effectively managing a correctional organization includes both roles and functions.*

Roles and functions, then, form a significant part of any successful managerial method, whether or not the role or function is made explicitly clear. Of course, as will be noted, the clearer the function, the greater the accountability:

> Managerial role includes behavior that is "expected," taking into consideration the *status* of the manager—a *status* specified by a *position description.* In the sense that the actual expectation is for this "performance" to be "played," the *position description* of a management status is also related to the theatrical definition of role. . . . Role then can be defined simply as the *performance of expected managerial functions.* . . . Managerial functions . . . become the most significant feature of managerial role. . . .[11]

To clarify the concept of role–function–method further, management methods are more effective when the role is evaluated and the function is measured. A manager could scarcely be held accountable for a role that consists of only vague expectations; but by clarifying explicit functions that can be measured, the manager can be held accountable for tangible results that are also measured.

Put another way, results-oriented correctional administration stands to gain greater accountability through measurement—through functional interfacing between managerial levels—than through evaluations.

## Functions and Interfacing

The term *interfacing* has been applied in so many differing contexts that it is necessary to clarify its definition in a system of goal-oriented management. Simply stated, the term *interface* in functionally systematic management means *enough overlap of management functions for communication but not enough to distort managerial roles.* Interfaces between managerial functions are obviously not functional when overlapped so much that roles are not clear—when questions of "who is accountable for which" can be raised. Having *no* overlap creates the same chaotic management pattern, by eliminating communication.

Either situation tends to distort roles and decrease incentive for the managerial level, thus "losing the managerial status." To minimize sensitivity to such status loss would be absurd in view of indications that

[11] Coffey, *Administration of Criminal Justice*, pp. 61–62.

even the automation of decision-aiding information can be perceived as threatening by managers:

> During the past few years, thousands of hard-working middle managers have looked on with rising uneasiness while theoreticians of all hues have been cheerfully debating what effects the inexorable spread of electronic data processing will have on their future. Has the death knell sounded for middle management? A good many authorities have intimated as much, forecasting that, with the widespread reorganization necessitated by EDP, a vast number of middle-management jobs will either vanish altogether or become so structured that for all practical purposes their incumbents will become mere supervisors, denuded of their decision-making powers and stripped of their status.[12]

Our definition of interfacing, since it involves the overlap of management functions, calls for a clear definition of these functions. But definitions of functions can vary widely, the only criterion being that, collectively measured, they produce "success"—that is, goal achievement.

For the purposes of this discussion, *interfacing* refers to the relationship between the managerial functions of defining *results*, defining *what* is required for achieving results, defining *who* is needed to achieve results, and defining *how* results are to be achieved. (See the accompanying diagram.)

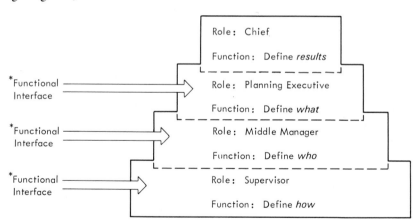

*Functional interface means sufficient overlap to insure communication, but not enough to distort roles.

CORRECTIONAL MANAGEMENT BY FUNCTION

[12] D. R. Shaul, "What's Really Ahead For Middle Management?" *Personnel*, November–December 1964, p. 8.

Correctional administration, then, is in need of dividing "success" into component parts, and calling each part a *function*. Each function, so defined, is assigned to a *role*—the occupant of the role being held accountable for the function or functions assigned.

The *role* of warden may or may not have various prison *functions* assigned, depending upon the size of the prison. In small prisons, the warden role might have assigned the functions of staff shift scheduling and group leader; in large prisons, these functions may be delegated to other managerial roles. So we see that role and function are not the same.

But just as important, the occupant of the role is also accountable for interfacing his assigned functions with other appropriate functions sufficiently to communicate without distorting roles. Only then does management by function become possible. And regardless of the managerial methods adopted, functional accountability is highly desirable if success is sought on an ongoing basis.

In the case of the functions depicted in the diagram ("Correctional Management by Function"), the managerial system is easy to describe regardless of the complexity of programming involved. For example, here are applied function interfaces within a large prison, or perhaps a large probation department:

   I.  Role: Chief probation office
      Function: Define *results*
      Method: A.  Interface with court
             B.  Interface with law enforcement
             C.  Interface with custody institutions
             D.  Interface with community
             E.  Interface with executive management
                 1.  Director of system management
                     a.  Managerial and staff development
                     b.  Research
                     c.  Cost–benefit analysis
                     d.  Organization systems
                 2.  Director of community services
                     a.  Sensor matrix
                     b.  Community analysis
                 3.  Director of field services
                     a.  Juvenile
                     b.  Adult
  II.  Role: Division director
      Function: Define *what*—*what* is required in the way of objectives to
                   achieve the goals set by the chief's interfaces; to plan
      Method: A.  Interface with chief
             B.  Interface with middle management
              C.  Interface with other planning executives
              D.  Formulate viable plans

III. Role: Middle manager
    Function: Define *who—who* within the organization is best suited to staff the programs called for by the planned objectives; to develop complete managerial expertise of available and projected staff resources
    Method: A. Interface with division director
           B. Interface with supervisor
           C. Interface with other middle managers
           D. Staff programs
IV. Role: Supervisor
    Function: Define *how—how* best to apply techniques and skills available through assigned staff; how best to achieve objectives
    Method: A. Interface with manager
           B. Interface with staff through methods known as *participatory management* (i.e., one facet of what will later be discussed in terms of staff influence upon organizational goals and objectives

### The Smaller Department

Although the example above is geared to the large correctional organization, note the ease with which a very small agency can adopt accountability by function:

I. Role: Chief probation officer
    Functions: A. Define *results*
             B. Define *what*
II. Role: Supervisor
    Functions: A. Define *who*
             B. Define *how*

Of course, these oversimplified examples fail to reflect the complexity involved in interfacing managerial functions in an effective manner. Nevertheless, they clarify a managerially significant aspect—that of the distinction between *efficiency* and *effectiveness:*

> Managerial roles can be evaluated as *efficient* on the basis of simply "doing what's expected"; managerial functions are measured in terms of results achieved, which is the definition of *effectiveness*. In other words, *efficiency* allows you to not be lost because you don't know where you're going. *Effectiveness* measures allow you to be lost only because you're lost.[13]

Not surprisingly, managerial methods that permit "knowing enough about where you're going to know when you're lost" have to do with *information*—management information.

---

[13] Coffey, *Administration of Criminal Justice*, p. 106.

## Management Information Systems as Part of Methods

Anything as general as "information" covers a broad scope—even when restricted to management information. In terms of how MIS relates to the systems model, its definition never encompasses that which is not directly related to management functions of *how, who, what,* and *results.* . . . Still admittedly broad . . . [it] nevertheless confines MIS to the specific function . . . to the degree that functions and roles are clear within an organization. . . . The complexity of information is never greater than any given function. . . . A well-designed MIS systematically provides specific decision-aiding data to specific functions—sorting relevant from irrelevant data. . . .[14]

One of the key words in these remarks about the MIS is "decision-aiding." Perhaps brief consideration of both the nature and the historical perspective of modern aids to managerial decisions would be useful before exploring the MIS further:

The twentieth century has provided us with many changes. The two that will probably have the most effect on mankind are atomic energy and the computer. Of these two, the computer will affect a larger number of individuals and may in the long run have the greatest impact on society.

Like atomic energy, new uses are discovered every day and the capability of the computer is expanding, while the costs per transaction are steadily declining. It is this increased capability and reducing costs per transaction that has resulted in the computer touching our lives in an ever-increasing number of ways. The futuristic probabilities as to each individual's daily contact are hundredfold. Management needs to understand the current capabilities and limitations and at the same time plan for the future capabilities. . . .

. . . Many people refer to isolated data as information. This is what has caused some of the past problems of one department not utilizing another's "information" data. For example, the name Henry Morgan, standing by itself, means very little; but when we combine it with another piece of data, such as "building permit," then it begins to have meaning and a value to others. Thus, the police, fire, utilities, license and permit, planning, and building departments *all* have an immediate interest. The recreation, transportation, civil defense and others *may* have an interest. The amount of interest is determined by what the accumulation of data, now referred to as information, reveals about the project. If the information indicates that it is to be a new bar or restaurant, then the police, fire, and others have a greater interest than if it is going to be a single-family dwelling. . . .

. . . The integrated information system has been presented as a tool for the working-level employee; the policeman on the beat, the desk sergeant, the clerk, the building inspector, the fireman, and others. What is in it for the management? The police captain is able to deploy his watch based

[14] *Ibid.,* p. 104.

on the information in a dynamic data base which shows where the activity is occurring or is likely to occur.

The question for management is not whether to automate. The question is a management question. If the manager wishes to maximize the resources of the organization, he should consider an integrated system. This system focuses and integrates the flow of information from a multiplicity of sources for coordinated efforts.[15]

The nature of and the historical perspective for aiding managerial decisions relates directly, then, to the *use* of data. But to be a genuine aid, the data must be selective. From our discussion of decisions and policy in Chapter 2, we can see that the sorting of relevant from irrelevant data emerges as the critical factor in aiding decisions—whether the correctional administration uses policy as the primary guide for the decisions, or uses policy as "fail-safe" for function breakdown.

Other noteworthy considerations related to MIS have to do with "impact":

> Since most organizational activity is centered around the acquisition, production, or transfer of information in various forms, employees are the targets of a conglomeration of data, information, and intelligence. Decisions are communicated by passing information to those with the delegated authority and responsibility for performance. Standards are established against which product quality, cost, and completion time are measured; evaluation procedures are developed for checking performance against the standards. The entire operation is continually monitored by a reporting system that communicates performance information to the manager, who uses a control system to feed back instructions to correct or prevent deviations from planned performance.[16]

But the MIS can also have impact in terms of confusion:

> In a day when words are used with no real attempt to define them, it should be no surprise to find that some people are puzzled by the term "management information system." For one thing, people tend to confuse a management information system with an electronic data processing (or computer) system. Are they the same? If so, are all computers management information systems? If not, can you have a management information system without a computer?[17]

MIS as a concept also has impact in terms of managerial control:

---

[15] Carl F. Davis, "Information Please: Integrated Information System," *Crime Prevention Review*, Vol. 1, No. 1 (October 1973), 25, 26–27, and 33.
[16] R. L. Johnson and I. H. Derman, "How Intelligent is Your MIS?" *Business Horizons*, February 1970.
[17] J. W. Konvalinka, and H. G. Trentin, "Management Information Systems," *Management Services*, September–October 1965, p. 27.

It is clear at this point of our discussion that control involves the communication of information. In an operational sense, information is that which can or does influence the comportment of another.[18]

Moreover, for a number of reasons, the impact of MIS seems to generate managerial enthusiasm—unfortunate enthusiasm, in many instances:

The growing preoccupation of operations researchers and management scientists with Management Information Systems (MIS's) is apparent. In fact, for some the design of such systems has almost become synonymous with operations research or management science. Enthusiasm for such systems is understandable: It involves the researcher in a romantic relationship with the most glamorous instrument of our time, the computer. Such enthusiasm is understandable but, nevertheless, some of the excesses to which it has led are not excusable.[19]

More serious consideration of the impact of MIS in terms of how such a system is installed may, however, redirect some of this dysfunctional enthusiasm:

Experience with any data-processing system will show that the success of any installation is dependent upon not only the design but also the implementation and control of the system. Many an installation has failed because of inadequate consideration of each of these components of management information systems. It is axiomatic to state that design is related to control, since within any system documentation must be available in order for management to accurately assess results against the planned objectives. Control is necessary during the design stage, during programming, as well as during the computer-operation stage.[20]

Returning to correctional applications of the MIS concept, we should consider the entire system of information in corrections—management and otherwise.

CORRECTIONAL USE. In terms of a correctional organization employing an MIS and the methods and functions discussed thus far, consider the system of information shown in the following diagram. The diagram depicts a correctional information system with subsystems for administration, for management, and for the operation of the correctional organization—all having in common the sorting of relevant from irrelevant data for decision aiding within a particular function.

[18] C. R. Dechert, "The Development of Cybernetics," *The American Behavioral Scientist*, June 1965, pp. 15–20.
[19] R. E. Ackoff, "Management Misinformation Systems," *Management Science*, December 1967, p. 147.
[20] P. P. Schoderbek, "Design, Implementation, and Control of the Management Information Systems," in *Management Systems* (New York: John Wiley & Sons, Inc., 1971), p. 356.

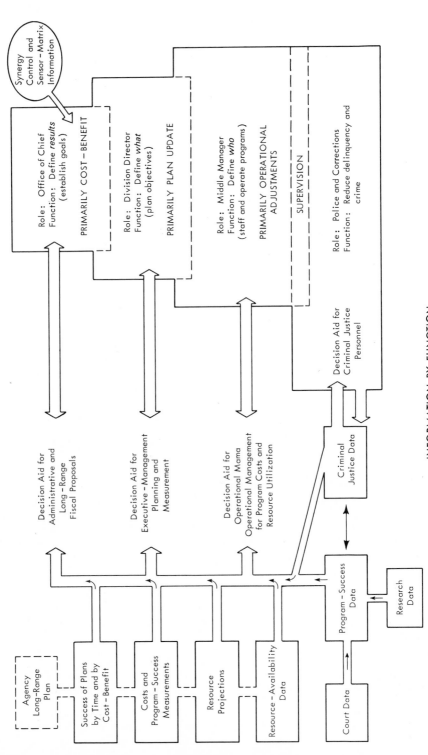

INFORMATION BY FUNCTION

Synergy Control and Sensor – Matrix Information

Role: Office of Chief
Function: Define *results*
(establish goals)

PRIMARILY COST – BENEFIT

Role: Division Director
Function: Define *what*
(plan objectives)

PRIMARILY PLAN UPDATE

Role: Middle Manager
Function: Define *who*
(staff and operate programs)

PRIMARILY OPERATIONAL
ADJUSTMENTS

SUPERVISION

Role: Police and Corrections
Function: Reduce delinquency and crime

Decision Aid for Criminal Justice Personnel

Decision Aid for Administrative and Long – Range Fiscal Proposals

Decision Aid for Executive – Management Planning and Measurement

Decision Aid for Operational Mama Operational Management for Program Costs and Resource Utilization

Criminal Justice Data

Agency Long-Range Plan

Success of Plans by Time and by Cost – Benefit

Costs and Program – Success Measurements

Resource Projections

Resource – Availability Data

Court Data

Program – Success Data

Research Data

60

Of course, such a system must be automated electronically, not only to retrieve records but to sort by function. Far less involved systems, however, can be made to produce many of the same results, once the following premise is accepted:

> All management methods improve in proportion to the relevant, decision-aiding information made available systematically.

The nature of some of the information varies between organizations, and between subsystems within organizations—a point that will become increasingly clear in the chapters covering management of probation, correctional institutions, and parole. Nonetheless, relevant, decision-aiding information remains critical.

## MANAGERIAL APPROACHES

Within the context of managerial approaches, there are any number of "packages"—combinations of elements in a given approach—that might be used in a correctional organization. The styles and the methods of correctional managers need not necessarily change in many of the available approaches.

Isolating the appropriate managerial approach is nevertheless more difficult than might be believed; let us examine some of the categories of managerial approaches.

### Theory X and Theory Y

The late Douglas McGregor evolved what many consider the most useful conceptual tool ever devised for examining managerial approaches in general:

> The conventional conception of management's task in harnessing human energy to organizational requirements can be stated broadly in terms of three propositions. In order to avoid the complications introduced by a label, I shall call this set of propositions "Theory X":
>
> 1. Management is responsible for organizing the elements of productive enterprise—money, materials, equipment, people—in the interest of economic ends.
> 2. With respect to people, this is a process of directing their efforts, motivating them, controlling their actions, modifying their behavior to fit the needs of the organization.
> 3. Without this active intervention by management, people would be passive—even resistant—to organizations' needs. They must therefore be persuaded, rewarded, punished, controlled—their activities must be di-

rected. This is management's task in managing subordinate managers or workers. We often sum it up by saying that magament consists of getting things done through other people.

Behind this conventional theory there are several additional beliefs—less explicit, but widespread:

4. The average man is by nature indolent—he works as little as possible.

5. He lacks ambition, dislikes responsibility, prefers to be led.

6. He is inherently self-centered, indifferent to organizational needs.

7. He is by nature resistant to change.

8. He is gullible, not very bright, the ready dupe of the charlatan and the demagogue.[21]

For the purposes of relating these observations specifically to correctional administration, consider them in the context of the following:

McGregor points out that from the framework of Theory X, management has outlined various means of accomplishing its task by either reward or punishment. As he saw it, management was confronted with two alternatives inherent in the concept of accomplishing work "through other people"; the "hard management approach"—relying on coercion and threat with stringent control as the mode of directing employee behavior; or the "soft management approach," which included satisfaction of employee demands through permissiveness and focus on harmony, hoping that people managed in this manner would accept organizational direction.

Placed in the context of criminal justice, many examples verify this part of McGregor's reasoning. Two state prisons may be nearly identical in terms of structure, size, design, programs, resources, and so forth. The management style of each warden may flow from Theory X. But one warden may operate on the "hard" principle, the other on the "soft" approach, each functioning from the framework of Theory X, but with very different results. The guards and treatment personnel working under the administration of the "hard" warden may report that "a man always knows where he stands on his staff." The personnel under the "soft" warden may report that "the staff really count in here."

But McGregor nevertheless conceived of both these extremes as flowing from the same management position. Moreover, he saw them as presenting major management problems.

The "hard management" approach appears to be related to such counterforces as restricted output, unionism, and antagonism toward organizational objectives. On the other hand, "soft management" has produced harmony performance or production. McGregor suggested what amounts

[21] D. McGregor, *Leadership and Motivation* (Cambridge, Mass.: The M.I.T. Press, 1966), pp. 5-6.

to a third alternative, beginning with a re-evaluation of managerial assumptions—inclusion of behavioral science, which in turn became the basis for McGregor's Theory Y. And as in the case of X, Theory Y also has great relevance to much of criminal justice management.

As McGregor developed Theory Y, the premises and assumptions of management emerged in terms of creating opportunities, removing obstacles, providing guidance rather than control, releasing potential, and, above all else, encouraging growth. McGregor interpreted research findings as evidence that Theory X assumptions were in error to the degree that Theory X management is dysfunctional. In this regard, Theory Y differs from Theory X in much the same way that Peter Drucker's "management by objectives" theory, to be discussed later in the chapter, differs from "management by control."

Theory Y management, according to McGregor, is not the "soft management" indicated by one extreme of Theory X. Instead, as an approach to accomplish work through others, it must take into account the employee's desire to "do meaningful work" when given the opportunity. Various difficulties involved in Theory Y were acknowledged by McGregor, but primarily in terms of the violation of managerial tradition—violation of the expectation of both management and employees to jobs that utilized small proportions of their capabilities have, according to McGregor, accustomed employees to ignore the possibility of work providing ego-need satisfaction of any kind. Although McGregor conceded difficulties generated by a history of Theory X management, he nevertheless maintained the position that managerial ingenuity and innovation could prevail.[22]

Now, within this context of McGregor's X and Y theory, the concepts discussed earlier in relation to the Grid® and managerial styles can be combined to form the basis of three categories of managerial approach: the "command approach," the "human-resources approach" and the "results approach." Of course, it must be emphasized that *each approach involves many characteristics of the other two;* classification here is based solely upon the predominant operation and philosophy.

### Three Managerial Approaches

Concerning these three approaches to criminal justice management, it has been said:

These three approaches, considered against the background of functional or dysfunctional system, are defined as follows:

[22] McGregor, p. 28.

*Command.* Command management is essentially what Douglas McGregor considered Theory X—whether "soft" or "hard." The command manager assumes responsibility for motivating and/or directing the activities and behavior of employees. Beyond the implications of McGregor's Theory X, a command manager also operates on the premise that continuous orders produce continuous achievement of organizational goals *independent* of concerns for production or morale.

*Human Resources.* The Theory Y that McGregor described also delineates a great deal of the human-resource management style. Concern for the frustrations, anxieties, and personal adjustments of employees goes beyond either the "soft X" or the ineffective Y manager. Human-resource approaches include integration of personal problems in the task of management, whether or not such concerns can be directly related to organizational goals of any kind. Although similar to the 1, 9, "country club" management style of the grid, human-resource styles establish happiness as a legitimate management task beyond the concept of employee morale.

*Results.* The approach to management referred to here means simply a reduction of *all measurements* used by management to predetermined, clearly defined, measurable results. The *only* measurement in this approach is the *accomplishment* of such results.

By *accomplishment* is meant the prison warden's success in programming early release through proven rehabilitation; the chief probation officer's success in programming a reduction in recidivism; the police chief's successful reduction of assaultive crimes—all presumably desirable criminal justice *results*.[23]

Once again placing the discussion in the context of *efficiency* and *effectiveness* will permit estimates as to the usefulness of each of these three approaches to the administration of corrections, as in the following table:

## SYSTEM AND APPROACH EVALUATION

|  | *System by Function* | *Nonsystem* | *System by Roles* |
|---|---|---|---|
| Command management approach | Little use to corrections | Little use to corrections | Great use to corrections |
| Human-resource management approach | Little use | Great use | Little use |
| Results management approach | Great use | Little use | Great use |

[23] *Ibid.*, p. 36.

Before elaborating on what is meant by "little use to corrections" or "great use to corrections," let us recall the earlier distinction between *efficiency* and *effectiveness*, then consider the following:

## STYLE AND APPROACH

| Command (9, 1 Grid $_{®}$) | Human-Resource (9, 9 Grid $_{®}$) | Results (9, 1 and 9, 9 Grid $_{®}$) |
|---|---|---|
| "Authoritarian" | "Democratic" | Accountability for well-defined, tangible, measurable functions that are goal-oriented as the *only* measure of management or staff "success"—communication both upward and downward, staff influence on goals; the "democratic" segment of administrative authority |
| "Downward communication" | "Upward communication" | |
| "Staff resist development" | "Staff creative" | |
| "Staff produce little" | "Staff produce much" | |

When the distinction between efficiency and effectiveness is not made clearly, human-resource management has what appears to be considerable advantage over the command approach. Once this distinction *is* made, however, it remains simply a matter of placing relative priority on one or the other—on effectiveness or efficiency. Some may argue that effectiveness and efficiency are actually the same thing; but think of an *efficiently* running automobile (engine tuned, transmission power column, rear axles proportionately aligned, and so on) that cannot *effectively* remove itself from the mud. Is the priority on the car's process, or on the outcome of riding in the car—that is, on results?

Assuming that correctional administration defines an outcome, or results to be achieved, the usefulness of the results approach to management is great, whether by function or by roles, as discussed earlier. (Of course, the results approach is of little use in a "nonsystem." Indeed, in light of the quoted description of the three approaches to management, the *only* useful approach in nonsystem is human-resource—a significant consideration that will be explored further later.) Let us use the desirability of effectively achieving results to explore the advantages of the results approach.

In combining the 9, 1 and the 9, 9 Grid $_{®}$ positions, however, the results approach tends to depend increasingly upon accountability for results achievement and, further, to depend in many ways upon clearly defined functions. A number of reasons exist for this, including what appears to be a mutually exclusive positioning of the 9, 1 and the 9, 9 styles —particularly when the two are isolated conceptually, as in a vacuum.

This being the case, the effectiveness of the results approach is much greater in the system by functions than in the system by roles, even though the effort to achieve results is valuable in the role system, where a manager's status is evaluated rather than measured.

But the functional systems model [24] is by no means the only organized approach. Consideration of two other organized approaches might be useful—management by objectives (MBO) and organizational development (OD), either of which can be evaluated in terms of the system for which it might be used—along with the categories of command, human-resource, and results.

## MANAGEMENT BY OBJECTIVES

The striking similarity between MBO and what has been referred to as the "functional systems model" is immediate:

> Peter Drucker was probably the first author and educator to specifically refer to the subject as Management by Objectives. He described it as a technique for effectively moving an organization in a growthful way. Numerous authors and educators followed Drucker. . . .
>
> . . . There is a vast array of nomenclature applied to the subject, some of which is on the following pages.
>
> > Standards of Performance
> > Management by Objectives
> > Objectives
> > Goal Setting
> > Expected Results
> > Measurement
> > Planning and Reviewing Performance
> > Planning and Reviewing
> > Performance Standards
> > Old Management [25]

Although many consider Peter Drucker the "father" of the MBO concept,[26] the correctional field itself is also responsible in part for the growing popularity of MBO:

[24] For a full-scale, technical elaboration of what is here being referred to as the "functional systems model," see Coffey, *Administration of Criminal Justice*, Chapters 4 through 8 and 13 through 15.
[25] G. H. Varney, "What is Management by Objectives?" in *Management by Objectives* (Chicago: The Dartnell Corporation, 1971), pp. 3–4.
[26] See, for example, Peter F. Drucker, *The Practice of Management* (New York: Harper & Row, Publishers, 1954).

Some of the larger correctional agencies are beginning to focus more sharply on the matter of *objectives*. Correctional administrators are combining *managerial* competence with *correctional* competence for the solution of pressing social problems. It is axiomatic that both the production and the use of tested knowledge tend to force increased attention to *ends* as well as *means*.

Specifying objectives and using these objectives as guides for conducting organizational activities is becoming increasingly characteristic of "modern" management in all fields. These techniques are elements of a new managerial model—"management by objectives."

Minimizing reliance on trial and error, rule of thumb, ideology, and tradition, this model provides rational guidelines for ordering and allocating manpower, equipment, and fiscal resources. It facilitates decision-making, simplifies the assessment of performance, and, ideally, encourages employees to become self-directing and self-motivating when they identify with organizational goals.

Management by objectives has not yet made significant headway in probation, in particular, or in correction generally. One reason may be the persisting conflict and confusion in society about how to deal with persons who offend against the law. A second may lie in the characteristics of correctional managers who tend to lack sophistication in the realm of management science. . . .

. . . The specification of objectives is simpler for some organizations than for others. Those with a profit orientation have an advantage over those whose function is service. The task of developing and implementing objectives in correction might be facilitated somewhat by regarding it as a problem of formulating, in economic and social terms, a profit-and-loss equivalent. . . .[27]

Other clear similarities between MBO and the functional systems model include significant concern with managerial style:

MBO is too useful a concept to be accepted blindly. Its difficulties must be squarely faced if management is to take full advantage of its strengths. Let me start out with the question of objectives, then describe the major problems which arise from MBO in practice, and finally suggest the realistic limits to MBO's use. . . .

. . . MBO is an umbrella concept covering a multitude of objectives. For some it is a means of introducing a Theory Y oriented form of autonomy in which managers are given freedom to set their own goals. Others approach it in terms of Theory X—as a means of tightening managerial control and getting subordinates to do exactly what management wants. . . .[28]

Moreover, the concern of Drucker with achieving a measurable outcome is identical with the functional systems model:

[27] C. Terwilliger and S. Adams, "Probation Department Management by Objectives," *Crime and Delinquency*, Vol. 15, No. 2 (April 1969), 227–30.
[28] G. Strauss, "Management by Objectives: A Critical View," *Training and Development Journal*, Vol. 26, No. 4 (April 1972), 10.

. . . Peter Drucker contends that the manager's authority is grounded in the objective responsibility of the job, based on performance standards which are objective and measurable. He contends that objectives are needed in every area where performance and results directly and totally affect the survival of the business.[29]

Versions of MBO other than Drucker's, however, begin to differ slightly from the systems model—particularly in terms of the differences between the results approaches and the human-resource approach:

> First is the classical one enunciated by George Odiorne. Odiorne holds that MBO is a process whereby superior and subordinate managers jointly identify common goals, define each individual's major area of responsibility in terms of results expected of him and use these measures as guides for operating the unit and assessing the contributions of each of its members. Odiorne would establish measures of organizational performance and definitions of unit measures and individual measures. He places his emphasis on economic survival, after which other goals may follow. . . .[30]

This difference is also subtly detectable in terms of the process of adopting a particularly managerial approach—of "installing" the approach:

> . . . In installing an MBO system, two factors are important: (1) achieving organization-wide acceptance of the MBO idea; (2) obtaining the necessary behavior that will allow an MBO program to be implemented successfully. . . .[31]

The functional systems model conceives of "installing" in terms of "components of success," preceding the definition of success; that is, functions that are measurable are isolated before success itself is defined, in order to ensure an ongoing functional system *after* success is defined. This, of course, is intended to retain a priority on effectiveness.

Replacing such priorities with priorities on "acceptance" as such and on "behavior" as such makes it possible to achieve the priorities without producing results. Moreover, when "acceptance" and "behavior" are the norm, one who accepts and behaves cannot easily be held accountable for what his acceptance and behavior fail to produce, since these are far less measurable than results not achieved.

*This by no means relegates acceptance and behavior to insignificance in the systems model.* Indeed, as the next chapter will elaborate, participa-

---

29 H. Levinson, "Management by Objectives: A Critique," *Training and Development Journal*, Vol. 26, No. 4 (April 1972), 3.

30 *Ibid.*

31 W. R. Mahler, "Management by Objectives: A Consultant's Viewpoint," *Training and Development Journal*, Vol. 26, No. 4 (April 1972), 16.

tory management is vital to managerial success. But it is far more useful to correctional success if participatory management emerges in significance *after* the measurable functions are clarified, and if the participation occurs instead in setting the goals objectives of the organization. The crew of a sailing ship accepts specific accountability for their specific functions only after there is consensus on the destination—at least, if reaching that destination is important.

Perhaps this analogy relates to the following:

As everyone in the field knows, management development's most chronic affliction has been one of being beguiled continuously by new concepts, systems or programs which often prove to be ineffective—if not counterproductive. It could be argued that any profession, so regularly victimized, is in part playing accomplice to its own victimization. However, that is another issue. . . .

. . . Though MBO emerges as a very attractive program for organizations that have the time, there are by common agreement important problem areas. The speakers identify important problem areas as being:

frequent failure by management to do the sustained follow-up work necessary to make MBO systems viable,

the continuing difficulty in reconciling organizational goals with personal goals,

the problem of how to relate MBO goal performance with the reward system . . .[32]

However, MBO holds a great deal of promise for correctional administrations that are unable to adopt the full, comprehensive systems approach.[33] For example:

. . . As internal consultants and trainers it was the responsibility of the authors to design an MBO program that would fit the needs of the adult probation department. There were no existing MBO programs in use among the rehabilitation agencies that could be used as a model. Therefore the business model that was familiar to the authors was retooled to meet the needs of the probation department.

The program was installed in three stages:

*Stage One:* a series of meetings to teach the MBO method of goal setting and objective writing to the top administration and throughout each level of the organization.

*Stage Two:* a total department workshop for team building and objective writing.

[32] W. Wohlking, "Management by Objectives: A Critical View," *Training and Development Journal*, Vol. 26, No. 4 (April 1972), 2.
[33] Coffey, *Administration of Criminal Justice*.

*Stage Three:* the installation of an evaluation and reporting system, and an ongoing program of updating the objectives through sessions with individual divisions and work units to revise their objectives or to write new ones. These ongoing meetings would then become a feedback mechanism to the top administration indicating the concerns and motivation of the working units within the department. . . .[34]

Of course so brief an overview scarcely does MBO justice. The scope of MBO is considerably wider than implied by so brief a discussion.[35]

The National Advisory Commission on Criminal Justice Standards and Goals sums up the correctional context of MBO rather succinctly:

Management by objectives (MBO) emphasizes a goal-oriented philosophy and attitude. Goal-oriented management focuses on results with less concern for method, as long as it is within acceptable legal and moral limits. Traditional management, on the other hand, tends to be task-oriented, with emphasis on task performance without adequate regard for results.

The purpose of management by objectives is to: (1) develop a mutually understood statement regarding the organization's direction and (2) provide criteria for measuring organization and individual performance. The statement is a hierarchical set of interrelated and measurable goals, objectives, and subobjectives. If properly conducted, the process may be as important as the objectives themselves because it improves vertical and horizontal communication and emphasizes interdepartmental integration.

For an MBO system to be implemented successfully, it must be based on a participative management philosophy and fulfill several specific conditions.

First, the full support of top management is essential. Indeed, at each level of management the superior's degree of acceptance of this managerial approach will determine substantially whether or not subordinates accept the system and try to make it work.

A second necessary condition is a goal-oriented management philosophy. The motivational value of an MBO approach depends in great part upon giving each manager and employee responsibility to carry out a job without constant supervision and then assessing him on his degree of accomplishment.

Third, each superior-subordinate relationship should be characterized by the highest degree of cooperation and mutual respect possible.

Fourth, managerial focus should be on any deviations from agreed-upon levels of goal attainment, not on personalities; and the evaluation system

[34] J. E. Taylor and E. Bertinot, "An O.D. Intervention to Install Participatory Management in a Bureaucratic Organization," *Training and Development Journal,* Vol. 27, No. 1 (January 1973), 18.
[35] See, for example, J. W. Humble, *Management By Objectives in Action* (New York: McGraw-Hill, 1973); See also *Management By Objectives* (Chicago: The Dartnell Corp., 1971); as well as P. Drucker, *The Practice of Management* (New York: Harper & Bros., 1954).

should report any such deviations to the manager or employee establishing the goal, not to his superior.

The fifth condition is feedback. If managers are to be evaluated on the results they obtain, they require timely and accurate readings of their progress to take corrective action when necessary. Further they need substantially accurate projections and interpretations of demographic, technical, social, legal, and other developments likely to affect their progress and performance.

Finally, to be successful, an intensive training program must precede organizational implementation. A followup consultative service should be available to organizational members or units requiring assistance in implementing this system.

Designing and implementing management by objectives requires the achievement of the following sequential steps:

1. An ongoing system capable of accurately identifying and predicting changes in the environment in which the organization functions.

2. Administrative capability through a management information system to provide data quickly to appropriate organizational members, work groups, or organizational units for their consideration and possible utilization.

3. Clearly established and articulated organizational and individual goals, mutually accepted through a process of continuous interaction between management and workers and between various levels of management. Unilateral imposition of organizational goals on lower echelon participants will not result in an MBO system but another bureaucracy.

4. An ongoing evaluation of the organizational and individual goals in the light of feedback from the system. Such feedback and evaluation may result in the resetting of goals.

5. A properly designed and functioning organizational system for effective and efficient service delivery. In such a system, goal-oriented collaboration and cooperation are organizationally facilitated, and administrative services fully support efforts at goal accomplishment.

6. A managerial and work climate highly conducive to employee motivation and self-actualization toward organizational goal accomplishments. Such a climate should be developed and nurtured through the application of a participative style of management, to be discussed shortly.

7. A properly functioning system for appraising organizational, work group, and individual progress toward goal attainment.[36]

For purposes of examining the comparative usefulness of managerial approaches to correctional administration, hopefully enough now has been overviewed to illustrate some of the great potential of MBO along with some of the limitations—limitations quite susceptible to adjustment on the same basis as the functional systems model.

[36] National Advisory Commission on Criminal Justice Standards and Goals, *Corrections* (Washington, D.C.: U. S. Government Printing Office, January 1973), pp. 445–446.

One more approach may complete the clarification of examining managerial approaches in terms of usefulness to corrections—organizational development or "OD."

Again the National Advisory Commission on Criminal Justice Standards and Goals sums up the correctional context succinctly:

> Managing a human resource organization is probably even more difficult than managing other public agencies because many traditional management tools are not directly applicable. Data describing effects of the correctional process relate to behavior or attitudes and are subject to subjective, frequently conflicting interpretations. The feedback loops necessary for judging the consequences of policies are difficult to create and suffer from incomplete and inaccurate information. There has not been in corrections an organized and consistent relation between evaluative research and management action.

> The management of corrections as a human resource organization must be viewed broadly in terms of how offenders, employees, and various organization processes (communications, decisionmaking, and others) are combined into what is called 'the corrections process' . . . .

> . . . Management by objectives (MBO), planning and organization analysis are elements of a relatively new concept called organization development (OD). Bennis defines it as a 'response to change, a complex educational strategy intended to change beliefs, attitudes, values, and structure of organizations so that they can better adapt to new technologies, markets and challenges and the dizzying rate of change itself.' Demands for innovation, the trend toward integrated services, and disagreement over objectives suggest that OD programs are applicable to the correction field. To specify how this could be done would require a separate book. Hence the discussion here will outline only the interrelations between basic elements of OD and will concentrate on three areas considered to be of top priority in corrections today: organization analysis, management by objectives, and planning. However, ideally and for completeness, any contemplated activity in these areas should not be considered apart from the broader concept of OD.

> Organization development is based on two sets of ideas: one relating to groups and organizations, and the other to individuals. Organizational development views organizations as many interrelated subsystems mutually affecting each other. Problem solving, therefore, is interdependent. In corrections, a simple example would be a change in the industrial production schedule that limited the time offenders could spend in counseling programs.

> A distinction is made between tasks or functions and the processes used to perform them. A planning function, for example, can be performed by a task force or a planning office, and it may begin at the operating level or the executive level. OD emphasizes *how* things are done, on the assumption that *what* is done will be determined in large part by the process. In turn, the work climate (e.g., the leadership styles discussed later) is a determinant of which processes are selected.

> Reflecting OD's social science origins, anonymous questionnaires and interviews are used to collect data on work group interrelationships, em-

ployees' attitudes, etc. Findings then are discussed with employee groups to improve their insights into such organization processes as line-staff and executive-staff communications, location of decisionmaking, and perceived roles.

Within the organization, individuals are encouraged to develop mutual trust, be candid, openly discuss conflict, and take risks. A premium is placed on the individual's self-actualization fulfillment of his needs within the organization's overall goals and objectives.

A variety of specific interventions are used to implement these ideas and are limited only by the creativity of the change agent. Team building, intergroup problem solving, surveys, reorganization, training in decisionmaking and problem solving, modifying work flows, and job enrichment are examples of the types or techniques frequently employed. An OD program usually involves an outside consultant to begin with, but it is essential to have (or develop) a capability for continuing the program within the organization. Generally, these techniques and processes are used in the work situation—the functions to be performed—to integrate the factors necessary for employee effectiveness (interpersonal skills, individual performance objectives, etc.) with the goals of the organization. OD practitioners feel that this complex process is necessary to relate organization design, planning, objectives, and employee performance.[37]

Clearly, then, "OD" is worthy of further consideration.

## ORGANIZATIONAL DEVELOPMENT

Bearing in mind the distinctions between command, human-resource and results managerial approaches, consider the following:

Some of the current enthusiasm in the field of administration is being generated from an area of applied behavioral sciences, called organizational development (OD). Managers who are keenly aware of the imminence of far-reaching societal change are beginning to think seriously of ways in which their own organizations can be more responsive, more compatible and more fully functioning in contemporary society. Organizational development, although a new and still vaguely defined field, holds promise for the practicing manager who is anxious to initiate successful change in his own organization and to be an integral part of that innovative process. Although the literature is building an inventory of cases and descriptions of techniques used to bring about important change in all types of organizations, there appear to be very little data so far about the effects of change over a period of time.[38]

The pity of it all is that it appears that some powerful technologies for the management of change do now exist. The challenge of creating an

---

[37] National Advisory Commission on Criminal Justice Standards and Goals, *Corrections* (Washington, D.C.: U. S. Government Printing Office, January 1973), pp. 442–443.

[38] N. Margulies, "Organizational Development and Changes in Organization Climate," *Public Personnel Management*, Vol. 2, No. 2 (March–April 1973), 84.

industrial democracy is realistically on the agenda in the affluent West. The primitive tactics of early capital accumulation are not needed in the present objective situation. In a different political-economic environment, the OD people could be a boon to the commonwealth.

Even now, unions or social movement organizations, student or parent groups could make use of the skills and insights of Burke and Hornstein et al. Yet the technological preoccupation evidenced in these articles results generally in a more privileged clientele. Without strong value or political criteria or perspectives, OD specialists become social scientists for hire. The ability to hire them, distributed as it is, too frequently puts them to work for those who need and deserve their aid the least.[39]

*Change*, then, is a key concept in OD, for at least two reasons: (1) the need for change in managerial approaches that no longer fit a social order that has already changed, and (2) the ethical ramifications of change isolated by the second critic cited. Before further examination of OD in terms of command, human-resource, or results approaches, a broader context for this key concept of *change* is needed:

> Most progressive managers today are deeply concerned with the problem of developing managerial strategies appropriate to the changing conditions. The word "change" is no longer even a buzz word. It has become part of our everyday language. Managers are continually working on the problems of how to develop a flexible organization which can move with changing requirements, which can be "proactive" (influencing the environment) rather than reactive. Managers are seeking ways to establish a work climate in which increasingly complex decisions can be made by people *with the information*, regardless of their location in the organization. Managers are looking for ways in which increasingly complex technologies can be managed and in which people who have an ever-higher sense of freedom and autonomy can be encouraged to want to stay and work in their organizations. . . .[40]

Change, when considered in this broader context, clearly becomes a significant part of *any* effective managerial approach—OD and otherwise.

Returning the discussion to correctional usefulness of managerial approaches, it is now clear that OD (like any legitimate managerial approach) is concerned with change, but perhaps more concerned with the *process* of change.

Of course, as noted at the outset of this discussion, any one approach has many of the characteristics of the other two—command has a great deal of human-resource and results, human-resource has a great deal of command and results, and the results approach is specifically designed to *combine* command and human-resource via functional systems.

39 R. Ross, "OD For Whom?" *Journal of Applied Behavioral Science*, Vol. 7, No. 5 (September–October 1971), 584–85.
40 R. Beckhard, *Organization Development: Strategies and Models* (Reading, Mass.: Addison-Wesley Publishing Co., Inc., 1969), p. 7.

Nevertheless, it is clear, from our brief sampling of OD literature and from more exhaustive reading,[41] that OD is a human-resource approach according to the definitions used in this chapter. This is particularly true in the correctional organizations that have engaged OD consultants with an emphasis on "sensitivity" and "training labs"—even though sensitivity, as such, is not emphasized by some of the more articulate OD advocates:

> . . . It should be clear by now that organization development is not simply *sensitivity training.* To be sure, many organization-development practitioners rely to a greater or lesser extent on experience-based educational programs, and some variant of sensitivity training is frequently used. But, as I have tried to show, a wide variety of programs can be effective, from data feedback sessions to confrontation meetings. The important thing about organization development is that data are generated from the client system itself. Frequently, these are the only data that count anyway, as there is sufficient evidence that data collected on "others" (no matter how valid) almost always lack the impact of self-generated data.[42]

Placing OD within what is here defined as the human-resource managerial approach further restricts its correctional usefulness to nonsystem. Before such positioning gains the appearance of relegation, however, the serious question must be asked, how systematic is corrections?

Even those claiming any kind of "local system" would presumably agree that gross, even contradictory, variations exist between jurisdictions, between government levels, and between corrections and other criminal justice subsystems—to a degree that constitutes non-system.

This being the case, it could scarcely be argued that human-resource, the *only* useful approach in nonsystem, has no place in correctional administration. And OD, as the most soundly developed of all human-resource approaches, may well be the very vehicle that brings about enough cohesion in corrections to permit results approaches. For it must be remembered:

> The process of introducing complex systems into organizations is still part science and part art. The science includes the comprehension and design of the technical parts of the system, and the art involves the process of introduction primarily with regard to the human element.[43]

[41] See, for example, C. Argyris, *Management and Organizational Development* (New York: McGraw-Hill Book Company, 1973); and the following six books, all published by Addison-Wesley Publishing Co., Inc., in 1969: Beckhard, *Organization Development;* L. Lawrence and L. Lorsch, *Developing Organizations;* Scheim, *Process Consultation;* Walton, *Third Party Consultation;* W. G. Bennis, *Organizational Development: Its Nature, Origins, and Prospects;* and, in particular, Blake and Mouton, *Building a Dynamic Corporation through Grid Organizational Development.*
[42] Bennis, *Organization Development,* p. 17.
[43] L. K. Williams, "The Human Side of a Systems Change," *Systems & Procedures Journal,* July–August 1964, p. 40.

The "human element" relates to the need to evolve a clearly *useful* system of corrections—a system in which pride can be taken and leadership demonstrated:

> Among the basic ingredients of sustained employee morale are understanding, interest, pride of accomplishment, and confidence in leadership. There are few workers whose interest and loyalty can long be maintained if they do not feel that their work is necessary and fruitful—that they are making a perceptible and worthwhile contribution to the affairs of the business. Moreover, they want to perform their work in an atmosphere of calm efficiency. Although occasional rush jobs may help to develop team spirit, continuously hectic operation and recurring crises quickly induce lunchroom speculation about "whether the boss knows what he's doing." There just cannot be much job enthusiasm or confidence among an embattled force of clerks struggling with red tape, antiquated methods, or complexity which defies comprehension.[44]

## SUMMARY

This chapter introduced the concept of managing correctional organizations as a process distinctly different from the administration of correctional organizations.

Variations in the styles of management were considered in terms of relative concern with production versus the employees who do the producing, along with other related organizational considerations.

Managerial methods were elaborated on in terms of the distinctions between role and function, as well as between efficiency and effectiveness. Managerial levels were related to this discussion.

The concept of managerial information was emphasized as significant to managerial methods.

Managerial approaches were introduced in the context of the now-classical Theories X and Y, then further detailed within the classifications of command, human-resource, and results approaches.

The functional systems model introduced in the preceding chapter was used to elaborate on distinctions between managerial approaches. The management-by-objectives approach and the organizational-development approach were also discussed in some detail.

[44] R. F. Neuschel, *Management by System* (New York: McGraw-Hill Book Company, 1960), p. 22.

## Discussion Topics

1. Distinguish between a managerial style and a managerial method.
2. Discuss some of the implications of the GRID℞ approach to examining managerial style.
3. Contrast managerial role and managerial function.
4. Describe functional interfacing.
5. Relate goal orientation to functions.
6. Elaborate on command, human-resource, and results managerial approaches.
7. Contrast the functional systems model with OD.

## Annotated References

ARGYRIS, C., *Management and Organizational Development.* New York: Mc-Graw-Hill Book Company, 1973. An outstanding overview of what was presented in this chapter as "OD," written by one of that approach's most articulate spokesmen.

*The Arts of Top Management: A McKinesey Anthology.* New York: Mc-Graw-Hill Book Company, 1973. A wide-scope anthology of managerial writing that affords an extremely broad context in which to consider this chapter.

BLAKE, R., and J. MOUTON, *Building a Dynamic Corporation through Grid Organizational Development.* Reading, Mass.: Addison-Wesley Publishing Co., Inc., 1969. Excellent elaboration of what this chapter presented as managerial style.

COFFEY, A. R., *Administration of Criminal Justice: A Management Systems Approach.* Englewood Cliffs, N.J.: Prentice-Hall, Inc., 1974. A comprehensive compilation of virtually all managerial ramifications of designing and implementing a complete system of management.

McGREGOR, D., *Leadership and Motivation*, eds. W. Bennis, E. Schein, and C. McGregor. Cambridge, Mass.: The M.I.T. Press, 1966.

————,*The Professional Manager*, eds. C. McGregor and W. Bennis. New York: McGraw-Hill Book Company, 1967. This and the preceding entry are two outstanding compilations affording excellent context for what was presented in this chapter as Theories X and Y.

# Supervisory Management in Correctional Administration

# Chapter 4

Just as there is great overlap between administrative process and managerial process, there is also considerable overlap between higher management and first-line supervision. For this reason, the position has been taken in this volume that correctional administration includes all three levels of management: administrators, managers, and supervisors.

Without going into a discussion of the theoretical development of public administration, it is worth noting that the material presented in the two preceding chapters is based upon managerial concepts that in some instances were fully developed well before World War I—Frederick Taylor's "scientific management," for example.[1] The conceptual differentiation between styles, types, approaches, and methods of management in terms of administrators, managers, and supervisors is a consequence of a vast number of contributions, such as Douglas McGregor's Theory X and Theory Y concepts; it is rooted in a rich developmental heritage.

[1] For a presentation of the theoretical development of public administration that bears on criminal justice, see, for example, Chapters 2 and 3 of A. R. Coffey, *Administration of Criminal Justice: A Management Systems Approach* (Englewood Cliffs, N.J.: Prentice-Hall, Inc., 1974).

But, as with the differences between the roles of administrator and executive or middle manager, there are also significant differences between the role of supervisor and that of any other managerial level in correctional administration. Moreover, significant differences exist between the functions customarily assigned to the various roles, making supervision a distinctive process in correctional management.

## THE GENERAL NATURE OF CORRECTIONAL SUPERVISION

Probably the most profound axiomatic observation that could be made about the nature of correctional supervision is that it is, or should be, a teaching position. Staff development directors, training officers, and personnel-orientation supervisors can at best *prepare* staff for training; the real training occurs on the job, for the most part by the first-line supervisor. This is true whether or not the supervisor involved calls his activities "training." For example, a supervisor may, without realizing it, be training in lethargy and cynicism, or perhaps in indifference—but he is still training.

In other words, staff members are learning *something* from each supervisor, whether or not he is intentionally teaching. Even the avoidance of training by a supervisor teaches the staff that training is not of value to the supervisor. If he shifts all training responsibility to the training division, the staff learns that he feels improvement in their work is not worth his time.

The training offered by supervisors varies widely, from a relatively structured, formalized training effort to the completely informal. An example of the structured type is suggested in this commentary on a learning need:

> If a staff member is able to write in a clear, effective manner, his worth, not only to himself but the institution, is greatly enhanced. There are many quasi-legal aspects to this profession. Accurate, clear reports and records play a key role in many important everyday decisions. If an agency or institution is extremely small, and verbal communication between all staff is easy, report writing takes on a lesser significance. In larger facilities, however, with hundreds of employees divided into divisions, sections, and units, written reports and communication take on a much greater significance and importance. Decisions must be made without personal knowledge of the subject or the writer. Decisions that are made with inaccurate or incomplete records can cause untold difficulty and harm.[2]

[2] E. Taron, "Correctional Report Writing and Recording," *Correctional Casework for Youth Counselors*, May 1967, p. 45.

In the category of informal or unstructured training offered by supervisors could fall virtually every contact between the supervisor and staff member: for example, case analysis, crisis intervention, and technique selection, along with myriad social, psychological, and legal ongoing interchange. In many instances, this unstructured training has far more to do with correctional career development than the training division's formal courses in family therapy, classification, transactional analysis, gestalt therapy, transcendental meditation, behavior modification, and a host of seemingly sophisticated treatment modes.

But beyond the factor of training staff, there are many other significant influences on the nature of correctional supervision. A brief discussion of the interest in and attitude toward supervision might serve to introduce some of these influences.

Optimism about the potential of supervising employees has been high for a long time: ". . . the solution to practically all . . . problems is just this: *improve your supervision*. . . ." [3] At least part of this interest in "improved supervision" regrettably relates to eliminating crisis management:

> . . . Strange as it may seem, some supervisors actually *enjoy* crises. In fact, a few of them even run their department in such a way that they are in a constant state of turmoil. They may not be aware of what they are doing; they may even proclaim loudly that the constant 'fire fighting' they have to do is driving them right up the wall. But they still enjoy them! If they didn't, they wouldn't have so many . . . the supervisor who is constantly fighting crises in his department is usually quite proud of his ability to handle the unexpected. . . . [4]

Regardless of the degree to which elimination of crisis management constitutes improved supervision gains, certainly most correctional administrators would agree that management of the organization is no better than the quality of supervision—and crisis management would in turn not be a significant part of the definition of *quality* supervision. But this raises the question of what constitutes quality supervision. In terms of defining quality, consider the following:

1. We still lack the techniques to synthesize a major system. Judgments are made by managers, usually on a very intuitive basis, with minimum influence by systems scientists.

2. There is a lack of appreciation of the disparities in knowledge, time, etc. between analysts and planners on the one hand and politicians and con-

[3] G. E. Halsey, *Supervising People* (N.Y.: Harper & Row, 1953), p. 1.
[4] "Crisis Management," *Dynamic Supervision*, No. 352(5B), Bureau of Business Practice, 1973, p. 143.

sumers on the other. All groups lack understanding of the basic societal forces which must be comprehended in order to be managed.

3. The system itself is rapidly changing and we are paying for the past mistakes, yet we lack an early-warning system to alert us of danger signs being ignored now.

4. We need a better conceptualization, expressed as curves, of the differential rate of change of awareness, public opinion, values, managerial and government response, etc.

5. The problems with which we must deal are getting tougher and the funds allocated to their solution more limited. This has a profound meaning for R & D management. The numbers and depths of findings will be limited, and the determination of what is good work and what mediocre perhaps much more difficult. Research is, after all, always a risky thing. For example, in an evaluation of the effects of operations research studies, we have estimated that 4 to 10% of studies have an immediate effect, 30 to 40% have a possible belated effect, and the remainder have no effect at all.

6. When we look at our present efforts we see vast expenditures of money yielding minuscule returns or even a worsening situation. This is particularly well exemplified in the case of welfare.

7. Criticisms of the social picture are common, but solutions, most usually from the extreme right or radical left, tend to be simplistic and naive.

8. Management will require much more problem-recognition as opposed to problem-solving and decision-making. This is illustrated by Curry's (1970, referenced in Chapter 9) classification of types of problems, and Livingston's (1971) look at successful and unsuccessful managers, and Libby's (1971) compilation of problems.

9. Societal decisions, in spite of industrial propaganda, seldom boil down to polemics such as 'jobs versus pollution,' 'homes versus redwoods,' etc. Behind each of these arguments lurk the spectres of oversimplification, obfuscation, and mismanagement. With an increasingly enlightened public, management will have to become more direct and more truthful (including with itself). And that's what this book is all about.

10. Industry has exploited both workers and the people, at least in the perceptions of an increasing number of people. Resistance is seen especially on the part of youth, who concretize an older generation's philosophies and theories and idealistically question gaps between what ought to be and what is. The behavior of youth and of disenfranchised groups should always be viewed by management as an early-warning sign of things to come, of emerging new patterns. This anticipatory behavior is a matter of acuteness of perception *and* selective perception, as well as biological brazenness.[5]

While these considerations appear to be restricted to *management* rather than supervision, and to private industry rather than the correctional field, even the briefest examination of factors that define *quality supervision* clarifies the relevance—supervisors must cope with these con-

[5] Kenyon B. DeGreene, *Sociotechnical Systems—Factors in Analysis, Design, and Management* (Englewood Cliffs, N.J.: Prentice-Hall, 1973), pp. 152–153.

siderations and their effect on the attitude of correctional practitioner and client alike.

Defining quality supervision, then, occurs in a very broad context for contemporary corrections. Bearing this broad context in mind, consider the following in terms of defining what constitutes quality in correctional staff supervision:

> Not long ago, the boss was a dictator to be feared. He was an ogre, an economic despot who ruled with an iron hand, and he was sole owner of the superiority complex. Today's supervisor makes quite a contrast. The upsurge of power in the hands of labor organizations has been a major reason for such a marked difference.[6]

It can be said, then, that like crisis management, the "dictator to be feared" is similarly not a part of the definition of quality supervision. Despite this fact, all organizations from time to time witness the spectacle of a newly promoted supervisor operating as though both these regrettable management practices defined quality:

> Some newly appointed managers just dive in cheerfully and without qualms. These are the ones who believe that the mere delegation of authority automatically equips and qualifies them to fulfill their new responsibilities. But, alas, the placing of the laurel wreath of authority on one's brow has no such magical effect. It will not immediately and automatically produce in others the correct response to such authority. A high hat does not make you taller; it only makes you look taller. Doors do not suddenly get lower; you just have to adjust yourself to new perils to your dignity.[7]

But the legitimate question emerges: If quality supervision is not simply wielding authority *nor* crisis management, what is it?

### Quality Supervision in Corrections

A chief probation officer, addressing a training class of first-line supervisors, said:

> . . . My task today is to try to help you examine some of the basic questions, which in my mind all boils down to one issue: how top administration views the role of staff supervisor. So my effort will be devoted to my telling you who I think you are, and what I think the expectations of staff and myself are or should be. Let me caution you that this is not a simple one-two-three discourse with easy answers. The probation department is

[6] J. J. Famularo, *Supervisors in Action* (New York: McGraw-Hill Book Company, 1961), pp. 12–13.
[7] D. Fuller, for Industrial Education Institute, *Manage or Be Managed!* (Boston: Cahners Books, 1970), p. 1.

a very complex organization, with many interlocking features and many diverse crosscurrents and pressures. Your actions as supervisors are intertwined with mine and mine with yours, and what we both do is closely intertwined with official and nonofficial actions and reactions in the community. . . .[8]

It might be assumed, then, that this top administrator conceives of quality supervision as including a strong relationship between what supervisors do and what top administrators do. His position is certainly clear that supervisory activities bear officially and nonofficially on the community; as we shall see later, the community is an extremely significant variable in corrections.

But in addition to strong, intertwining relationships with top administration, what else goes into quality supervision in corrections?

An analysis of what is required for a supervisor to become a better leader is sometimes delimited, or restricted, to an analysis of what it takes to secure the satisfaction, happiness, or acceptance of the supervisor's subordinates. In other words, the criterion—or measure—of what is good supervision in such an analysis may be stated as the happiness or satisfaction of subordinates, or their acceptance of the supervisor. Such limited approach has value if it is realized that good leadership by no means depends *wholly* upon the reaction of subordinates, but that this is just one facet of supervision. . . .[9]

Leadership, then, might be considered at least one dimension of quality supervision, and certainly a segment of the nature of correctional supervision—particularly in light of the following:

The fire of inspired leadership is a contagious thing. It usurps the role of command and leads men to go on beyond the call of duty to new levels of performance. Many books have been written on the psychology of leadership. They are to be found in every library and await their use by those interested in improving their capabilities in this important area of the profession.[10]

But important though leadership may be, it is only one of many dimensions of quality supervision. Moreover, there are certain limitations on leadership, which emerge in the very process of efforts to develop leaders:

[8] James D. Callahan, chief of Alameda County (California) Probation Department, addressing training class of agency supervisors, January 19, 1972. Full text of address in "The Role of the Supervisor," *Training Reference No. TR 60*, Alameda County Probation Department, Oakland, Calif.

[9] A. Q. Sartain and A. W. Baker, *The Supervisor and His Job* (New York: McGraw-Hill Book Company, 1965), p. 4.

[10] V. A. Leonard and H. W. More, *Police Organization and Management* (Mineola, N.Y.: The Foundation Press, Inc., 1971), pp. 43–44.

In summary, our data as well as the underlying theory suggest methods which lead to a more effective utilization of managerial and leadership training, as well as a more efficient approach to rotational policies in business and military organizations. Current training programs may well have failed to yield the desired results, not because the training was insufficient or inappropriate but because we have looked for a direct relationship between human relations skills or technical training and performance. Leadership training or leadership experience need to be viewed as means for improving the situational favorableness. True, these leadership experiences in part moderate the relationship between the leader's personality and organizational performance, a relationship which the Contingency Model has explicated.[11]

In his reference to moderating the relationship between the leader's personality and organizational performance, Fiedler brings out another element of quality supervision—that of motivation. In a sense, leadership itself affords a kind of motivation; but what is referred to here is more of a generalized situational kind of motivation, somewhat removed from the supervisor's direct leadership, even though generated by the manner in which the supervisor goes about his business.

Regarding this variety of motivation, another authority has said:

The secret of how to motivate people to work as efficiently as they are capable is a problem as old and as complex as society. There are no universal or simple answers. There are only theories and principles which need to be individually applied in much the same manner that a physician cures each patient of his illness.[12]

Of course, the individual application called for here requires in most cases a certain degree of leadership—once again reinforcing the significance of leadership in the nature of correctional supervision. But in motivating people to work efficiently, particularly on a consistent basis, the challenge is not so much to lead as it is to create an atmosphere conducive to efficient work—to motivate. Time spent by the supervisor in probation, correctional institutions, and parole in creating such motivational environment is time well spent—a "high-yield" form of time management.

[11] F. E. Fiedler, "On the Death and Transfiguration of Leadership Training," abstract, *University of Washington*. Address to Division 8, 14 and 19 for which he received the 1971 Research Award of Division 13 (Consulting Psychology) of the American Psychological Association, Washington, D.C., Sept. 3, 1971. It is a revision and extension of Technical Reports 70–16 and 71–21 of the Organizational Research Group, University of Washington, Seattle.
[12] H. G. Zollitsch, "Motivation for Productivity," *Proceedings of the 7th Annual Midwest Management Conference*, Business Research Bureau, Carbondale, Illinois, 1964, p. 63.

## Quality Supervision and Time Management

When leadership is combined with the motivational environment that encourages efficient work, an assumption can be made that quality supervision is in existence, and that the supervisor is making excellent use of his managerial time:

> Time spent on trivial activities provides a low pay-off. In contrast, certain time expenditures yield a high pay-off. Time spent in *learning* usually results in high and continuing pay-off. Some examples of low pay-off time for managers are: time spent in fire-fighting, time spent on routines, time spent in supervising or checking and time spent on day-to-day operations.
>
> In contrast, high pay-off time is any time spent on looking for opportunities and challenges, discovering new goals, thinking creatively and innovatively, building a management system, delegating authority, planning the future, developing people. Most managers know the difference between low and high pay-off actions. Their problem is to do something about it. The difficulty is that managers are restricted by the system within which they work.[13]

The *management of time*, usually associated with higher levels of managers, is nonetheless a significant part of quality supervision. After all, the higher managerial levels are involved with the management of the entire organization—not just time—whereas in correctional supervision, the matter of time management centers almost entirely on how the supervisor applies his time.

This distinction, although somewhat generalized and vague, gains some dimension by consideration of the similarities and differences among public organizations overall:

> The management of agencies in the administration of justice isn't essentially different from the management of a public works agency, a fire department, or a unit charged with the collection of taxes. Agencies charged with law enforcement, the trial of offenders, and the rehabilitation of convicted persons are only a small portion of the full spread of services a successful government must provide for its citizens. However, administration-of-justice agencies differ from other units in public administration in three ways: (1) they produce services their "clients" or "customers" fail to understand or ask for; (2) there are many opportunities for corruption; and (3) the environmental influence resulting from daily contacts with criminal offenders is a process of corruption.[14]

[13] F. D. Barrett, "Everyman's Guide to Time Management," quoted as excerpts from "Time Analysis Is an Important Managerial Function," in *Notes and Quotes*, No. 408 (June–July 1973), 2.
[14] P. B. Weston, *Supervision in the Administration of Justice* (Springfield, Ill.: Charles C. Thomas, Publisher, 1965), p. 3.

A further distinction in time management between higher management levels and supervisory management lies in what Barrett referred to as "time spent on looking for opportunities and challenges." Unlike the fiscal, budget, planning, and other administrative activities of concern to the administrator and executive manager, time management for the correctional supervisor, as Weston says, can focus upon:

1. Services clients fail to ask for
2. Opportunities for corruption
3. Corrupting environment

Therefore, supervisory management finds that time spent seeking "opportunities and challenges" focuses primarily on the recognition that correctional "customers" do not volunteer, and the nature of criminal justice itself generates both the possibility and the situation for corrupting influence—all of which is readily perceptible at the supervisory level of management, but frequently obscured at higher levels.

There is risk here of acknowledging the potential for corruption in a manner that suggests cynicism. However, supervisory recognition of that potential not only *can* but *will* reduce or eliminate the problem. High-yield time is what *makes corrections possible*, because it can result in correctional philosophy influencing the offender instead of the offender's philosophy influencing corrections. This is the key in the "nonvoluntary" environment of corrections.

Therefore, regardless of what else constitutes high-yield time for correctional supervisors, it must incorporate a greater degree of concern for the nonvoluntary nature of the work, as well as for the opportunity and situations that create a potentially corruptive environment—particularly significant variables in defining quality supervision in corrections.

### The Nature of Correctional Supervision and the Question of Control

In assigning greater significance to time management at the supervisory level, the question is raised as to what degree of control is involved in the nature of supervision—that is, of immediate control of those correctional personnel who deal directly with the "nonvolunteer" "customer" in the corrupting environment.

The late Douglas McGregor, creator of Theories X and Y, reviewed a number of managerial changes that he considered necessary, and predicted:

Perhaps the primary change will be in a deep-seated and long-standing conception of managerial control. This conception concerns the necessity for imposing direction and limitations on the individual in order to get him to perform the work for which he is hired. It is, however, an observable characteristic of human beings that they will exercise *self*-direction and *self*-control for externally imposed controls. The movement, if any, appears to be in the opposite direction, because this concept of self-control is erroneously associated with "soft" management.[15]

The high-yield time of quality supervision, then, may well reduce itself to exhibiting leadership in combination with motivational self-direction—more specifically, to generating self-control. The nature of supervision, then, is such that quality increases in proportion to supervisory time committed to leading and motivating staff to self-control, in coping with the problems of "nonvolunteer" clients in a potentially corrupting environment. Reduced to the simplest considerations, this becomes a matter of supervisory *communication*.

### Supervision and Communication

Although virtually all that will be presented later in this chapter requires effective communication, the concept of communication itself is so fundamental to supervising in the correctional field that it deserves brief elaboration here.

A publication of the American Management Association expresses this point of view:

> The fundamental objective of most face-to-face communications on the job is to *sell an idea*. The do-this-or-else-and-never-mind-why type of order is a thing of the past in enlightened organizations: It went out with the realization that people are different from machines. People need to *understand* a communication in order to give their best support to it. They need to *accept* an idea before they will do more than simply go through the motions.[16]

Whether or not everyone would agree that "selling an idea" is the *fundamental* objective, most would presumably agree that face-to-face communication is certainly required if ideas are to be "sold." In light of the preceding discussion of quality supervision, it becomes clear that both leadership and motivation are virtually dependent upon face-to-face communication—between supervisors and managers, as well as between supervisors and employees.

The first effort to analyze the content of this face-to-face communica-

---

[15] D. McGregor, *Leadership and Motivation* (Cambridge, Mass.: The M.I.T. Press, 1966), p. 28.
[16] D. Emery, "How to Plan Your Communications," in *Effective Communication on the Job* (New York: American Management Association, Inc., 1963), p. 55.

tion between supervisors and employees is, for most supervisors, relatively easy:

> What do your employees want to know? First, they want to know their conditions of employment, rates of pay, hours, holidays, sick leave, pension and so on. Then they are concerned with their job security: They want to feel confident that their job will be there next week, next month and next year. Consequently they want to know how the business is going, whether you have landed a large contract, if you are expanding, going into a new field, moving to new premises, building an annex, what new products you are developing. They want to know company policies and company history and they want to know "why." A man will do almost anything if you tell him why you want him to do it. The same goes for possibly unpalatable things you may have to do. Explain why you have had to make an unpopular decision and it will be accepted with far better grace.[17]

Moreover, the location, time, and format of much of this communication can be greatly simplified—at least, initially—through the customary supervisory-staff meeting:

> Most management experts say there's no inflexible set of rules that insure success for a staff meeting, but some general principles should be followed.
>
> 1.  Hold staff meetings regularly, but not more often than necessary for worthwhile communication.
>
> 2.  Balance the agenda with both performance reporting and information reporting.
>
> 3.  Make the staff meeting a vital link in an action system. In other words, what's decided there should be put into practice.[18]

In regard to the true nature of supervision, however, these simpler facets of communication are collectively only one factor—an important one, but only one of many in communication. When leadership and motivation are considered, many other factors immediately emerge; for example:

> Every man carries his own context with him. The past experience and the character, intelligence, and interests of each individual affect the meaning—the real significance to him—of what he hears or reads. A kind word will arouse the suspicions of one worker while it encourages another. An admonition stirs bitter resentment in one worker and stimulates another to greater effort. Announcement of a reduction in piece rates makes one worker quit and another work harder. A campaign for cost reduction and

[17] M. Bosticco, *Creative Techniques for Management* (London: Camelot Press Ltd., 1971), pp. 40–41.

[18] U.S. Chamber of Commerce, "Why Staff Meetings Fall Flat," excerpts from "Effective Communication," *Notes and Quotes*, No. 408 (June–July 1973), 3.

greater productivity provokes some employees to resist, even to "soldier," while others cooperate willingly.[19]

So, no matter how the facts are presented to employees, results may in some cases be negative. However, the proportion of negative to positive results can be greatly reduced through attention to the context as well as the content of communications:

> . . . The manager who states that the world is flat may find many who disagree with the *content* of his message. But assuming that there exists an otherwise healthy working relationship within his organization, even those disagreeing with the content of his message should agree on its *context—* that an individual has the right to express whatever content he believes. . . .[20]

This does not imply that correctional supervisors are tied into communications for communications' sake. On the contrary, the *achievement of results* is the *total* purpose of communication:

> . . . The *amount* of communication is determined by the relevance of communication to results, and not to any capricious individual variations in preference for communication . . . just enough openness in communication to achieve managerial results . . . the manager seeking overall communication improvement through changes in his personality [must then] search *outside* the organization . . . [and] when results are involved, managers who may not *like* the communication process [must nevertheless] participate sufficiently to insure performance of role and function . . . to insure achievement of results. . . .[21]

In relating communication to the nature of correctional supervision, this brief discussion has barely introduced the extremely complex subject of human communication.[22] Indeed, within the context of information

---

[19] W. Exton, Jr., "The Semantics of Managing," *Effective Communication on the Job* (New York: American Management Association, Inc., 1963), p. 44.
[20] Coffey, *Administration of Criminal Justice*, pp. 149–150.
[21] *Ibid.*, p. 153.
[22] For information on this subject, see Coffey, *Administration of Criminal Justice*, Chap. 7; P. Watzlawick, J. H. Beavin, and D. Jackson, *Pragmatics of Communication* (New York: W. W. Norton & Company, Inc., 1967); I. D. Yalom, *Theory and Practice of Group Psychotherapy* (New York: Basic Books, Inc., Publishers, 1970); E. H. Schein, *Process Consultation: Its Role in Organizational Development* (Reading, Mass.: Addison-Wesley Publishing Co., Inc., 1969); J. Luft, *Group Processes: An Introduction to Group Dynamics* (this is the "Johari Window" approach) (Palo Alto, Calif.: National Press Books, 1970); W. G. Bennis, *Organizational Development: Its Nature, Origins and Prospects* (Reading, Mass.: Addison-Wesley Publishing Co., Inc., 1969); C. Goldberg, "An Encounter with the Sensitivity Training Movement," *Canada's Mental Health*, September–October 1970; and J. H. Grossman, "Are Your Messages Provoking Conflict?" *Supervisory Management*, Vol. 10, No. 2 (November

systems, discussed briefly in the preceding chapter, it should be clear that communication is the critical factor in virtually *everything* complex in correctional administration. But it is also clear that the very nature of supervision in corrections tends to increase the significance of communication—particularly face-to-face communication involved in the supervisor's responsibility to connect management and staff.

Against this brief background of the general nature of correctional supervision, we turn our attention to the *process* of supervising in the field of probation, correctional institutions, and parole.


## THE PROCESS OF CORRECTIONAL SUPERVISION

The role definition of supervisors in the correctional field is far less clear than the role definition of higher levels of correctional management. The titles of Supervising Parole Agent or Senior Probation Officer or Sergeant of the Guard suggest far more role clarity than actually exists in many organizations. However, we can say that there is at least one expectation accompanying this role, regardless of function or variety of organization: that *the supervisor "connects" the management process and the operational process.*

A wide range of approaches to this connection are possible, but the connection itself can be said to be much like pregnancy, in that it is un-equivocal—it either does or does not exist. When such managerial connection does not exist, (1) higher managers by-pass supervisors; and/or (2) there is no cohesive force to focus budget, law, courts, community, government, and staff into a goal-oriented organizational operation. In the first case, there is also a loss of "cohesive force"—that of focusing all elements of the correctional organization. Both considerations dramatize the consequences of supervisors' not connecting management and operations. And these consequences in turn lead to a sharp reduction in supervisory accountability, since the supervisor is accountable for no more than he is allowed to supervise, and by-passing prevents him from supervising.

The expectation that correctional supervisors "connect" the organization might be viewed as in the accompanying diagram. This diagram goes

---

1970). For basic information on communication—most important to knowledge of its more specialized aspects—see S. I. Hayakawa, *Semantics Et Cetera: A Review of General Semantics 9* (4) (1952), 243–57 (also available as a Bobbs-Merrill Reprint, *Language 43*); P. Watzlawick, *Anthology of Human Communication* (book and tape) (Palo Alto, Calif.: Science & Behavior Books, Inc., 1964); and A. Nehrabian and A. Weiner, "Non-Immediacy between Communicator and Object," *Journal of Consulting Psychology*, 30 (1966), 420–26.

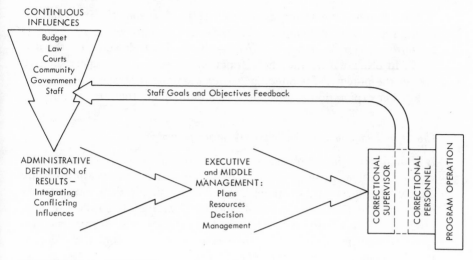

**CORRECTIONAL SUPERVISOR CONNECTION**

beyond merely identifying the supervisor's responsibility to clarify managerial plans and expectations. Note in particular the feedback of staff goals and objectives. In effect, this method of conceptualizing the role of correctional supervisors makes possible a *system* of ongoing organizational communication—of participatory management.

### Participatory Management

In light of the discussion in the preceding chapter of the functional systems management model, consider the following description of the *function* assigned to the *role* of supervisors—the "how function":

> . . . The *how* function is of course the final key managerial function of the model—it is the "how it's done" management function. . . . Distinction between what is to be done and who is to do it focuses on this third distinction of *how* it is to be done, provided administrative and executive management have retained more concern for what gets done than for who is doing it and how. . . .[23]

If this premise is accepted—that the key *function* of the supervisory *role* is "how things get done"—the value of the supervisor to correctional administration increases manyfold. For one thing, this function is lifted from the shoulders of higher management, which in turn becomes free to manage instead of continually learning new correctional techniques.

[23] Coffey, *Administration of Criminal Justice*, p. 73.

*But far more important, administratively permitting the interface between supervisors and staff to determine how results are to be achieved establishes a system of staff feedback*—the feedback depicted on the diagram. In other words, the "how function" as part of the supervisor role creates the potential for ongoing *participatory management.*

Further exploration of this "how function" might then be useful.

## The How Function and Participatory Management [24]

It should again be emphasized that the role of supervisor has no universal definition. In some correctional organizations, supervisor roles are clearly "management"; in others, a supervisor is simply the senior member of a unit. But this is the value of isolating *functions.* Regardless of how obscure the supervisor role, clarity of the function performed permits goal-oriented management. Consideration of the how function independent of supervisory role is therefore useful.

Staff meetings, mentioned in the discussion of communication, are capable of communicating not only what management expects of employees, but also what employees expect of management—two-way communication, in other words:

> With the assumption that has already been made in terms of the *how* function being ideally suited for a first-line supervisor role (although possibly in another role level in a smaller department), the interface between *how* and the staff function of *how much* readily lends itself to the kinds of activities likely to occur in a typical staff meeting. Of course, against the background of management functions, "how much" refers to the degree of staff willingness to provide resources. . . .[25]

"Staff willingness to provide resources," though frequently overlooked, is the key element of supervisorial communication that relates to what employees expect of management.

There are any number of techniques to establish this two-way communication feedback, one of which is a relatively simple chart that can be posted routinely at regularly scheduled staff meetings:[26]

---

[24] Much of this section is taken from Chapters 3 through 6 of Coffey, *Administration of Criminal Justice.* Virtually all the material on the technology of reflexing synergetics, ergonetic analysis and energy assessment are removed here in order to isolate the concept of participatory management rather than the science of operating cybernated systems.

[25] Coffey, *Administration of Criminal Justice,* p. 88.

[26] A procedural device used by the author in training supervisory staff the how function.

## STAFF MEETING

TASK OR PROBLEM: _____

|   | *Staff Options* | *Solves* | *Possible* | *Appropriate* |
|---|---|---|---|---|
| 1. | | | | |
| 2. | | | | |
| 3. | | | | |
| 4. | | | | |
| 5. | | | | |

A parole unit, for example, may have a number of problems and tasks related to geographical distances. The parole supervisor may begin a staff meeting by communicating what management expects to occur in the geographical area, but can then use this chart to "negotiate" how these expectations are to be met. Moreover, what staff expects of management as a result of these negotiations can also readily emerge, as illustrated in the following:

The parole agent asks that the supervisor declare, say, "Driving time" as the problem to be written at the top of the chart. Five members of the parole unit then list options that can solve the problem. Once this is done, each staff member rates each option on a scale of 1 to 5 in terms of solving the problem. Next, each option is rated from 1 to 5 as to whether it is even possible, and finally each is rated as to how appropriate it may be. The highest score determines how the problem of driving time (or any other unit problem or task) will be handled, the staff involved participating directly in how managerial expectations are met.

Of course, the understanding is that *the staff accepts with the supervisor the accountability for achieving results.*

The supervisor then systematically gives feedback to administration, in a context that is *not* a suggestion-box approach, but instead one that insures direct as well as current operational information on the programs management seeks to sustain.[27]

Some of the other managerial advantages to this relatively simple technique are these:

1. The managerial role of correctional supervisor is clarified through this how-function demonstration.
2. Administrative acceptance of correctional-staff feedback occurs in that part of managerial process *most directly* impinging on staff—supervisor judgment relating to staff.
3. The technique establishes a system of judging staff enthusiasm for various programs.
4. *Most important:* The staff learns to distinguish between notions that solve problems and notions that *cause* problems.

[27] See Coffey, *Administration of Criminal Justice*, Chaps. 3–5.

It would be difficult to overestimate the administrative value of number 4—having the staff learn through firsthand experience just how many great-sounding solutions actually cause more problems than they solve. Indeed, it may well be that unless the correctional staff is permitted to participate in these operational determinations of its members' activities, it may come to believe that every administrative program has less merit than one that some particular staff member may prefer—an obvious disadvantage to correctional continuity.

Of course, this approach to staff meetings, with the chart suggested, is but one of an infinite variety of participatory management techniques available to the correctional organization. The key concept, however, is that the participation be both systematic and relevant, through operations immediately perceptible to the staff participating—*directly* involving the interface between staff and supervisor.

## Other Concepts of Supervision in Corrections

Obviously, this limited discussion of the nature and the process of correctional supervision by no means exhausts existing views on the subject. A great many correctional administrators, for example, conceive of a supervisor as merely a senior member of his particular unit, responsible for transmitting the administration's desires and monitoring and reporting violations of policy. It may well be that many correctional supervisors themselves see the supervisory role in this manner; perhaps even more supervisors are functioning in this manner.

Still another construct for the correctional supervisory role is as a kind of coordinator—somewhat more involved in management than simply carrying messages and monitoring reaction, but still without accountability for a management function or correctional outcome. Stripped of misleading titles and tables of organization, this supervisory construct, except for its organizational permanence, is similar to the position of chairman of an ad hoc committee.

There are any number of variations involving combinations of these two concepts. Indeed, there may be in the correction field so much variation in the *process* of supervision that there may also be variations in the *general nature* of supervision—a regrettable possibility, in view of the need for a reduction in fragmentation.

The position of this volume is that the role and function of supervisor are critically important elements of *management*, since managerial success frequently hinges on the clear managerial identity of first-line supervisors. To whatever degree management of a correctional organization occurs without the aid of those managers closest to the operational problems, to that same degree management is creating an enormous deficit of lost talent and incentive, as well as lost system continuity.

The remainder of this volume, therefore, will approach administering the correctional field in terms of a full management team that includes supervisors—the acknowledged variations in this construct notwithstanding.

## SUMMARY

This chapter presented the role of supervisory management in correctional administration, making the distinction among administrative management, executive and middle management, and supervisory management. These distinctions were made in the context of overlap and interrelationships within correctional administration.

The nature of correctional supervision was explained in relation to training staff on the job and discussed in terms of influences upon quality supervision—leadership, motivation, time management, control, and communication.

The process of correctional supervision was presented in terms of the functions most appropriately assigned to the role of supervisor, with the function of creating participatory management carried out through functionally determining *how* results are to be achieved. Managerial feedback was emphasized in this context.

The techniques and rationale of assigning supervisors the primary responsibility of participatory management was presented, along with a discussion of the managerial advantages involved. Acknowledgement was made of other constructs for the supervisory role in this connection, with a final position taken that supervisors must be conceived of as a part of the managerial process in corrections.

### Discussion Topics

1. Explain how on-the-job training defines much of the nature of correctional supervision.
2. Discuss the relationship between supervisory management and higher management.
3. Discuss the relationship between supervisory management and staff.
4. Contrast leadership and motivation.
5. Contrast time management and control.
6. Elaborate on the significance of communication.

7. Discuss the rationale for the how function.
8. Relate the how function to feedback.
9. Discuss the advantages of participatory management through supervision.
10. Elaborate on the contrast between the how function and the two other constructs presented at the close of this chapter.

## Annotated References

ARGYRIS, C., *Interpersonal Competence and Organizational Effectiveness*. Homewood, Ill.: Dorsey Press, 1967. Also, Argyris, *Organizations and Innovation*. Excellent in-depth context for what this chapter discussed as the influence of communication upon supervision in a correctional organization.

COFFEY, A. R., *Administration of Criminal Justice: A Management Systems Approach*. Englewood Cliffs, N.J.: Prentice-Hall, Inc., 1974. Chapters 3–9 and 13–15 exhaustively cover the supervisor role in the system of criminal justice management.

COFFEY, A., E. ELDEFONSO, and W. HARTINGER, *Introduction to the Criminal Justice System and Process*. Englewood Cliffs, N.J.: Prentice-Hall, Inc., 1974. An overall context for the managerial process discussed in this chapter as relating to supervision. See also Coffey, Eldefonso, and Hartinger, *Human Relations: Law Enforcement in a Changing Community*. Englewood Cliffs, N.J.: Prentice-Hall, Inc., 1971; and Coffey, Eldefonso, and Hartinger, *Police–Community Relations*, Englewood Cliffs, N.J.: Prentice-Hall, Inc., 1971.

FAMULARO, J. L., *Supervisors in Action*. New York: McGraw-Hill Book Company, 1961.

HALSEY, G. D., *Supervising People*. New York: Harper & Row, Publishers, 1953.

LUFT, J., *Group Processes: An Introduction to Group Dynamics*. Palo Alto, Calif.: National Press Books, 1970. Good context for this chapter's discussion of limitations on communication. See also Luft, "The Johari Window," *Human Rights Training News*, 5 (1961), 6–7. For deeper exploration of this concern, see references in footnote 21 of this chapter.

McGREGOR, D., *Leadership and Motivation*. Cambridge, Mass.: The M.I.T. Press, 1966. A well-edited overview of the late Douglas McGregor's views on what this chapter presented as the distinction between leadership and motivation.

SARTAIN, A. Q., and A. W. BAKER, *The Supervisor and His Job*. New York: McGraw-Hill Book Company, 1965.

WESTON, P. B., *Supervision in the Administration of Justice*. Springfield, Ill.: Chas. C. Thomas, Publisher, 1965. Good elaboration of the role of supervising criminal justice activities.

# OPERATING THE
# FIELD OF
# CORRECTIONS

# TWO

# Probation Operations

# Chapter 5

Although probation is the first organizational structure on the "correctional continuum," organizational structure as such is not extremely significant within the context of correctional administration, because the principles of administration are essentially the same whether the organization is structured at the state, county, or city level. For consistency, then, probation will be examined primarily in one context—in this case, the county model. Keep in mind, however, that many other organizational structures exist and that any could serve equally well, since the emphasis of this chapter is on the administration, rather than the practice, of probation.[1]

As a partial context for this discussion, consider the following:

It has become obvious to both criminal justice professionals and the lay public that there are some fundamental problems with corrections and the

[1] For more detail on organizational considerations in criminal justice, see Alan R. Coffey, *Administration of Criminal Justice* (Englewood Cliffs, N.J.: Prentice-Hall, Inc., 1974), particularly Chap. 9, but also Chaps. 10–12.

criminal justice system in America. However, as to exactly what the problems are and what to do about them, there is less unanimity of opinion.

From the public sector and from some inspired but not necessarily enlightened elected representatives come cries for more and better law enforcement, for quicker justice and for more tranquil prisons. From the better informed segments of the public there are also concerns that these measures should be coupled with more humane and effective confinement.

From the professional side the recommendations are somewhat different: screening fewer people into the system in the first place, providing more legal safeguards for both the accused and convicted, and for a greater involvement of the community in the correctional process. But professionals are also concerned with more humane and effective confinement.[2]

Concern with "more humane and effective confinement" refers of course to correctional-institution administration, which will be the subject of the next chapter. But in terms of reducing the system fragmentation, the approach to the administration of the probation operation must be from the same perspective as the approach to administering prisons and parole. This administrative perspective begins with the recognition that *negative* public and political attention focused upon prisons (or law enforcement, or courts, or prosecution, for that matter) is hardly an advantage to probation administrators; the administrative plight of any subsystem of criminal justice ultimately accrues to the administration of all its subsystems.

It is frequently stated that prisons deal in large measure with probation failures; and, regardless of procedural and situational differences, probation is in the same system as prisons and parole and closely related to them.

And so the increasing public and political concern with prisons (as well as law enforcement and courts) is of sufficient moment to probation administration to constitute a major segment of the context in which probation operations are administered.

The corrections system can be diagrammed thus:

If the correct definition of *output* is rehabilitated offenders, the procedural and situational variations in achieving this output are merely incidental, from the administrative perspective. This point will be clarified further in the discussion of community-based corrections in Chapter 8.

[2] H. C. Quay, "What Corrections Can Correct and How," *Federal Probation*, Vol. 37, No. 2 (June 1973), 3.

Before exploring the concept of administering probation operations, however, let us consider the *nature* of probation—a nature that accounts for its appearance of being somewhat unrelated to other correctional subsystems.

## THE NATURE OF PROBATION

The nature of probation and that of prison and parole are in most respects significantly different. There is, however, a common nature, that of "people work"—work with people having difficulties.

One source of confusion regarding this relatively simple commonality is the frequently overlooked distinction between probation and parole activities: Probation occurs before institutional care, and parole occurs after institutional care. But it is common practice for a sentencing judge in some jurisdictions to make a jail term a condition of probation, thus literally requiring probation to occur *after* institutional care—making probation become parole. And many probation organizations are structured in such a manner that juvenile institutions are included, thereby again making the probation services that occur *after* institutional care become parole.

This obstruction to a clear understanding of the similarities in the "people-work" nature of probation, prisons, and parole is reduced by the use of probation officers for *both* probation and parole in the federal correctional system, and in many other jurisdictions following the same practice. (Aside from reducing confusion, there are great administrative advantages to such a combination, not the least of which is staffing flexibility and correction continuity.) Such a combination does tend to clarify the similarity in the nature of all corrections, a similarity we should remember while discussing the *differences* in their operations.

For purposes of discussion, then, the nature of probation will be defined as partially the same as that of prison and parole, this partial common nature being that of "people work." And to account for differences in the nature of the three correctional components, emphasis will be placed upon the nature of probation occurring *prior* to institutional care —the exceptions already noted notwithstanding.

### Probation Defined

In approachng the definition of *probation*, many factors must be considered. For example, juvenile probation occurs both before and after court, whereas adult probation occurs primarily (but not always) during and after court:

. . . The individual is released, if he so desires, and is offered "high-support" counseling, job development, job training and other services with the dual aim of stabilizing his behavior so that he will avoid further criminal activity and obtain dismissal of his charges. At the end of his "probationary" continuance he returns to court where: (1) the charges may be dropped; (2) another trial continuance under program supervision may be imposed; or (3) trial may be set. This current federal proposal deviates slightly from practices of the pilot programs. In contrast to the Boston Court Resource Project, for instance, the current federal plan provides: (1) persons charged with crimes of violence would be excluded (whereas the BCRP has found such offenders "good or better prospects" with equal or lesser recidivism ranges); (2) a continuance of six months, rather than three months, is required; (3) all discretion about continuance lies with the program administrator, eliminating any discretion on the part of the committing officer or judge, who is responsible for the final decision in Boston based upon the BCRP recommendation.

Thus, although the concept of deferred prosecution probation and diversion from the criminal warrant process is and can be operationally initiated in some different ways and with some different variations for practical purposes, yet the laudable ideological and social goals of such programs (i.e., to reduce crime, to better protect society, to facilitate the operation of the criminal justice system, to run that system both more efficiently and less expensively, etc.) remain consistent, undeviating, worthwhile, and common to all such programs.[3]

So we see that a simple definition of probation is not possible. All correctional components are complex, and probation has more components than have institutions and parole.

Despite its complexity, however, there are certain elements of probation operations that offer an approach to defining this pre-institutional segment of corrections:

An analysis of the definition of probation which we have given here will reveal that its basic elements are (1) a suspension of sentence, (2) a period of trial for the offender in the community, (3) the offender's observance of the law and adherence to the conditions imposed by the court, and (4) the supervision of the offender by a probation officer. Some writers urge that the concept of probation be divorced entirely from that of the suspended sentence so that the constructive and rehabilitative aspects of probation will be emphasized. Although it is recognized that this side of probation must be clearly understood, and that some other phrase, such as "postponement of final judgment" instead of "suspension of sentence," might better describe the action of the court, it is also believed that it would be wholly unrealistic not to see probation as a substitute for commitment

[3] National District Attorneys Association, "Alternatives to the Criminal Warrant Process: The Prosecutor's Discretionary Decision to Charge," *Screening of Criminal Cases,* Chicago, pp. 47–48.

to an institution, to which the court must usually resort when probation fails.[4]

Probation functions fill three social needs, each as specific and demanding as the needs filled by penal institutions:

(1) There is a social need created by mere acceptance of the idea that the "eye-for-an-eye" philosophy should be tempered by the "reasons" an act occurs. Clearly there is no way to completely reconcile the philosophy of government by "laws-not-men" with the philosophy of "mitigating circumstances." But probation is the instrument by which the society attempts to sustain these incongruent and often conflicting doctrines. Here there is need of note that probation should not, indeed cannot, combine these conflicting doctrines entirely. Instead, there is a theoretical basis comprised of interpreting behavior in terms of statute, on the one hand, and recognizing that identical acts can have different causes, on the other. Beyond this, probation does not relate to the opposing philosophies.

(2) There is a social need filled by probation in the somewhat unique therapy that it contributes to those individuals deemed to be in need of "correction." The role of probation within the range of corrective measures can be considered unique in that the "second chance" philosophy prevails. Contrasted against the generally punitive overtones of other treatment techniques, even the most restrictive measures of probation are defensible as mere support for the probationer's own efforts to justify his "second chance." Few authorities would care to defend incarceration or parole on these grounds, semantic confusion notwithstanding.

(3) Probation provides the potential to modify behavior without the attack on dignity that is associated with liberty deprivaton. Unlike the prison inmate facing the social reality that his personal behavior forces his removal from the group, the probationer needs only focus on modifications required to remain with the group.

Sustaining self-respect permits the corrective program to function at the optimum community-adjustment level. Those programs which initially deprive the offender of dignity must include in a later phase and as a separate stage a program of community adjustment.

Clearly, the need filled by probation relates primarily but not exclusively to adults. This is the assumed personality support gained by saving the community the cost and responsibility of the offender and his dependents. When an offender is spared the psychological need to rationalize the burden imposed by his unacceptable behavior, he should be able to approach his missing *insight* with less interference. But the financial savings here is only a fortunate by-product and not a distinct advantage. Indeed, if the probation program fails within its own theoretical framework, the later costs of corrections would erase any such savings. The single need served in this connection remains the psychological variable of an offender not forced to feel he is not responsible for himself and his dependents. In the case of

[4] R. G. Caldwell, *Criminology* (New York: The Ronald Press Company, 1965), p. 462.

juveniles, similar personality support may be gained by saving parents the cost of correctional alternatives.[5]

The definition of probation, then, while not simple, can nevertheless be conceptualized in concrete terms. The conceptual clarity can be increased even more by placing probation in the context of *law*—particularly when law is considered in terms of its value to society in general:

> It is commonly accepted that laws are intrinsic to a just society: No one denies that it is wrong to injure one's neighbor, or to take that which is his neighbor's. This part of justice, the substantive law, is what we usually think of as the law. And while there may not be unanimity on all laws—there are good laws and bad ones—most disputes about substantive laws involve arguments that the ordinary citizen can appreciate. Procedural laws, however, often involve a subtlety and complexity which are not readily understood by the ordinary, law-abiding citizen. If it is wrong to harm one's neighbor, then he who does so should be apprehended and punished. The good citizen often cannot understand certain principles of fair procedures which seem to him to restrict the application of substantive law. The popularity or lack thereof of recent high court decisions on due process testifies to the confusion and wariness of a large part of the population. It becomes necessary to remind ourselves that fair procedures are necessary for the protection of the innocent as well as the guilty from unfair treatment.[6]

Beyond this concrete dimension of law, probation gains clarity through consideration of crime and delinquency on the basis of both scope and severity, quickly bringing into focus the theoretical potential of pre-institutional corrections. Regrettably, such enlightenment still seems more in the future than immediately at hand, since current crime thought tends to be in terms of either severity *or* scope, choices relating more to political philosophy than to criminology. Not surprisingly, dividing the thinking on severity from the thinking on the scope of crime tends to generate further fragmentation not only of the correctional functions, but of the criminal justice system overall—and at a time when increasing demand for solutions is emerging:

> Every responsible citizen, as well as every judge, is deeply concerned, indeed shocked, by the crime wave sweeping the country like a deadly plague to threaten the very life of our ordered society. From the pulpit to the Halls of Congress, from the fireside of the responsible parent to the local civic clubs, from the sociologist and welfare worker to the employer of labor, comes the cry for protection from the marauding criminal. Crime and criminals are denounced everywhere, but any attempted discussion of

[5] A. Coffey, "Correctional Probation: What Use to Society," *Journal of the California Probation, Parole and Correctional Association*, Vol. 5, No. 1 (Spring 1968), 29–30.
[6] California Council on Criminal Justice, "Issues Concerning Fair Procedures for Making Decisions," *A Project of the State Bar of California: Law in a Free Society* (Sacramento, Cal., 1972), p. 12.

remedial measure leads inevitably to an irreconcilable conflict of opinion. With every atrocious crime, the affected community clamors for harsher punishment. And, unfortunately, most of those who clamor for more stringent penalties as a solution to criminality seldom have the responsibility for enforcing the law or imposing the sentence, and know nothing of the background or mental capacity of the offender.[7]

An additional influence on the definition of probation is the variation between adult and juvenile probation, to be taken up later in this chapter.

For our present purposes, and with a warning against concluding that its complexities can be simplified, probation will be defined here as *legally defined activities for children and adults that serve both correctional rehabilitation and justice prior to institutional treatment.*

Of course, like any simplified definition of a complex process, this one suffers many inadequacies, among them the implication that institutional treatment will indeed follow—a paradox, in light of the common belief that institutional care after probation proves that probation did not work.

Nevertheless, for purposes of this chapter, this definition of probation affords a context for the discussion of administering probation operations. Moreover, it allows for a relatively simple concept by which to relate probation to both prison and parole—that, in part, the *nature* of all three correctional functions is "people work."

Among the many advantages of utilizing a definition and nature that permit a conceptual relationship among all three correctional functions is the obvious reduction in fragmentation of thought, in the sense that they have in common a nature that is precisely the same except for the situation in which the "people work" occurs. Indeed, conceiving of the nature of all corrections as "people work," varying only with the correctional situation, permits administrators to relate correctional operations in a functional manner, goal-oriented and geared to reducing the problem of crime and delinquency.

## PROBATION ORGANIZATION

One need not share the cynical outlook for probation organizations to concede the validity of the ensuing commentary:

> . . . It is questionable whether bureaucratized probation organizations with their stress on routinization and their centralized decision-making processes are flexible enough to meet the change occurring within the environment of the community. . . .
>
> . . . Having been created in periods when the rate of change was relatively

[7] A. Murrah, *Journal of Criminal Law, Criminology and Police Science*, 47 (1956), 451.

slow, bureaucratic-type organizations such as probation departments are accustomed to functioning in a fairly undifferentiated and stable environment and under conditions of predictability. Today, however, the very texture of the social as well as the physical environments has changed. The rate of change itself has changed, accelerating at an ever-increasing rate. . . .[8]

The *organization* of probation, then, is of critical importance, rather than merely of administrative interest. As the rate of social change continues to accelerate, the organizational implications of delivering traditional services grows:

> . . . Probation may be viewed both as a sentence of the court and as a correctional process. In the former sense it combines the suspension of a punitive sanction against convicted offenders (ordinarily a prison or jail term) with orders for treatment under conditional liberty in the community. In the latter sense it includes the conduct of presentence investigation as an aid to court dispositions and the personal supervision and guidance of selected offenders in accordance with the conditions that the court establishes. It should be observed that probation usually involves the following elements: the conviction of a crime, the specified period of time and the avoidance of imprisonment, the imposition of conditions as a limitation on the freedom of the offender and as a basis for possible revocation, and the control and treatment of the individual in the community. . . . Probation differs from the suspended sentence in that the latter, taken alone, does not require supervision, though conditions may be attached and it is subject to revocation. It differs from parole in that it is a court sentence rather than a board determination and it is a substitute for, rather than a consequence of, imprisonment. Like parole, however, freedom on probation is subject to conditions, revocation, and imprisonment. Both imply supervision. Both imply supervision in the community.[9]

Note in particular that, in this classical explanation of probation, there is implied a considerable demand on the organization required to deliver these (adult) services—"treatment under conditional liberty in the community," "supervision and guidance"—both in addition to pre-sentencing demands that are also placed upon it.

Moreover, even without expressed demands as to how these services will be provided, the probation organization facing the accelerating rate of social change can scarcely ignore the problems related to change, even though virtually all explicit demands were also formulated in an era when probation departments were "accustomed to functioning in a fairly undifferentiated and stable environment and under conditions of predictability."[10]

Compounding the complexity of the problem, of course, is lack of

[8] D. C. Sullivan, *Team Management in Probation: Some Models for Implementation* (Paramus, N.J.: NCCD Training Ctr., 1972), p. 6.
[9] P. W. Tappan, *Crime, Justice and Correction* (New York: McGraw-Hill Book Company, 1960), p. 539.
[10] Sullivan, *Team Management.*

uniformity in organizational structure from one jurisdiction to the next, along with almost incredible variation, even inconsistency, in court sentencing practices. In addition, the organization of a system of probation, to be effective in crime *and* delinquency, must incorporate services for juveniles as well, thus increasing the demands upon the organization still more.

But it is these very demands that justify the functional-systems approach to correctional administration that was introduced in the three preceding chapters. The functional management system model, it will be recalled, isolates goal-oriented administration as the context in which clearly defined managerial functions are assigned to equally clarified managerial roles for the purpose of permitting effective managerial interfacing.

Recalling this system model, see the following diagram. The classical TO (table of organization) for the functions in the diagram is shown on the next page.

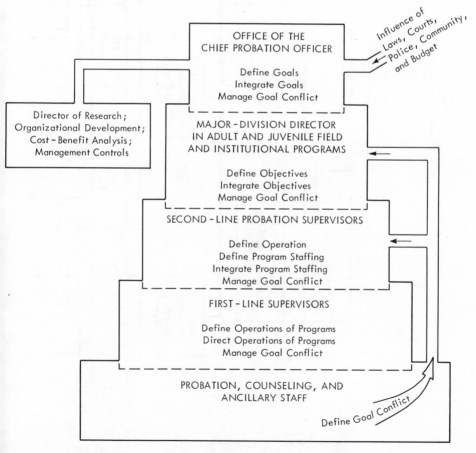

**PROBATION ORGANIZATION BY FUNCTION**

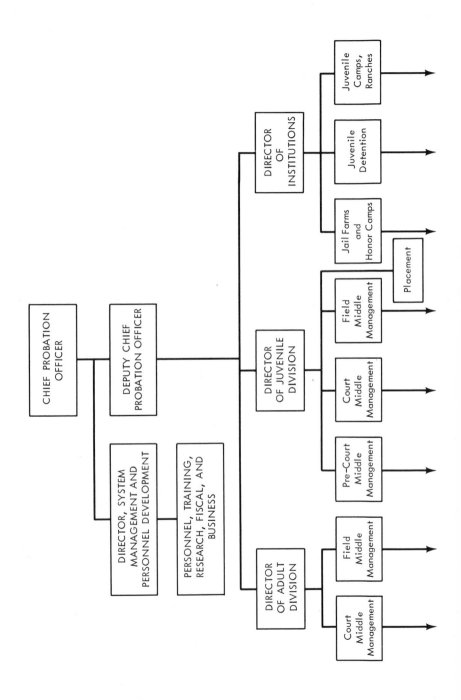

## Flow Process

Of course, any one segment of the TO has a "flow process"—a chartable flow of probation functions and subfunctions, and activities that have "options."

Moreover, these functions flow in a manner that of necessity cuts across other functions. Indeed, in matters that are not screened out of the system or diverted away from the system, more than one organizational function is invariably involved. And when there is institutional treatment involved, there is a kind of cutting-across of the entire TO. Consider the following example of flow process involving the juvenile segment of probation.

The actual organization within which the probation flow process occurs is, in most cases, somewhat military, in the sense that the line-and-staff method of organizing around levels of authority is used. Accountability for specific functions tends to reduce the need for authority, at least until the functions for which probation managers are accountable are *not* performed—at which point authority and administrative policy come into play. Organizationally, then, the managerial approach has considerable influence on the kind of organizational structure required.

There is a particular relationship between flow process and policy in terms of organizational structure. Therefore, although administrative policy was discussed in Chapters 2 and 3, policy as it relates to the flow process of the organization is worthy of note in a discussion of probation organization—particularly since the organizational structure and managerial approach influence administrative policy, in such matters as "the offender versus the community." This, although its implications are but one policy consideration, serves as an excellent example of how the organization, management approach, and policy are related.

Vincent O'Leary and David Duffee have devised an impressive method of conceptualizing various categories of correctional policy relating to organizational positions—in particular, the organizational position on "offender-versus-community." [11] Whatever its other merits, their approach proves beyond doubt that it is possible to conceptualize such things as a probation department as being organized, or "structured," for the community and programmed for the offender—a kind of administrative version of the contradictory influences of punishment and rehabilitation.

Although somewhat less dramatically contrasted, another such influence upon the flow process of a probation organization is the courts themselves. These are the embodiment of the effort to integrate punish-

[11] V. O'Leary and D. Duffee, "Correctional Policy—A Classification of Goals Designed to Change," *Crime and Delinquency*, 17, No. 4 (October 1971), 373–86.

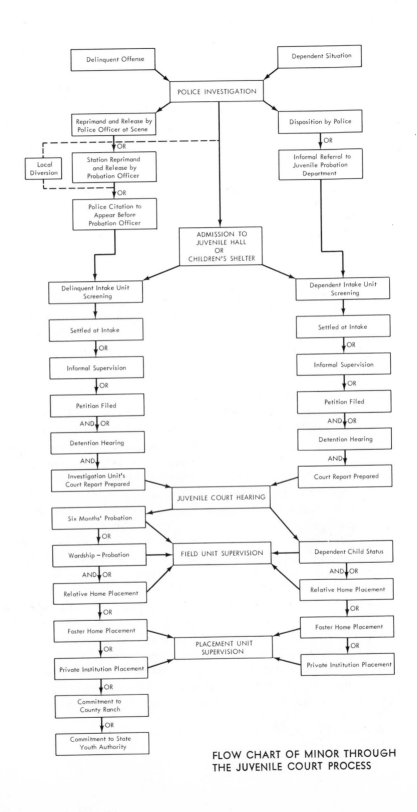

FLOW CHART OF MINOR THROUGH
THE JUVENILE COURT PROCESS

ment and rehabilitation through, at times, corrections in general, and, at times, probation in particular.

## The Courts

To establish a context for considering the relationship of the courts to probation, consider the following:

> . . . The most common approach to organizing a probation department is to form the county department in which the state writes the law and the county administers the roles, functions, and activities. The variation from this approach is the centralized state probation system, from which a "superagency" administers role and function throughout all counties of the larger jurisdiction. . . .[12]

There are still other variations, such as in the federal and certain state jurisdictions where the probation and parole functions are combined. This combination of probation and parole, operated by the same staff, may in fact be modeling a trend for what amounts to a *local* superagency. This local version combines at the county level all correctional services—adult and juvenile probation, institutions, and parole—all with virtually no dependence upon a state system.[13]

The court, then, relates to a much larger correctional system in all cases when the superagency emerges. The directness of the courts' relationship to corrections in general is usually confined to probation in any event, but this is particularly the case in terms of the superagency.

Larger correctional organizations incorporate probation as a single organizational element, then tend to minimize the directness of court involvement in correctional administration overall. Conversely, the more isolated probation is, the greater the judicial involvement in purely administrative matters—or at least, the greater the risk of such involvement. Put another way, the probation agency without institutional and post-institutional responsibilities is likely to have more judicial decisions than administrative decisions, regardless of what those decisions may be called.

Indeed, even when overwhelmingly complex administrative programming and fiscal problems confront a probation agency, judicial influence may well supersede administrative planning if there are no institutional responsibilities. The significance of this judicial influence could scarcely be overlooked in view of the practice in many jurisdictions of having the court appoint the top administrator in probation, with the appointment remaining "at the pleasure of the court."

Enlightenment on the major distinction between the administrative

[12] Coffey, *Administration of Criminal Justice*, p. 229.
[13] An example of such a system is reflected in the TO on page 31.

process and the judicial process continues to reduce the seriousness of this organizational problem. But it would be grossly premature to say that the problem is being resolved.

Of course, the relationship between probation administration and the court has many constructive facets, particularly in aligning judicial and correctional policies toward effective correctional outcome. When such alignment is developed, the activities of court and probation are mutually complimentary and facilitate correctional success. Administrative effort to bring such alignment about is, therefore, "high-yield time."

## ADULT PROBATION

The distinction between adult probation and juvenile probation is somewhat comparable to the distinction between responsibility and accountability. Perhaps an example will prove useful:

> Timmy is an eight-year-old who was taken into custody when police were summoned to a home in which Timmy was surprised by unexpectedly returning occupants.
>
> Randy is a fifteen-year-old who was taken into custody by deputy sheriffs who observed him exiting from a darkened home through a window.
>
> Orlando is an eighteen-year-old who was taken into custody by detectives staked out on a house that had been burglarized on numerous occasions prior to their observing Orlando leaving the house with a portable television.[14]

Juveniles, as legally defined minor children, are not *responsible* for crime, but are nonetheless *accountable* for delinquency. Young Timmy, although somewhat accountable, is less accountable than fifteen-year-old Randy. Yet neither juvenile is *responsible* for the offense for which he was taken into custody.

Adults, as legally defined mature individuals, are *responsible* for their offenses. Orlando is a legally defined adult and, if convicted of the offense for which he was arrested, is a criminal. The criterion by which Orlando can be identified as an adult and therefore a criminal is essentially the same criterion that distinguishes between adult and juvenile probation: Adult probation deals with clients considered legally responsible for their offenses; juvenile probation deals with clients considered to be, at most, accountable for their offenses.

Operationally, there are still other differences between adult and ju-

---

[14] A. R. Coffey, *Juvenile Justice as a System: Law Enforcement to Rehabilitation* (Englewood Cliffs, N.J.: Prentice-Hall, Inc., 1974). Chapters 1–4 elaborate on many dimensions of this distinction.

venile that are of relevance to the management and administration of probation departments.

## Adult Operations

In its broadest terms, adult probation operations divide into two general areas: court and supervision. "Court" refers to the probation activities directly related to the court process, and "supervision" refers to typical probation activities occurring after the court process.

Of course, the many additional probation operations of many jurisdictions complicate the simplicity of this division—in particular, such activities as collecting money, in the form of alimony, child support, restitution, and, in some jurisdictions, outright debts. For purposes of discussing the overall administration in probation, however, we will use the simple division between court and supervision.

Adult Probation in Court. As might be expected, the activities of probation officers in (and for) the criminal court vary from one jurisdiction to the next. Yet most of these officers perform a relatively uniform function that is commonly referred to as the "pre-sentence investigation report":

> The presentence investigation report is a basic working document in judicial and correctional administration. It performs five functions: (1) to aid the court in determining the appropriate sentence, (2) to assist Bureau of Prisons institutions in their release and planning, (3) to furnish the Board of Parole with information pertinent to its consideration of parole, (4) to aid the probation officer in his rehabilitative efforts during probation and parole supervision, and (5) to serve as a source of pertinent information for systematic research.
>
> The primary objective of the presentence report is to focus light on the character and personality of the defendant, to offer insight into his problems and needs, to help understand the world in which he lives, to learn about his relationships with people, and to discover those salient factors that underlie his specific offense and his conduct in general. It is not the purpose of the report to demonstrate the guilt or the innocence of the defendant.
>
> Authorities in the judicial and correctional fields assert that a presentence investigation should be made in every case. With the aid of a presentence report the court may avoid committing a defendant to an institution who merits probation instead, or may avoid granting probation when confinement is appropriate.
>
> Probation cannot succeed unless care is exercised in selecting those who are to receive its benefits. The presentence report is an essential aid in this selective process.[15]

15 Division of Probation, Administrative Office of the Unitel States Courts, "The Presentence Investigation Report, Its Functions and Objectives" (Washington, D.C.: U.S. Government Printing Office, February 1965), p. 1.

It would be difficult to expand on this succinct summary of the pre-sentence reporting process without including local variations, since the bulk of the administrative implications of the pre-sentence investigations that are common to most jurisdictions were covered rather adequately. Of course, a great deal more could be said on the subject if the discussion were focused on adult operations as such; but let us now shift our attention to the second operational segment of adult probation: Supervision.

ADULT PROBATION SUPERVISION.   Against the background of the probation activities in and for the court, let us try to establish a relationship between probation supervision and the pre-sentence investigation:

> As the literature of probation demonstrates, a thoroughly eclectic discipline possesses an almost infinite capacity to generate the most diverse forms of theory. Probation students' published attentions to supervision include everything from after-dinner speeches to decision models. Speeches tell the reader a good deal about the speaker and decision models tell a good deal about the officer, but neither seems to capture what probation supervision is. Decision models cannot be considered inappropriate, since knowledge of decision making is certainly of legitimate scientific concern. The speeches, as well as the dozens of articles which discuss the question of what probation supervision "ought to be," can be sympathetically interpreted as teaching theories. One cannot object to the treatment of probation problems at this level either. . . . Our intention is to provide a description and analysis of the standard form of probation supervision. To do so, four elements must be considered. The first is the working philosophy of the officer—the way he sees his job and duties. The second is the organizational context in which the officer finds himself. The third is the legal and logical definition of revocation, and the fourth is the psychological approach of the probationer. It is our observation that each of these four components responds to movement in the other. As a result, any theory of probation supervision must not only cite each of these components but also specify the nature and mechanics of their interaction.[16]

Now, within the context of this conceptual approach to relating the pre-sentence segment of probation to probation supervision, consider the implications of the following remarks on probation supervision:

> Probationary supervision has developed from a relatively simple process in which probation officers "advise, assist and befriend" probations, to a skilled operation on which an extensive body of theoretical knowledge is brought to bear. This distinction between benevolent assistance and skilled treatment is of great practical significance. Without the necessary training and understanding, "there is a temptation to rely on temporary palliatives, such as gifts or money, or on other measures which may keep the probationer out of mischief but will not prove a permanent cure." Similarly, the finding of employment and other auxiliary forms of assistance can only be fully

---

[16] C. B. Klockars, Jr., "A Theory of Probation Supervision," *The Journal of Criminal Law, Criminology and Police Science,* Vol. 63, No. 4 (December 1972), 550.

utilized in the interests of the probationer's social rehabilitation if done with an adequate understanding of his personality needs and his likely responses. Above all, refined understanding and skill are required for the constructive utilization of the personal relationship between officer and offender.[17]

The term *supervision*, in this context, could scarcely have the same meaning as the term *supervision* used in the preceding chapter (as in "supervisory management"). Indeed, relating pre-sentence probation activities to supervision, and in turn emphasizing treatment, tends to define supervision in a nonsupervisorial manner. In other words, pre-sentence investigation geared toward the appropriate probation treatment necessarily reduces the demand that the supervision be limited to supervising.

Nevertheless, probation administrators must conceive of probation supervision as including a great deal of supervising, if for no other reason than the legal structure and the implications of the penal sanctions within which probation operates. But besides concern for the supervising involved in probation supervision, administrators must consider treatment as an increasingly significant segment of the probation process. Methods and techniques of treatment within the probation supervision program include conjoint family therapy, transactional analysis, gestalt therapy, fight training, paradox intervention, crisis therapy, and a host of variations in behavior modification. Increasingly, these treatments and techniques are practiced within a growing number of sophisticated classification systems combining variables of personality, maturity, and behavior.

From an administrative point of view, the treatment classification that bears directly upon behavior, rather than feelings and emotions, affords greater advantage:

> The implementation of what we already know regarding behavior therapy would almost certainly result in a substantial improvement in our rehabilitative efforts. It was shown earlier in the article that principles of learning theory have been successfully applied in situations where all other approaches which were tried failed. There is little question that our correctional facilities are merely penal institutions—we are failing to rehabilitate offenders. A learning theory approach in the correctional setting seems promising. In the short run, a behavior modification program would probably be more economical than present programs in terms of time, money and effort.[18]

Beyond the correctional implications for institutional treatment referred to here is the probation application of isolating behavior as *the* significant variable: Behavior breaks the law, feeling cannot break laws.

---

[17] B. A. Kay and C. B. Vedder, eds., *Probation and Parole* (Springfield, Ill.: Charles C. Thomas, Publisher, 1963), p. 84.
[18] M. J. Hindelang, "A Learning Theory Analysis of the Correctional Process," *Issues in Criminology*, Vol. 5, No. 1 (Winter 1970), 54.

The significance of establishing this axiom in the field of corrections grows with each additional contact made by the offender with criminal justice. Probation is, to all intents and purposes, the first chance the correctional field has to establish that *behavior is optional*, even though feelings and emotions may not be—a significant consideration for probation administrators attempting to choose between behavior-oriented treatment and emotion treatment. The staff-training implications will be explored in subsequent chapters.

As one training director in a large probation agency stated, *"Behavior treatment and emotional treatment cannot be mixed. You can't tell a man not to hit his wife and then ask him how he feels when he hits her."*

## JUVENILE PROBATION

The most common concept of juvenile probation in the United States is as an arm of the juvenile court. At one time, this was appropriate: Following the opening of the first juvenile court, in Cook County Illinois, in 1899, the initial approach to probation placed probation officers in the position of being the judge's staff. Since that time, however, the expanding role of probation has reached proportions that force many jurisdictions to recognize the contradiction implicit in the judiciary's attempting to perform, simultaneously, the judicial function and the administrative functions of probation.

Since it remains common practice for the court to appoint probation officers, the juvenile court judge usually makes or strongly influences these appointments. Probation administration overall can, therefore, scarcely ignore the juvenile court.

### Juvenile Court and Juvenile Probation

Although there are many variations around the country in how the relationship between the juvenile court and probation is structured, there is a relatively simple concept that can be used to make this relationship functional and systematic. This concept is called a *linear system*.[19]

When stripped of the complex considerations needed for sophisticated systems analysis, a functional linear system is simply some configuration of input, process, and output. This can be diagrammed as follows:

[19] For more elaborate and technical discussion of the linear system than will be presented here, see Chapters 1, 3–9, and 14 of Coffey, *Administration of Criminal Justice*. See also A. R. Coffey, E. Eldefonso, and W. Hartinger, *Introduction to the Criminal Justice System and Process* (Englewood Cliffs, N.J.: Prentice-Hall, Inc., 1974), Chap. 1.

Juvenile justice, including juvenile probation, can be conceived of this way:

Compare this to criminal justice for adults:

Note in particular that the court, in both juvenile and adult matters, is only one of many functions of the system—an important function, but still only one. In adult matters, the court's influence over the administration of prosecution is virtually nonexistent. Juvenile court influence over the equivalent of prosecution for juvenile matters, however, is often all but overpowering.

The reasons for this juvenile court influence are many; but the administrative aspects are relatively few:

1.   The court's appointment of probation officers

2.   The legally sanctioned differences in dealing with delinquency and with crime (i.e., responsibility vs. accountability)

3.   The common practice by probation staff of performing essentially the same screening function for juveniles that criminal prosecutors perform in adult matters

In other words, the juvenile court influence on screening court cases exists in most cases because this function is assigned to the probation staff that works for a Chief Probation Officer appointed by the court, and thus the screening staff virtually works for the court at the time the cases are being screened. This screening, or "intake" function, is worthy of further consideration in the administrative context.

### Juvenile Probation Intake

In effect, the typical juvenile probation intake process actually changes the linear-system diagram of juvenile justice. This can be seen by isolating the "PROCESS" segment:

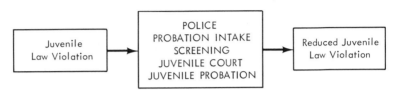

Note in particular that the probation intake function is performed *before* the screening, and the screening occurs *before* juvenile court—just as in the case of the functions of police and prosecutor in adult matters. The only difference between adult and juvenile matters in this regard is that juvenile intake is in many instances virtually controlled by the court, whereas the determination of adult prosecution is made somewhat independent of court.

However, in spite of the reality that the adjudication function frequently all but controls that which is to be adjudicated, discussion of the juvenile intake and screening remains in the administrative context, shifting away from existing reality toward a system that operates as though the screening function for juveniles operated as freely as in the case of adults. In other words, we approach the functional components of the juvenile justice system on the same basis as we do the components of the adult justice system.

*Emphasizing these functional aspects of a relationship between court and screening in no way reduces the significance of major differences between adult criminals and juvenile delinquents.* Such emphasis merely isolates the systematic approach to aligning functions toward outcome rather than toward each other—that is, to police, probation, and courts gearing their activities toward the specific outcome of reduced crime and delinquency, rather than to influence over each other. This "ideal" will be the context in which the following discussion of juvenile intake will be presented.

JUVENILE INTAKE AND THE POLICE.[20]   To understand the juvenile intake process as a functional component of the juvenile justice system overall, the relationship between police and probation must be examined. This does not minimize the significance of probation–court relations; it merely elevates the significance of police–probation relations.

[20] Some of the material used in this discussion has been treated in depth in Coffey, *Juvenile Justice as a System.*

Police discretion in determining whether or not to take a juvenile into custody does *not* in most jurisdictions include the discretion of whether to "bring the matter before the court." The actual petitioning of the court is customarily a matter for the juvenile probation staff.

But to be functional, the juvenile justice system requires police to operate independently and within the context of public safety, their own function, rather than in terms of the criteria probation officers use to determine court cases. And probation should, if it can, examine the case in the context of probation, rather than in terms of the judicial criteria used by juvenile courts to adjudicate the cases presented. In other words, a functional system brings three different perspectives to bear on delinquency rather than upon each other.

The systematic nature of functionally interfacing the three key elements of the juvenile intake screening process—police, probation, and court—will not be detailed here. But in the administrative context, the significance of bringing the three key perspectives to bear on delinquency rather than on each other cannot be overemphasized, particularly since many jurisdictions virtually prevent separating these elements functionally. From this situation arises a kind of mythology that two elements can be interchangeable. Indeed, many probation administrators find that the juvenile court control over what the court will hear is greater than control by a state supreme court over what appeals will be heard; the state supreme courts customarily refrain from active influence over the selection of cases they hear.

DIVERSION. The administrative relevance of the intake screening process is embodied in the "system discretion" to prevent youthful offenders from penetrating the system—in diverting predelinquents. Chapter 8 will elaborate on community-based correctional activities that involve prevention and such diversion. But in the current context of the ideal intake and screening function, the three key elements of the justice system for juveniles must be permitted to function independently in order to permit either diversion or prevention of delinquency. Our discussion in Chapter 1 of "system versus nonsystem" emerges as exceedingly relevant to the administration of the intake screening process, if the correctional system is to be effective.

## Juvenile Supervision

Although there are many significant differences between the probation supervision of adults and that of minors, probation administration as such can conceive of the budgeting, planning, and directing of both in much the same way. The differences lie in references to schools instead of jobs, parents instead of employers, runaways instead of divorces, and a host of similar situations of administrative concern. But even these situational differences tend to be reduced from the administrative perspective when treatment methods are considered. There are far more similarities than differences in probation supervision of adults and juveniles, situational exceptions notwithstanding, as we shall see in Chapter 10.

Perhaps this point is made more eloquently in the related implications of the following:

> Perhaps the most creative innovation of all would be for us to really work toward professionalism. None of us—be he probation officer, parole agent, or correctional worker—is simply a county, state, or federal employee. We must reach the point where it is generally acknowledged that we are professionals who simply happen to be working for this county, that state, or the federal government. When this occurs—and it won't unless we make it occur—we'll be able to elevate standards, enrich programs, and develop staff, having achieved such things as federal and state registration and licensing, standardization of salaries, and exchange of staff at the same levels, temporarily or permanently, among our different agencies.
>
> The potential for our budding profession is phenomenal. But accepting the challenges of our role as pioneers means increasing our involvement, committing ourselves to viewing our work as much more than eight-hour shifts, forty-hour work weeks, four-week vacations, and other assorted fringe benefits.[21]

## ADMINISTRATIVE SUCCESS IN PROBATION

One final but vital consideration in the administration of a probation department is the concept of administrative success. Fundamentally, probation success occurs whenever crime or delinquency has been reduced as a result of probation effort. Administrative success, of course, includes this definition of success in probation. But administrative success in probation must also include some measures of reducing crime and delinquency *on a systematic basis*, and doing so *at the least possible cost*.

In essence, the roles and functions presented for administrators, managers, and supervisors in the three preceding chapters interrelate (at least in the ideal) to cope with the following problem:

> There is no question that the offender is a consumer of resources, nor is there any doubt that the costs he incurs will increase as new and expanded correctional programs and services are developed for his benefit and so-

[21] P. Stein, "Are Probation Officers Really Professionals?" *Crime and Delinquency,* Vol. 17, No. 3 (July 1971), 301.

ciety's. The central question now becomes: How can greater returns be produced by the resources that are consumed? [22]

The administrative obligation to ensure that this question gets answered can be approached from many perspectives—from the functional system model, from management by objectives, from organization development, or any number of others. But regardless of the perspective, administrative success in probation demands constant emphasis on research in answering this question and continuous assessment of progress.

There are many methods and techniques for systematically assessing administrative success in planning and accomplishment. *Program Evaluation and Review Technique* (PERT) is one device used. It is geared to planning but strategically valuable in assessing the success of plans as well.

## PERT AND PROBATION

PERT is an acronym for Program Evaluation and Review Technique, a planning and control technique devised for large complex projects. Like other great "revolutionary" techniques it too had its predecessors. It is generally admitted that PERT owes much to the Critical Path Method and to the now famous Gantt Chart Method. However, as a refinement of previous methods it has effected significant changes in planning and control, so much so that some enthusiastic advocates look upon PERT as a panacea for all that ails management. A more sobering exposition would undoubtedly reveal that PERT was originally conceived not as a nostrum for management fevers but as a rationally based total system approach to the planning and control aspects of research and development projects currently in vogue.[23]

As implied in this somewhat cynical comment, PERT is less than utopian in nature for probation administrators. But without losing sight of its limitations, consider the probation administrative potential of PERT in terms of integrating complex programs of adult–juvenile probation, court–probation, polic–probation, detention homes, and even correctional facilities that include probation aftercare:

PERT, as a dynamic program tool, uses linear programming and statistical probability concepts to plan and control series and parallel tasks which appear only remotely interrelated. Many tasks involve extensive research and development which itself is difficult to schedule, least of all to find a "one best way" of doing it. PERT's objective is to determine the optimum

[22] M. S. Richmond, "Measuring the Cost of Correctional Services," *Crime and Delinquency*, Vol. 18, No. 3 (July 1972), 252.
[23] P. P. Schoderbek, "PERT and PERT/Cost," *Management Systems* (New York: John Wiley & Sons, Inc., 1971), p. 445.

way by which to maximize the attainment, in time, of some predetermined objective that is preceded by a number of constraints—hence its linear programming feature. A measure of the degree of risk is predicted in probabilistic terms to foretell the reasonableness of accomplishment on scheduled time—hence its statistical probability feature.[24]

Although it is unlikely to generate the wholehearted enthusiasm of managers attracted to the probation field through behavioral interests, PERT, as one of many methods to assess administrative planning and accomplishment success, puts to rest the belief of many that plans and programs cannot be continuously updated, evaluated, and even measured. And once the premise is accepted that administrative success in probation (and in corrections in general) requires such evaluation, even a statistical technique such as PERT can gain a significant place in managerial activities.

## SUMMARY

This chapter began with a comment on the need to recognize the relationship between probation and correctional institutions as being particularly significant, as public and political concern appear to mount with regard to prisons.

The nature of probation was described as pre-institutional, as opposed to the post-institutional nature of parole.

The complexities of defining probation were explored at length; the definition reached was *legally defined activities for children and adults that serve both correctional rehabilitation and justice prior to institutional treatment.*

Probation organization was elaborated upon from the administrative perspective, and examples of a TO and flow process were presented. The relation of probation to the courts was emphasized, particularly through the typical juvenile court influence over the top probation administrator.

The operation of the probation organization was administratively divided into *adult* and *juvenile,* and each was discussed in terms of managerial considerations and related activities.

The chapter was concluded with a brief discussion of probation administrative success, with emphasis on the complexity of the various programs under probation that require evaluation on an ongoing basis.

[24] D. G. Boulanger, "Program Evaluation and Review Technique," *Advanced Management,* July–August 1961, p. 8.

## Discussion Topics

1. Elaborate on the need for probation administrators to remain sensitive to public concern with prisons.
2. Discuss the many influences on defining probation.
3. Relate the organization of probation to the administrative management of probation.
4. Relate flow process to administration.
5. Elaborate on the influence of the court on probation.
6. Contrast adult operations and juvenile operations in terms of responsibility versus accountability.
7. Discuss probation administrative success.

## Annotated References

COFFEY, A., *Criminal Justice Administration: A Management Systems Approach.* Englewood Cliffs, N.J.: Prentice-Hall, Inc., 1974. Chapters 3–9 and Chapter 11 explore all that was presented in this chapter as administrative responsibility in probation.

———, *Juvenile Justice as a System: Law Enforcement to Rehabilitation.* Englewood Cliffs, N.J.: Prentice-Hall, Inc., 1974. In-depth elaboration of what was presented in this chapter as juvenile operations and court influence on probation administration.

———, E. ELDEFONSO, and W. HARTINGER, *Introduction to the Criminal Justice System and Process.* Englewood Cliffs, N.J.: Prentice-Hall, Inc., 1974. Comprehensive elaboration of what this chapter presented as the relationship between probation and prison as well as other criminal justice subsystems.

———, and V. RENNER, eds., *Criminal Justice as a System: Readings.* Englewood Cliffs, N.J.: Prentice-Hall, Inc., 1974. Supportive collection of articles bearing directly upon the relationships between probation and all other criminal justice functions.

Fox, V., *Introduction to Corrections.* Englewood Cliffs, N.J.: Prentice-Hall, Inc., 1972. Good overview of correctional practice as opposed to this chapter's emphasis on managerial perspective. See also W. Hartinger, E. Eldefonso, and A. Coffey, *Corrections: A Component of the Criminal Justice System.* Pacific Palisades, Calif.: Goodyear Publishing Co., Inc., 1973.

MacCORMICK, A. H., "The Potential Value of Probation," *Federal Probation,* 19 (March 1955), 4–5. Clarifies the concept of probation as it existed two decades ago in the same context as this chapter.

ROBINSON, J., and G. SMITH, "The Effectiveness of Correctional Programs," *Crime and Delinquency,* 17 (January 1971). Good transitional material relating this chapter to corrections overall.

# The Administration
# of Correctional
# Institutions

# Chapter 6

Although the trend in corrections appears to be clearly toward the "community-based," the role of correctional institutions nevertheless remains significant. Indeed, many consider the role of prisons even more critical than in the past. One of the reasons presented is the protection of the public:

> Prison contribution to public protection is twofold. First, for the most serious felonies, including homicide, sale of heroin, receiving stolen property, robbery and other dangerous, violent crimes, prison protects simply by isolating the criminal for long terms. The public should be protected by sentencing all such offenders to state prison to be retained for substantial terms.
>
> Second, prison can contribute to public protection against all felonies by punishing offenders who are convicted, and deterring those who are potential offenders. For this purpose, it is more important that the sentence be swift and certain rather than be severe. In other words, it is more effective if 25 to 35 percent of burglars average 14 months in prison than if 8 percent average 36 months. . . .
>
> Felony probation tends to be a method to keep criminals out of state prison.

Many criminals for whom probation is considered should be sentenced to state prison. To that end, any aspect of probation subsidy which provides a financial incentive for not sentencing criminals to state prison should be eliminated.

Probation should be returned to its original function of providing a defendant who is a good risk a chance to prove that he has learned his lesson and deserves not to go to prison. Regardless of other factors such as background and seriousness of the crime, a defendant should not be granted probation unless the judge believes he has a reasonable chance to remain free and without violation for at least five years.

Probation should not be regarded as keeping the probationer out of prison but rather emphasize that the probationer keeps himself out of prison. If he violates probation, probation should be revoked and he should be sentenced to prison. There has been an excessive tolerance of violations of probation which should be eliminated. . . .[1]

In spite of this significant argument in favor of retaining prisons as a vital part of corrections, however, concern with prison administration has appeared to be on the rise in recent years. The following remarks are typical of the concerns that have been expressed:

The failure of prison rehabilitation programs to achieve their stated purposes is becoming increasingly well documented. Typically, treated and untreated inmates have similar rates of return to crime after release from prison. This appears also to be true for treatment programs administered in halfway houses or in community treatment situations. Poor methodology makes it difficult to interpret occasionally reported successes as unambiguous indication of effectiveness of treatment; on at least one occasion, it was possible to demonstrate that the "success" of a treatment program was an artifact created by differential parole revocation policies for the treated and control groups.[2]

Of course, the implications of these critical comments cannot be taken out of the context of the "severity" of the inmate population with whom correctional institutions must deal. Prisons typically hold cases of far greater severity than do probation caseloads, for example, and this severity must be taken into consideration when examining the success of correctional institutions:

Deciding whether to place an offender on probation or to imprison him is not determined by the relative rehabilitative efficacy of the two approaches. The courts place only their "best risks" on probation; the persons who are

[1] *Report of the Governor's Select Committee on Law Enforcement Problems, Protecting the Law-Abiding,* "Controlling Crime In California," Sacramento, August 1973, pp. 67–68.
[2] David F. Greenberg, "A Voucher System for Correction," *Crime and Delinquency,* Vol. 19, No. 2 (April 1973), 212–13. See also "Justice on Trial," *Newsweek,* March 9, 1971, pp. 16–19.

imprisoned differ in many ways from those given probation. Hence a simple analysis of the difference in recidivism rates between prison and probation cases will not answer questions about their relative effectiveness. Exploring this difference requires control for case differences.[3]

Stated more bluntly, prisons in effect deal with either probation "failures" or cases too severe for probation. Not surprisingly then, many "successes" in prison turn out to be more apparent than real. Severity is one of the major concerns in administering correctional institutions, as well as in judging the success of such administration.

## OFFENDER SEVERITY

For a number of years, a trend has been developing toward "community-based" correctional approaches. (This trend will be elaborated on in Chapter 8 in terms of a correctional-prevention approach to programming, with various levels of such prevention shown as vital to the future success of the correctional field overall.) The steady rise of the "release on own recognizance" (O.R.) replacing bail, of the serving of sentences on weekends, of work furlough, delinquency prevention, and offender diversion, along with a host of other specially designed intensive programs, have marked the progress of this trend.

As a result, there has been a gradual change in the prison population. The once heterogeneous inmate population that ranged from "extremely dangerous" to "model honor trustees" has gradually evolved toward a somewhat homogeneous population of severely criminalistic offenders. The "model honor trustees" are now the offenders being channeled through community programs to probation and other alternatives to imprisonment. In other words, *prisons are increasingly populated by the most severe of those offenders apprehended in criminal justice.*

Administrative effort to cope with this reality takes many forms—some effective, some not so effective. Compounding the frustration of many administrators is the articulate criticism from some who feel that severity is not the key issue, and may not even be relevant—at least not as relevant as certain other changes that are occurring:

Fogel, former prisons director in Minnesota and now director of the Illinois Law Enforcement Commission, conceptualized the philosophy shared by a distinct number of innovators inside and outside of corrections.

First of all, said Fogel, the treatment–rehabilitation approach to corrections has failed, and what we are left with is what we essentially began with:

[3] James Robinson and Gerald Smith, "The Effectiveness of Correctional Programs," *Crime and Delinquency*, Vol. 17, No. 1 (January 1971), 68.

"The angry and inappropriate protagonists—keeper and kept—playing out a drama of escalating confrontation which promises to reach epic proportion.

"Human dignity is reaching a new plateau which some administrators have fearfully mistaken for a widespread conspiracy among a 'new breed' of inmates," said Fogel. "Our history is full of such excuses and alibis. Let's finally realize and say out loud that we have in this society . . . witnessed a belated human rights explosion which promises to continue. This means more, not less people, are willing to use the system.

"Almost all the people we have incarcerated don't know how, have tried to manipulate, or have demonstrated that they haven't been willing to use the system. The period of incarceration can be conceptualized as the time in which we try to reorient a man in a prison to how to lawfully use the system by example.

"Perhaps the most fruitful way of teaching non-law abiders to be law-abiding is to *treat them* in a lawful manner. The entire effort of the prison should be brought into an influence attempt based upon teaching by program and example. This is called the 'justice model' of rehabilitation." [4]

The claim that attacks upon prisons are merely "fashionable" is of little comfort to prison administrators:

It has long been fashionable, both in this country and abroad, to attack as corrupt and inefficient the staid political and economic institutions upon which an industrial society is built. And in this age of computerized, Madison Avenue megalopolis, sacred cows can be slaughtered wholesale by anyone with enough money or influence to command a headline. Recently, dissatisfaction has centered around the glaring inadequacies of our penal institutions, considered by most to be the weakest link in the system's chain. Unfortunately, responsive measures taken by those in positions of authority, as evidenced by the killings at San Quentin and Attica, have served to crystallize rather than dissolve this dissent.[5]

Add to the implications of these remarks the subsequent Oklahoma prison riots and similar disturbances, and it becomes clear that severity is both relevant and not readily perceived by the critics of correctional institutions.

On the other hand, there are those who show sensitivity to the criminal severity of inmate populations as compared to probation caseloads:

Among these problems which cry out for solution is the condition of corrections in our country: brutal jails, festering prisons, inadequate parole and

---

[4] "Corrections: Justice Model of Rehabilitation Explained," *Criminal Justice Newsletter*, Vol. 4, No. 14 (July 9, 1973), 6.
[5] University of Kentucky, "Transcendental Meditation and the Criminal Justice System," *Kentucky Law Journal*, Vol. 60, No. 2 (1971–72), 1. See also Russell Oswald, *Attica—My Story*, ed. Rodney Campbell (Garden City, N.Y.: Doubleday & Company, Inc., 1972.)

probation services, the whole false economy of warehousing men without making any effort to train or rehabilitate or educate them, or, sometimes, even to treat them with minimal human decency. It is as though upon the imprisonment of an offender we expect never to see him again, and consider the problem settled.

When there is a tragedy such as Attica or San Quentin, or when the "Tombs" Prison in New York explodes in violence, or when juveniles are raped in prison vans on their way to court, or when a runaway child is murdered while being held overnight in a common cell with older, brutal prisoners in a Dade County, Florida, jail, the public is horrified. But it soon forgets in the distraction of tomorrow's headline about something else. There seems to be a barrier between public concern and this other world of corrections that does not seem to involve most of us directly.

Aside from these occasional warning signals of disaster which are forgotten so soon, many thoughtful men in our profession have warned us that in permitting public apathy to let corrections sink into its present condition, we build a monster which threatens our whole society.[6]

Correctional administrators may acknowledge the absolute validity of this criticism, but they are often powerless to undertake the changes called for. Nor can comfort be gained from the repeated assertion that criticism of prisons is simply in vogue with the times:

The decade of the 1960's ushered in an era in which criminal law, public institutions and a host of penological "sacred cows" were subject to searching criticism. A reordering of priorities in certain specific areas was widely discussed, and, especially in the legal field, direct judicial intervention to effect this reordering was not only theoretically contemplated, but was actually realized in practice.[7]

The lack of recognition that severity relates directly to prison problems is understandable from many quadrants. It remains surprising, however, when even some of the more scholarly, research-oriented criticisms tend to avoid explicitly acknowledging that prisons are increasingly populated by inmates on whom all else has been tried.

The following comments—again, absolutely valid—clarify severity as a major impediment to institutional success:

To the best of our knowledge at this point in the development of criminology, the organizational structures of many correctional institutions are the major enemy of effective correctional programs. It is the enemy because

[6] Richard J. Hughes, "Corrections Reform: A Mission for the Lawyer," *Judicature*, Vol. 55, No. 8 (April 1972), 315.
[7] Charles S. Prigmore, Ph.D., and John C. Watkins, Jr., "Correctional Manpower: Are We 'The Society of Captives'?" *Federal Probation*, Vol. XXXVI, No. 4 (December 1972), 12.

of its direct relationship with the type of inmate society which emerges within these institutions, and because the attitudes, values, and norms which are transmitted during each inmate's socialization to this minisociety can make or break any program. Yet we ignore this body of research far more than we openly recognize it. We ignore more than 15 years of well-conceptualized, often very well executed, research. A major reason for this inaction appears to be that it does not fit dominant preconceptions held by correctional practitioners about how individuals may be resocialized. But the dominant preconceptions are not resulting in effective programs and they never have. So we look for subtle differences among the trees and never at the forest.[8]

It would be absurd to ignore the value of any of these criticisms. All are relevant, and all include significant considerations in bringing the administration of correctional institutions to grips with the obvious reality that changes *must* occur—indeed *will* occur, one way or the other.

Equally absurd would be to approach institutional administration as though modern inmate populations even resembled the average severity of those at the time these institutions were built—even if maximum-security institutions are being considered.

Our discussion of administering correctional institutions, then, will be carried out with the recognition of the validity of mounting criticism, as well as awareness that solutions must include the reality of inmate populations made up—often *entirely*—of the severest cases in criminal justice.

## OPERATING CORRECTIONAL INSTITUTIONS

From the perspective of criminal justice, a correctional institution is any facility to which the criminal court or the juvenile court sends offenders. Notice that physical custody in itself does not necessarily qualify as "corrections." Something else is needed—*direction* by the criminal court or the juvenile court that an offender be detained. Even with this provision, however, this definition is extremely broad in scope. With such a scope, a correctional institution is any of the following:

| | |
|---|---|
| Prison | Training school |
| Reformatory | Camp |
| Penitentiary | Ranch |
| Jail | Detention hall |
| Jail farm | House of correction |

[8] Charles W. Thomas, "The Correctional Institution as an Enemy of Corrections," *Federal Probation*, Vol. XXXVII, No. 1 (March 1973), 12.

The names for such facilities vary from one jurisdiction to the next, and there is a vast number of jurisdictions: [9]

The federal system
The systems of fifty different states
Variations within each state by counties
Variations within each state by cities
District of Columbia
Puerto Rico

The enormous diversity in operating these myriad correctional institutions is compounded by yet another variable—the enormous volume involved in the inmate population. On a typical day, correctional institutions around the country are responsible for between a million and one and one-half million inmates, with the average number of admissions annually between two and three million. Not surprisingly, the collective annual budget for correctional institutions is well over $1 billion.[10]

Even though this tremendously diverse and expensive operation does not readily lend itself to description, there are certain categories of correctional institutions that do provide a conceptual framework within which correctional administration can be considered. For example, all correctional institutions fall into one or more of the following classifications:

Juvenile institution
Women's institution
Men's institution
Minimum-security institution
Medium-security institution
Maximum-security institution

### Jails as Correctional Institutions

Perhaps one source of confusion in the simplification of institutional categories is the jail as a correctional institution. Given the definition of the correctional institution as any facility to which the court sends an offender, many jails qualify, in that courts often send offenders to adult jails and juvenile detention facilities for correction. Thus, in effect, the very same facility used for detaining individuals *before* court becomes

[9] President's Commission on Law Enforcement and the Administration of Justice, *Task Force Report: Corrections* (Washington, D.C.: U.S. Government Printing Office, 1967), p. 5.
[10] *Ibid.*

the institution in which correction is to take place—mixing law enforcement and correction.

On the one hand, detention before court is legitimately a function of law enforcement, rather than of corrections:

> . . . From an administrative point of view, the issue is not whether a person taken into custody is to be punished or dealt with constructively, but concern for the safety of society regarding the ability of the accused to escape before his guilt or innocence can be established. From this particular frame of reference, administering jails as part of the police subsystem is amply justified, the assumption being that an arrest would not be made unless the community was in some danger requiring the custody of the accused. . . .[11]

On the other hand, however, corrections, as a systematic process occurring *after* court, is no longer an appropriate function of police. To clarify this, recall the discussion of court influence over probation. In much the same way that the potential of probation administration diminishes to the degree that it becomes a judicial function, so also does the correctional potential diminish to the degree that it is made a police function rather than a correctional function—unless, of course, punishment as such is the extent of corrections.

But even if punishment *is* the extent of the correction desired, the criminal justice function designed to find and arrest the offender is scarcely the appropriate function to punish and release him:

> . . . If this interpretation is correct, many of the psychological pains of imprisonment are revealed most clearly at time of release rather than entry. It suggests a basis for a cyclical fluctuation of attitudes as the offender sheds the culture of the prison, experiences social rejection, finds support among other former inmates, returns to crime and to prison, reincorporates prison values, and so on. If true, it points to another possible reason for the organization of therapeutic efforts around the time of release, as well as to the limitations of such efforts unless they can bring about a change in the response to the offender on the part of those in his parole environment. And it suggests that sociological research should be as concerned with the process of re-entry into the community as it has been historically with the problem of assimilation in prison. . . .[12]

Finding and arresting, when considered in the context above, is scarcely the same thing as punishing and releasing, even if no "therapeutic effort" nor "sociological research" is added to the punishing imprisonment.

Be all this as it may, many jails are correctional institutions and fall

[11] Alan R. Coffey, *Administration of Criminal Justice* (Englewood Cliffs, N.J.: Prentice-Hall, Inc., 1974), p. 253.
[12] Stanton Wheeler, "Socialization in Correctional Communities," *American Sociological Review*, Vol. 26, No. 5 (October 1961), 711.

within the categories to be considered: institutions for juveniles, women, and men, and all with security either minimum, medium, or maximum.

## INSTITUTIONAL SECURITY

From the administrative viewpoint, the security of a correctional institution has to do with a number of variables, one of which is severity, as already discussed—the degree of severity in part determining the degree of security.

Another influence upon security is the nature of the inmate population. In addition to the severity of criminality, the nature of the criminality is also significant in terms of security:

Violently assaultive
Potentially assaultive
Property offenses

These three crude classifications may serve to conceptualize the general nature of criminality to be judged in terms of severity. Of course, a given offender may be violently assaultive in an institution even though the crime for which he was sentenced is a property offense.

Inmate populations also include offenders who are severe mental, emotional, physical, or psychiatric problems:

Mentally ill inmates
Mentally defective inmates
Epileptic inmates
Drug-addicted inmates
Physically or mentally abnormal inmates
Inmates with chronic disorders

All these considerations bear directly upon institutional security. Ideally, the bearing would be so direct that institutions would be structured, organized, and administered totally in terms of the nature of the inmate population. This would make security only one of many important considerations. Regrettably, this is not the case and does not appear to be likely for some time to come in many jurisdictions. Institutional security remains, therefore, critically significant.

### Security and Risk

Having related the degree of security to the severity of criminality and to the nature of the inmate population, we can think of security as simply the degree of *risk* involved in retaining the inmate population.

Administratively, then, when the risk of losing custody of inmates is minimal, the institution can have minimum security. In other words, if the severity and nature of the inmate population pose little risk of losing custody, the administration of the institution need not focus on security.

This, of course, brings into focus the *selection process*—the methods through which inmates posing minimal security risks are chosen. This process of classifying inmates in terms of risks, increasingly difficult in view of the trend already mentioned toward selecting offenders for community programs, is still a significant segment of correctional administration.

One approach is the attempt to determine through an offender's record the nature and severity of his criminality, and in turn relate this to the particular type of institution. An infinite variety of screening committees and classification boards function for this purpose.

Administratively, however, the most systematic approach appears to be the reception center.

### The Reception Center

The reception center provides a great deal more correctional service than selection of the institution that offers the proper degree of security for the risk involved:

> The reception and classification center, whether it is a separate institution or part of an existing institution, is administratively operated on the basis of an offender as being committed by a court to the correctional process rather than to a specific prison. It is used as a method of individualizing the offender, with the treatment program and the specific correctional institution designed to fit the specific needs of the offender. Although the court making the commitment has frequently been exposed to an exhaustive study of the offender through the probation department's presentence report, few judges are completely acquainted with the various institutions and programs to which an individual can be committed, including the reception classification center.

> One of the keys to having a good correctional program within the state is provision for an orderly diagnosis and treatment of offenders by classification into appropriate treatment categories. Administratively, this can best be effected by statutes permitting the courts to commit convicted offenders to the process of corrections rather than to a given institution or program.[13]

Note in particular the use of the reception center for *diagnosis*—which implicitly concedes that the appropriate correctional process is difficult to determine even by those specializing in the correctional system. Moreover, there is an implicit acknowledgment that such diagnosis is virtually impossible when undertaken on the basis of legal procedure or court pro-

[13] Coffey, *Administration of Criminal Justice*, pp. 248–49.

cedure alone. Indeed, the acknowledged validity of the criticisms cited early in this chapter *may relate more to the absence of sophisticated reception centers than to inadequate prison administration.*

Ideally, then, the categories of minimum-, medium-, and maximum-security institutions should encompass a great deal more than degree of risk.

### Minimum Security [14]

The absence of guards and fences is the most conspicuous characteristic of the minimum-security correctional institution—at least those that are typically located in remote areas. More often than not, inmates are housed in dormitories. A wide variety of minimum-security institutions exist in the United States. Two examples may illustrate the nature of the program administered in these institutions.

CAMPS.  The least restrictive of the minimum-security institutions is the camp. Administratively, the cost of all minimum-security institutions is substantially lower than that of higher-security institutions for two primary reasons:

1.  Dormitories instead of cells
2.  Smaller staff without guards

In the case of camps, the cost is still lower, because of the reduced overhead. Camps are often located strategically to provide forestry or forestation services or similar programs by which the jurisdiction receives services from the inmates, at a fraction of ordinary service costs even where the inmates are paid.

RANCHES.  A slightly more structured version of the minimum-security institution is the ranch, sometimes called, in the case of adult offenders, the jail farm. The same fiscal advantage accrues to ranches as to camps, with the services to the jurisdiction usually in agriculture and livestock rather than forestry. Although the principal inmate housing is dormitory-style, administration of the typical program customarily includes additional facilities for education, medical services, and, in some instances, "security cells."

### Medium Security

The administrative costs of the medium-security correctional institution increase over camps and ranches in the very structural facet that dis-

[14] The institutional programming involved is treated in greater detail than here in A. Coffey, E. Eldefonso, and W. Hartinger, *Introduction to the Criminal Justice System and Process* (Englewood Cliffs, N.J.: Prentice-Hall, Inc., 1974), Chap. 11.

tinguishes a medium-security from a minimum-security institution: a double 12-foot fence, guards, and, typically, cells instead of dormitories.

The medium-security cell is customarily on the outside wall of a building that is never closer than 35 feet to the inner security fence. Perhaps because of increasing dependence upon the medium-security institutions in most states, cells have been replaced in some places by dormitories, thereby lowering the administrative costs substantially. Nevertheless, the operational cost of a medium-security institution is enormous compared to that of minimum-security institutions.

Unlike the case with camps and ranches, the inmate activity is completely programmed to the institution, rather than to forestry, agriculture, or similar activities. Occasionally, minimum-security "satellites" provide specialized-program tracts for the medium-security institution, but by and large, the correctional program is administered on the basis of the institution itself.

### Maximum Security

Although some maximum-security institutions are enclosed by the same kind of double fence that characterizes the medium-security institution, the more typical approach to maximum security is the 18- to 25-foot-high stone or brick wall with guard towers.

By far the most expensive of correctional institutions, maximum-security structures are on the decline. The costs of building cells on interior walls alone constitute enormous fiscal outlay. This overwhelming financial burden may account for the increasing expectation that such institutions will be continually replaced with medium-security operations in most jurisdictions as the severity and nature of inmate population permit.

An additional administrative responsibility in many maximum-security institutions is the maintenance of facilities for imposing capital punishment. In jurisdictions permitting the death penalty, the electric chair, gallows, gas chamber, or firing squad is customarily housed in the most secure segment of the maximum-security institution.

## INSTITUTIONS FOR JUVENILES, WOMEN, AND MEN

The inmates in the overwhelming majority of correctional institutions are segregated by both age and sex, but such segregation is not *necessarily* the case:

> In a number of smaller states as well as in many county and municipal jails, men and women are housed together within the same institution. This causes problems when men and women attend joint movies or other entertain-

ment, and religious services. These problems make separate institutions for males and females seem more and more desirable.

However, at the juvenile level, thirteen of a total of two hundred and twenty institutions are designated as coeducational. Obviously, the institutions being so designated are not detention homes. They are what is commonly referred to as training facilities.[15]

Many exceptions notwithstanding, however, most correctional institutions *are* administered on the basis of sex and age, and are clearly distinguishable as institutions for juveniles (male or female), men, women, and, at times, "young offenders."

### Juvenile Institutions [16]

TRAINING SCHOOLS. Until the elimination in Massachusetts of state-operated "training schools," there was at least one such institution in every state jurisdiction. The significance of the Massachusetts program would be difficult to overestimate; its impact will prove profound throughout the field of juvenile justice.

Closing of these training schools is generally attributed to Dr. Jerome Miller, whose position has drawn both praise and criticism. Here is a sample of the former:

> Dr. Miller has dealt a death blow to training schools in this country. The movement to store delinquent kids in institutional warehouses is dead. For that, we are also in Miller's debt.
>
> Miller has given tremendous impetus to the community-based services movement, which while already working in Florida, California, Kentucky and elsewhere, has yet to get off the drawing boards in many states. Then there is also the comprehensive purchase-of-care programs that Miller put together in Massachusetts which will hopefully be the precedent of each state's approach to community-based services.
>
> Whether or not one accepts Dr. Miller's premise that the training schools in Massachusetts were unsalvageable . . . there can be no question but that he has changed the course of the juvenile justice system. . . .[17]

Whether or not one agrees with the Massachusetts position, it remains clear that there is growing interest in alternatives to training schools. But

[15] Walter Hartinger, Edward Eldefonso, and Alan Coffey, *Corrections: A Component of the Criminal Justice System* (Pacific Palisades, Calif.: Goodyear Publishing Co., Inc., 1973), p. 209.

[16] Beyond the administrative context presented here, the entire correctional system for juveniles is treated in considerable detail in A. Coffey, *Juvenile Justice as a System: Law Enforcement to Rehabilitation* (Englewood Cliffs, N.J.: Prentice-Hall, Inc., 1974).

[17] Editorial, "Miller Maligned," *Impact* (Raleigh, N.C.), Vol. 1, No. 5 (June/July, 1973), 2.

since training schools are still the most commonly used juvenile institutions, they remain of significant administrative concern.

The typical training school in most states is equivalent to at least the medium-security and sometimes the maximum-security adult institution, except for the elimination of the armed guards—although it frequently includes design characteristics used for nothing other than retention of custody of residents.

The term *training* suggests much of the rationale for the programs offered in these institutions, considered by many to be more appropriately called "*retraining*" schools. The programs usually include vocational courses and shop skills in the context of secondary (high school) education. Local training schools tend to generate greater emphasis on the educational, and state-level training schools greater emphasis on the vocational courses:

> In further meeting our need for residential placement, the court is fortunate in having the Cleveland Boys' School and the Blossom Hill School for Girls, operated by the Cuyahoga County Welfare Department, available to us. The majority of the children we place in these two schools are unruly children who have not responded to probation efforts and who demonstrate a real need for placement outside their homes to control their deviant behavior and to meet their educational needs which are generally unrealized in the normal school setting. The academic programs of the two schools are geared to the educational requirements of these children who, for the most part, have a record of consistent school failure and chronic truancy. The advantages of the educational systems of both schools include: small classes, usually 10 or 12 students in a class; teachers who are able to cope with deviant behavior; assignment at appropriate grade levels; and, of course, the total elimination of the problem of truancy. Another advantage offered by these schools is their accessibility to the families of the children; the location of both schools in the Greater Cleveland Area allows for regular family visitation to the schools, and periodic weekend and holiday visits by the children to their homes. While both schools have excellent physical facilities, they both have a need for additional social workers for counseling purposes within the schools and for aftercare service when the children are returned to their homes.[18]

The administrative costs of the training school in this broader context that includes both academic training and counseling are, of course, higher, because of a counseling staff in addition to the educational staff.

JUVENILE CAMPS AND RANCHES.   Juvenile camps and ranches are quite similar to those for adults; variations exist only in programs.

As in the case of training schools, camps and ranches located far from the juvenile's home tend to minimize family ties, which are thought by

[18] Walter G. Whitlatch, "Toward an Understanding of the Juvenile Court Process," *Juvenile Justice*, Vol. 23, No. 3 (November 1972), 7.

many to be a prime ingredient in successful juvenile rehabilitation. Unlike the case with security institutions, correctional administrators operating juvenile camps and ranches customarily enjoy greater flexibility in the location of their facilities, which may in turn promise a trend toward localized camps and ranches.

JUVENILE HALLS AND DETENTION HOMES. Although the juvenile hall is primarily the facility in which children are detained *pending* court, many jurisdictions commit minors to juvenile hall *after* court, and so such detention facilities may be considered correctional institutions. Moreover, many jurisdictions detain juveniles for extended periods while foster-home placements are being sought or arranged.

Juvenile halls frequently have medium-security construction except for the absence of armed guards. When used as a correctional facility, the typical juvenile hall affords education as the core of whatever is administratively defined as "the program."

Inasmuch as individual rooms (cells) are often used instead of dormitories, the use of juvenile halls for corrections is administratively more expensive than camps or ranches, treatment programs being equal.

DAY-CARE CENTERS. Most juvenile courts would consider the availability of a controlled educational and counseling program in the daytime, with "home on probation" at night, a particularly appropriate disposition for many juvenile cases. Administratively, the day-care center is just that—controlled education and counseling in the day, with the juvenile returning to his home at night.

Correctional administrators charged with operating juvenile day-care centers find that staffing and other costs are substantially lower than in any form of 24-hour-a-day institutional care, even when staffed with higher-level professionals.

It is conceivable that the restricted use of day-care centers will change and develop into a trend when more is known about staffing and administering such facilities. They are certainly worth administrative interest in a time of escalating criticism of the effectiveness of correctional institutions.

### Women's Institutions

Because it has been not much more than a century since women were jailed with men, it is in some respects amazing by historical standards how completely distinctive the administration of women's institutions has become.

Security at the typical women's institution is in the low–medium range, even with populations of inmates having violently assaultive histories. Reducing the emphasis on security even more are a number of program variations that tend toward minimum security in their operation.

In spite of major differences, however—for example, violence within the institution is not nearly as common—administration of women's institutions has some of the same problems typically associated with men's institutions. One example of many problems common to both is homosexuality:

> The number of sex-starved women who yield to homosexuality *faute de mieux* as a result of their close association within prison walls is much greater than one might suppose. Joseph Fishman, former Inspector of Federal Prisons, observed there were more lesbians in women's institutions than on the outside. While this conclusion is disputable, it does indicate the prevalence of homosexuality among women prisoners.[19]

Also as common as with male institutions is the administrative difficulty, stemming from the same areas of institutional operations, in determining the degree to which homosexual practices occur:

> Once having determined what is meant by homosexual behavior, it is still very difficult to determine accurately the amount of homosexual behavior at Fontera. Homosexuals, like others engaging in any kind of deviant behavior, have a variety of reasons for concealing their activities. Some inmates are fearful that prison staff members will inform their families of their affairs. Many inmates feel that staff knowledge of homosexual involvement hurts chances of early parole and draws extra staff surveillance. Such concerns are not groundless, for the label of homosexual by a staff member has important consequences for the inmate. The designation becomes a permanent part of her file information, available to all the staff. It may affect decisions about her housing and work assignments and other activities in prison, and as a violation of prison rules it calls for an appearance before the disciplinary committee. Being adjudged guilty means punishment and designation as a rule violator in addition to being labeled homosexual. Homosexuality, like other sexual behavior, is private behavior which takes place, for the most part, behind closed doors with only the participants knowing what actually transpires.[20]

Also in common with those of male-institution administration are the problems of contraband and related difficulties in operating any correctional institution. Indeed, when the problems of program continuity in a correctional setting are isolated administratively, many facets of male and female institutions are precisely the same.

One distinction that does exist between male and female institutions is

[19] Frank S. Caprio, *Female Homosexuality: A Psychodynamic Study of Lesbianism* (New York: Citadel Press, Inc., 1954), p. 76.
[20] David Ward and Gene G. Kassebaum, *Women's Prison; Sex and Social Structure* (Chicago: Aldine Publishing Company, 1965), pp. 88–89.

the variation in public concern; the public seems less concerned with institutions for women, possibly because the violence within them gains less publicity. But regardless of the reasons, this comparatively small public concern for women's institutions has both advantage and disadvantage—advantage in the reduced criticism, and disadvantage in the competition with male prisons for budgets.

Most correctional administrators agree, however, that this disadvantage is more than compensated for by relative freedom from riots and other forms of institutional violence.[21]

### Conjugal and "Co-ed" Institutions

As we have noted earlier, in some places men and women are housed together within the same institution. Moreover, the concept of conjugal visiting, as practiced in other countries, is becoming less foreign to American penology. *Both these concepts pose many problems for institutional administrators; but both also afford considerable promise.*

Isolating only the administrative responsibility to define organizational goals (discussed as "results" in Chapters 2 and 3), at least one institutional goal would presumably be: Prepare the inmate to return to the community better able to cope with life in a law-abiding manner. Now, the community in which this "coping" occurs is made up of men *and* women. Even when the institutional program is completely relevant to a changing social structure outside, it is artificially irrelevant when "learned" in an irrelevant context—in a context totally different from the community.

The legal, judicial, political, and legislative barriers to bringing this simple reality into correctional practice appear overwhelming at present. And yet the significance of recognizing that rehabilitation exists only to the degree that the inmate can "cope" requires all conscientious administrators to look long and hard at anything whatever that is learned in a community totally unlike the one to which the inmate returns.

Those who would dismiss this idea in favor of the "deterrence of imprisonment" might study national tables of recidivism, then consider the following:

> An effective penal system must aim for the re-integration of prisoners into society. In the last resort this is because there is a moral argument for aftercare. It is simply that no man is so guilty, nor is society so blameless, that it is justified in condemning anyone to a lifetime of punishment, legal or social. Society must be protected, but this is not done by refusing help to those who need it far more than most of their fellow citizens.[22]

21 Burton M. Atkins and Henry B. Glick, eds., *Prisons, Protest and Politics* (Englewood Cliffs, N.J.: Prentice-Hall, Inc., 1972).
22 J. P. Martin, "After-Care in Transition," in *Criminology in Transition* (London: Tavistock Publications, 1965), p. 107.

## INSTITUTIONAL PROGRAMMING

*Institutional programming* refers to what the administrator defines as the overall activities of the institution. Programming might be thought of as having three parts: (1) custody, (2) program, and (3) treatment.

Inasmuch as the counseling, guidance, and therapy methods in treatment are virtually the same for probation, institutions, and parole, discussion of treatment will be presented in the general context of the administrative responsibility for training correctional personnel, the subject of Chapter 9. For purposes of exploring institutional administration, then, custody and program will be the basis of the present discussion.

Beyond the obvious significance of programming is the less obvious reality that modification in programs may well be the only viable alternative that administrators have in answering their critics. Administrative priority for programming is, therefore, warranted:

> An ideal correctional system would be one in which types of offenders were matched successfully with types of programs. On one hand, society must be protected against the incorrigible offender but, on the other, it should not make the problem worse by locking up those who would do better in the community. The need to isolate types of offenders works both ways. As well as identifying those who must be kept out of community programs, it is equally important to identify those who should be kept in them.[23]

This suggests that a good program is one in which the inmate population is *appropriate*—"those who must be kept out of the community."

This is not a minor point; it may be crucial. By acknowledging that the population *is* appropriate, the negative implications of offender severity are reduced. The question of how to deal with the most severe criminality can be changed to the question, *Where else would they go?*

### Good Custody as Part of Good Program

The administrative programming concern that follows efforts to ensure that the population is indeed appropriate is to *retain custody until the program succeeds*. Combining custody and program, however, is something less than easy:

> We have seen that keeping men confined is a complex and difficult task, not simply because some men are ingenious in devising ways to escape but also, and more importantly, because the variety of functions which the custodians must perform are often in conflict. Internal order, the organiza-

[23] LaMar T. Empey, "Alternatives to Incarceration," in *Studies in Delinquency*, U.S. Department of Health, Education and Welfare, Office of Juvenile Delinquency and Youth Development, 1967, p. 79.

tion of prison labor, punishment, and rehabilitation—all must be pursued along with custody within a framework of sharply limited means.[24]

The difficulty in retaining custody "within a framework of sharply limited means" is problem enough. And yet the whole idea is the relationship between this custody and the program—the idea that whatever the program is to accomplish requires the presence of the inmate. The significance of this concept cannot be overstated, because it is the presence of the inmate during the program that permits *predicting change* as a result of the program—assuming that the program is to bring about change:

> That inmates change in prison has always been assumed. . . . Parole and the indeterminate sentence are predicted, in part, on the assumption that change can be discerned while a man is in prison; that is one reason why it is contended that the optimum time to release the inmate can be determined more adequately after he has been confined than at the time of sentencing. Similarly, designation of an appropriate institution and an optimum program for an inmate involves, in part, some assumptions that one can predict if or how the man will change while confined. . . .[25]

Custody, then, is something more than a simple exigency of correctional administrators. Indeed, in a correctional field created to both punish and rehabilitate, a security institution that cannot retain custody can do neither.

There is a significant difference between the *practice* of corrections and the *administration* of corrections. But in the case of correctional institutions, the concept of security tends to reduce this distinction for many reasons, not the least of which is the common concern for safety of inmates and staff, whether practicing or managing.

But the administrative concern with custody is primarily a matter of combining programs with security. And beyond combining custody with programming, successful institutional administration requires the full support of the administrative and appropriate organizational structure.

### Administrative and Organizational Structure

Thinking of programming in terms of predictable change while in custody brings into focus the presence or absence of complete support from both administration and organization. Look at the partial TO below:

[24] Gresham M. Sykes, "A Postscript For Reformers," in *The Society of Captives: A Study of a Maximum Security Prison* (Princeton, N.J.: Princeton University Press, 1958), p. 130.
[25] Daniel Glasser and John R. Stratton, "Measuring Inmate Change in Prison," in *The Prison: Studies in Institutional Organization Change* (New York: Holt, Rinehart & Winston, Inc., 1961), p. 381.

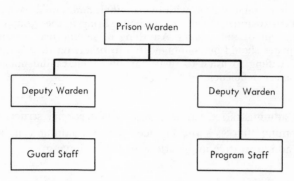

Nothing is really wrong with that structure, but contrast it with this one:

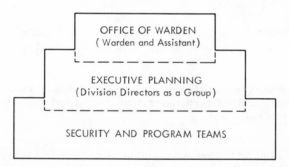

Obviously, this second diagram draws upon the functional management system model presented in Chapters 2, 3, and 4. But note the shift in emphasis away from organizationally splitting custody and program. This by no means relieves division directors of their divisional accountability. On the contrary, such accountability is emphasized by their interfacing directly with other division directors.

More important, such an approach emphasizes the integration of functions toward some outcome, and does so in a far more viable context than simple line-and-staff, quasi-military organizational concepts. Here is an excerpt from a concept known as the "Correctional Community":

In addition to the necessity for some assurance of top administrative support, there is also need for a definite organizational structure within the correctional community. There should be a direct line of responsibility from the staff engaged in the unit's operations. The supervisor should have primary responsibility for the selection and removal of staff.

The purpose of this organizational structure is to create a consistent treatment philosophy. The supervisor of the unit should be able to develop a total network of staff communication, and integrate the management of the correctional community. The staff members who supervise the inmates should be in communication with one another, and should have conferences to implement treatment plans. They should bring to the group observations of the behavior of the inmates. Anything of significance revealed to them by the inmates should be communicated to others on the staff. Supervisors should be willing to listen to their staff and their candid opinions and be able to correct deficiencies.[26]

Bringing administrative support and organizational structure to bear on programming increases the chances that something can be done to modify the administrative implications of the following:

Will the clients act differently if we lock them up, or keep them locked up longer, or do something with them inside, or watch them more closely afterward, or cut them loose officially?—*Probably not.*[27]

From a managerial point of view, to modify the implication of this assertion we must consider one further administrative reality:

. . . Institutional necessities include a continuous flow of prisoners, personnel, and money; statutory permission to operate and maintain a physical plant and program. . . .[28]

Institutional administrators have no choice but to realize that a "continuous flow of prisoners" is *required* if an institutional program is to exist at all. The trick, of course, is not to allow this obvious reality to interfere with programming efforts intended to drastically reduce this continuous flow. Although the administrative approaches to doing this are many, one of the most powerful is the adoption of programming efforts to *increase services* by *decreasing recidivism*—to approach correctional success in an administrative framework that permits reduced recidivism to be welcome.

With the profound implications of this approach in mind, let us turn our attention to some of the typical institutional program approaches.[29]

26 Floyd A. Chamlee, "Administrative Considerations in the Correctional Community," in *The Correctional Community*, eds. Norman Fenton, Ernest G. Reimer, and Harry A. Wilmer (Berkeley and Los Angeles: University of California Press, 1967), p. 31.
27 Robinson and Smith, "The Effectiveness of Correctional Programs," p. 80.
28 Donald Cressy, ed., *The Prison* (New York: Holt, Rinehart & Winston, Inc., 1961), p. 5.
29 See Chapter 11 of Coffey, Eldefonso, and Hartinger, *Introduction to the Criminal Justice System and Process,* for further elaboration of what will now be discussed briefly in the administrative context of programming.

## Work Programs

In their efforts to program work for inmates, institutional administrators have long been supported by penologists, politicians, and the general public. To administrative program efforts, the concept of work goes far beyond the "puritan ethic" cited by some criminologists in reviewing the history of penitentiaries, presumably to influence correctional administration. The correctional value of inmate work, it will be seen, touches many spheres in terms of administration. But beyond this correctional value, there are administrative advantages in terms of security and discipline, not to mention inmate and staff morale.

The correctional value of a program, *from an administrative point of view*, relates primarily to inmate attitude. Attitudinally, work is intended to prepare inmates for productive lives by providing skills and work habits, both seen as desirable in the community to which the inmate must ultimately adjust. In addition, self-supporting offenders contribute to the economy rather than draining it. Work, then, has a number of administrative implications in the correctional institutions.

Work programs include *maintenance* (internally maintaining the institution itself, etc.), *industrial, farming, forestation,* and *conservation,* and a host of variations or combinations of these.

MANAGEMENT VS. PRACTICE: STATE, COUNTY, CITY. It should be emphasized that the distinction between the management and the practice of corrections remains significant even during a discussion of correctional functions in which such a distinction is difficult. For example, descriptions of the industrial, farming, forestation, and conservation programs may sound similar whether in terms of practices or of management. But practices may remain similar in *any* organizational structure, whereas management varies (at least in terms of program implications) between state, county, and city organizations. Such organizational variations are common to American corrections.

Moreover, the distinction between the practice and the management of correctional programming increases still more when combinations of approaches, increasingly common in correctional administration, are used.

## Work-Furlough Programs

The work-furlough program, at present, is customarily operated in minimum- or medium-security institutions.

Work furlough, or "work release," [30] has been a part of corrections for some time. Administratively, it is primarily geared to inmate employ-

[30] S. E. Grupp, "Work Release and the Misdemeanant," *Federal Probation,* Vol. 29 (June 1965), 6–12.

ment outside the institution, with the inmate returning to the institution after each work day.[31]

Although the use of the work-furlough program continues to expand, vast numbers of institutions are still not using this approach—a significant consideration in the context of solutions for the problems posed in the criticism cited early in this chapter. And by traditional practice, work furlough is limited even further by being virtually restricted to county and municipal institutions for misdemeanants.

However, awareness of the potential tax savings through a decrease in welfare recipients when men can support their families, combined with improved methods of recognizing security risks, may cause an expansion of the work-furlough concept into institutions housing felons. The pace of this expansion will be slow, because of the problems of severity discussed earlier, but the tremendous rehabilitative potential of work furlough should prove sufficient inducement to keep progress going.

### Educational Programs

The concept of providing education as a segment of correctional programming is by no means new. In recent years, however, the scope and intent of such programming has expanded to include more than the traditional high school diploma goal. Sophisticated technology along with the arts and other facets of science can be found incorporated in an increasing number of correctional programs.

### Recreational Programs

Managerially staffing recreation programs does (or should) require recruitment of specialists in channeling leisure time constructively—a specialty sometimes foreign to prison staff who specialize in either security or counseling as such.

Recreational programs should be staffed by specialists because relief from monotony and pent-up emotions and energies are of critical administrative concern whenever human behavior is restricted. An effective program of recreation can lessen the tensions and improve the behavior of inmates, bringing benefits to everyone involved in the criminal justice system.

### Treatment Programs

As we have noted, the techniques and methods of counseling, guidance, and therapy that are involved in changing attitude and behavior are more

[31] E. H. Johnson, "State Work-Release Programs," *Crime and Delinquency*, Vol. 16, No. 4 (October 1970), 417–26.

or less the same for probation, prison, and parole, and will for this reason be presented in a single administrative context in Chapter 9.

In the institutional setting, however, it is worth note here that the need for sophisticated diagnosis and classification in probation and parole is amplified manyfold when inmates are compacted and their liberty severely limited. Administrative concern with the treatment segment of the institutional program may in the past have been somewhat secondary to that with other institutional problems. But as creative solutions are sought to the criticism cited early in this chapter, it appears destined to gain an ever-increasing significance.

## SUMMARY

This chapter introduced the administration of correctional institutions in the context of the increasing severity of institutional populations, combined with mounting concern over institutional effectiveness.

The correctional institution was distinguished from detention by the fact that the inmate is housed in the facility by direction of the court.

The operation of a wide variety of federal, state, and local institutions was discussed in terms of distinctions in security level, sex, and age, concluding with a brief discussion of the potential of conjugal and "co-ed" institutions.

Correctional-institution programming was presented as including custody, program, and treatment, with the concept of treatment deferred to Chapter 9, to be considered with probation and parole. Administrative support and organizational structure were considered. Institutional programming was then discussed as custody and program—citing work programs, work-furlough programs, educational programs, and recreational programs.

### Discussion Topics

1. Elaborate on offender severity.
2. Relate increases in community diversion to institutional severity.
3. Relate severity to mounting concern over institutional effectiveness.
4. Discuss the difference between pre-court detention and correctional institutions.
5. Relate police to the discussion in Topic 4.
6. Elaborate on problems connected with the operation of correctional facilities by police.
7. Contrast the three levels of security: minimum, medium, and maximum.

8.  Contrast institutional considerations involving offenders of different ages and sexes.

9.  Discuss the implications of the various programs presented, in terms of the criticisms of correctional institutions that were cited early in the chapter.

## Annotated References

ATKINS, BURTON M., and HENRY B. GLICK, eds., *Prisons, Protest, and Politics*. Englewood Cliffs, N.J.: Prentice-Hall, Inc., 1972. The emphasis of this extremely comprehensive work is suggested in this excerpt from its introduction: ". . . Despite . . . change in the content and direction of prisoner protest, responses to prisoners' grievances have not changed appreciably over the years."

COFFEY, ALAN R., *Juvenile Justice as a System: Law Enforcement to Rehabilitation*. Englewood Cliffs, N.J.: Prentice-Hall, Inc., 1974. Chapter 11 elaborates on what were discussed briefly in this chapter as juvenile institutions.

———, EDWARD ELDEFONSO, and WALTER HARTINGER, *Introduction to the Criminal Justice System and Process*. Englewood Cliffs, N.J.: Prentice-Hall, Inc., 1974. Chapter 11 elaborates on correctional institutions as a subsystem of criminal justice. See also Alan Coffey and Vernon Renner, eds., *Criminal Justice: Readings*. Englewood Cliffs, N.J.: Prentice-Hall, Inc., 1974.

COOPER, JOHNATHAN D., *American Criminal Justice: The Defendant's Perspective*. Englewood Cliffs, N.J.: Prentice-Hall, Inc., 1972. Elaborates on a key dimension of what this chapter presented as severity of criminality—the perspective of the offenders involved.

FOX, VERNON, *Introduction to Corrections*. Englewood Cliffs, N.J.: Prentice-Hall, Inc., 1972. Comprehensive context for the correctional institution in America.

HARTINGER, WALTER, EDWARD ELDEFONSO, and ALAN COFFEY, *Corrections*. Pacific Palisades, Calif.: Goodyear Publishing Co., Inc., 1973. In-depth study of the rationale and operation of the institution in the context of corrections overall.

OSWALD, RUSSELL G., *Attica—My Story*, ed. Rodney Campbell. Garden City, N.Y.: Doubleday & Company, Inc., 1972. Good treatment of the internal difficulties of prison operation that are beginning to gain public attention.

# Parole Operations

# Chapter 7

Parole was born in this country a century ago, intended as a reform to avoid having prisoners rot away in their cells. The theory was that rehabilitation would be fostered if the offender served the last portion of his sentence in the community, free but supervised. Yet, of more than 50,000 convicts released from prison on parole every year, at least one third and perhaps as many as two thirds—statistics are poorly kept—will be returned to prison for new crimes.

And what of those convicts who do not win parole? The official New York commission investigating the 1971 prison uprising at Attica labeled inequities in the parole system as a primary source of the tension and bitterness that climaxed in the killing of 11 correctional employees and 32 prisoners.

Conclusion: Parole is a bankrupt institution that we can no longer tolerate; a hypocritical, confused and capricious system on which we spend $60 million annually. On paper, it is humane. In practice, it is hamstrung by flaws that cripple its three basic premises.[1]

As we can see from these remarks, the growing concern with correctional effectiveness is related to parole as much as to any other segment

[1] Herman Schwartz, "Let's Abolish Parole," *Reader's Digest*, August 1973, p. 185.

of corrections. This is understandable, since parole is in many respects an extension of the correctional institution; and administration of the parole functions and corrections is in many respects simply an extension of the administrative considerations presented in the preceding chapter. However, parole does constitute an explicit function requiring administrative consideration.

There is wide variation in the organization of parole in the United States,[2] which in turn produces variations in the administration and management of parole. It would therefore be useful to list the *objectives* of parole before examining the administrative considerations:

1. Release of each person from confinement at the most favorable time, with appropriate consideration to requirements of justice, expectations of subsequent behavior and cost
2. The largest possible number of parole completions
3. The smallest number of new crimes committed by released offenders
4. The smallest number of violent acts committed by released offenders
5. An increase of general community confidence in parole administration [3]

These objectives clearly distinguish parole from probation, but let us clarify this distinction further:

Parole is to be distinguished from probation in that the latter is granted by the court as an alternative to incarceration. Parole is also to be distinguished from pardon, which is an act of forgiveness and remission of punishment, freeing the individual from responsibility to the State with respect to the remainder of his sentence.[4]

## AFTERCARE AND REINTEGRATION

Even though many of the same treatment methods are appropriate for both probation and parole (as we shall see in Chapter 9), the "aftercare" concept in parole differs from probation in many ways—beginning with the fact that parolees are *re*integrated into communities, and probationers *remain* integrated in them.

The concept of reintegrating offenders back into communities from which they were removed was slow in development:

[2] Vincent O'Leary and Joan Nuffield, *The Organization of the Parole System in the United States* (Hackensack, N.J.: National Council on Crime and Delinquency, 1973).
[3] M. Martin, ed., "Corrections in the United States," *Crime and Delinquency*, 13 (January 1967), 210.
[4] Barbara A. Kay and Clyde B. Vedder, eds., *Probation and Parole* (Springfield, Ill.: Charles C. Thomas, Publisher, 1963), pp. 93–94.

After-care for offenders originated in the relief work for discharged prisoners. The possibility of parole changed the favor of aid and support, which could be bestowed upon a discharged prisoner, into a necessity, which had to be organized. Although in the beginning conditional release was designed primarily as a measure to hold the released prisoner under control, it is clear that the development of conditional release under control into parole under supervision and with after-care was inevitable.[5]

This by no means suggests that modern parole has fully evolved into "social work"; on the contrary, parole today is frequently more similar to law enforcement than to social work.[6] Nevertheless, aftercare and reintegration are significant variables in achieving the five parole objectives cited earlier.

In some respects, the relationship between aftercare and reintegration has to do with the administrative relationship of parole staff and parole organization—particularly the *variations* in organizations that are so common to the field of corrections. One of the many considerations involved here is the potential conflict generated by such variation:

The relation of the staff to the formal organization involved in parole is mentioned last here because that relationship is so highly variable. The staff in an integrated, statewide organization consists of one or two assistants for the director of parole, a statistician, a fiscal officer, a personnel director, and a secretarial staff that is adequate. Obviously, only the largest parole departments can afford to hire separate people for these jobs. In smaller departments, however, one person may perform several of these functions.

In many organizations a conflict develops between the staff and the "line," which consists of those who carry out the actual operations of the organization. This conflict arises whenever the staff perceives itself as more qualified to advise top management than are the line personnel, and/or whenever staff personnel try to initiate activity for line personnel. This type of conflict apparently does not arise in most parole organizations because (1) staff personnel generally are no better educated than the line personnel, so they do not perceive that it would be appropriate for them to initiate activity for the line, and (2) staffs are small and thus would have little chance of influencing top management if they tried to do so. . . .[7]

The impact of such conflict is administratively significant, if for no other reason than that neither effective aftercare nor reintegration is likely to occur in the presence of such conflict. And the resultant absence

[5] *Ibid.*, p. 107.
[6] Elliot Studt, *People in the Parole Action System: Their Tasks and Dilemmas* (Los Angeles: Institute of Government and Public Affairs, University of California, 1971), p. 131.
[7] William R. Arnold, *Juveniles on Parole—A Sociological Perspective* (New York: Random House, Inc., 1970), p. 65.

of either aftercare or reintegration virtually prevents achieving the five parole objectives referred to earlier, particularly since successful aftercare *includes* reintegration into the community. A government commission stated the following:

> The general underlying premise for the new directions in corrections is that crime and delinquency are symptoms of failures and disorganizations of the community as well as the individual offenders. In particular, these failures are seen as depriving offenders of the contact of institutions that are basically responsible for assuring development of law-abiding conduct: sound family life, good schools, employment, recreational opportunities, and desirable companions, to name only some of the more direct influences. The substitution of deleterious habits, standards, and associates for these strengthening influences contributes to crime and delinquency.
>
> The task of corrections therefore includes building or rebuilding solid ties between offender and community, integrating and reintegrating the offender into community life—restoring family ties, obtaining employment and education, securing in the larger sense a place for the offender in the routine functioning of society. This requires not only efforts directed toward changing the individual offender, which has been almost the exclusive focus of rehabilitation, but also mobilization and change of the community and its institutions, and these efforts must be undertaken without giving up the important control and deterrent role of corrections, particularly as applied to dangerous offenders.[8]

"Mobilization and change of the community" will be the subject of the next chapter. But the thrust of all effective parole programs is "reintegrating the offender into community life—restoring family ties, obtaining employment and education . . . without giving up the important control and deterrent role of corrections."

This, then, is the context in which parole operations seek to achieve the five parole objectives.


## PAROLE OPERATIONS

The administration of the parole function is part of "post-institutional" programming. However, although there are persuasive arguments in favor of such uniform procedures, not all offenders are under parole supervision upon leaving the institution.[9] Moreover, in many cases, the length of time of parole supervision is controlled outside this sphere of parole adminis-

---

[8] President's Commission on Law Enforcement and the Administration of Justice, *Task Force Report: Corrections* (Washington, D.C.: U.S. Government Printing Office, 1967), p. 7.
[9] David Dressler, "Parole Today," *Practice and Theory of Probation and Parole* (New York: Columbia University Press, 1959), p. 63.

tration; parole boards frequently retain significant influence over both the length of institutionalization and the length of parole.

Some of the concerns that have already been noted with regard to release determination gain a singular significance in the specific context of parole influence over the length of institutionalization:

> In many jurisdictions the average parole hearing takes less than ten minutes. The prisoner then returns to prison routine and awaits the decision in a state of anguish.

> To be denied parole is frustrating. But to be denied parole without any explanation for the decision is embittering and rancorous.

> Because no rationale is given, the prisoner, comparing his case to that of others who were granted parole, may see the denial as a capricious decision. He is often at a loss to understand what he has done wrong or how he can improve his performance. Parole board silence compounds his cynicism and his hostility to authority.

> At the very least, unexplained parole denials obstruct rehabilitation. Yet they are quite common in many state and local jurisdictions.

> Good correctional practice requires that denial of parole be explained to the offender so that he can be in no doubt as to his shortcomings. A practice of explanation might well produce more rational decision-making. It would highlight and expose poor decisions or politically motivated decisions. It would provide a basis for litigation by prisoners who think they have been unfairly denied parole.[10]

Moreover, the law itself in governing parole also removes administrative influence in certain categories:

> In addition to denying parole to certain categories of offenders altogether, most states specify that minimum time to be served before eligibility occurs for those who may be considered.

> 1. It might be the minimum of the sentence less good time allowance. For example, if the sentence is five to ten years, the prisoner is eligible in five years less the time he earns for good behavior and work willingly performed.

> 2. It might be a specified part of the maximum. Some laws require service of half the maximum; others, one third; and so on.

> 3. There are many other formulas. There may be, for instance, a one year minimum, regardless of the maximum; of one third of the term or ten years, whichever is less. A Federal prisoner (other than a juvenile delinquent or youthful offender), if serving more than 180 days, is eligible for parole after completing one third of the sentence. When a life sentence is imposed by a Federal court, the earliest possible release is in fifteen years.[11]

[10] Board of Directors, National Council on Crime and Delinquency, "Parole Decisions, A Policy Statement," *Crime and Delinquency*, Vol. 19, No. 2 (April 1973), 137.

[11] *Ibid.*

To gain the administrative significance of this "external control" of the length of parole programming, a comparison with probation might be useful.

Like parole, probation is often designated for a specified time. But in the case of probation, courts are often willing to consider modifications, even dismissals, prior to completion of the term. More important, the laws that control probation usually grant the courts this prerogative.

In contrast, laws controlling parole usually relate directly to the criteria used by the jurisdiction in determining how long the offender remains in the institution. When this prerogative is turned over to a parole board, the administrative criteria for program success are far less flexible. Exceptions to the law that imposes control over parole tend to tighten rather than relax such control, if for no other reason than that the release-determining body functions outside the sphere of administrative accountability.

In terms of program flexibility, the administration of parole is generally far more restricted than the administration of probation, not only in terms of the law and the release-determining process, but also in terms of the somewhat restrictive reality of parole organization.

### Parole Organization [12]

The contrast with probation may again serve to clarify the organization of parole.

Although it is true that the federal government and a few other jurisdictions assign probation officers to both probation and parole, most jurisdictions segregate parole as a separate function organizationally. To compound whatever administrative difficulty arises out of such organizational "splitting," many jurisdictions structure the organization of the correctional institution so as to incorporate the parole function, and place parole under the institutional administration.

PAROLE AS AN EXTENSION OF THE INSTITUTION. The rationale for organizationally structuring parole under institutional administration has to do with the relationship between institutional programs and parole itself.

Successful institutional programming, as we have noted, requires by definition that the offender be successful in the community to which he returns; reintegration is the measure of success for both the institution and parole. In this context, parole becomes an extension of the institutional program. Indeed, the laws governing parole in most jurisdictions tend to organize it in such a fashion that the offender's rights, civil and

[12] This section adopted from O'Leary and Nuffield, *The Organization of the Parole System.*

otherwise, are virtually the same as when he was in the institution: There is "institutional control" of his total life activities, including residence, possessions, associations, and leisure time while on parole.

COMPARATIVE POWER. To shift briefly from the administration to the *practice* of parole, it should be noted that the parole officer is the individual embodiment of all the power and authority of the parole system. In other words, the relatively diffused power of institutional staff is in practice focused sharply in the individual parole agent, whose *actual* power is awesome.

*This does not, however, detract from the administrative impact of parole boards' controlling the operation of parole externally.* But independent of external control, the actual practice of parole involves enormous ranges of power and authority on an individual basis. It is conceivable that this power factor may prove to be a key consideration in administrative effort to cope with mounting concerns with correctional effectiveness.

As we have seen, the conditions of parole encompass what amounts to the total life of the offender; probation conditions usually impinge on only some areas of it. Moreover, the consequence of violating probation conditions is the possibility that the sentencing court may consider institutional care; violation of parole, however, establishes the *probability* of imprisonment—of returning the offender to the same program until it works.

Functioning as an extension of the institution, of course, provides parole the administrative advantage of program continuity. Furthermore, conceiving of parole as an extension of the institutional program tends to encourage awareness of the goal of both institution and parole: *offenders successfully reintegrated into the community.*

But isolating parole from probation has some administrative disadvantages as well. For one, in "criminogenic neighborhoods" (a sociological term for ghettos), a probation officer and a parole agent often pursue the correctional function in a manner suggesting that neither knows the other exists. Practicing precisely the same correctional casework techniques, parole agents may in effect follow probation officers into the same house, to the same family, over and over again. Many clientele are *routinely* called upon by, in turn:

    Police patrolmen
    Police detectives (adult)
    Police detectives (juvenile)
    Investigating probation officers (adult)
    Investigating probation officers (juvenile)
    Supervision probation officers (adult)
    Supervision probation officers (juvenile)

Probation officers for females
Probation officers for males
District Attorney's investigators
Social workers
Parole agents

It doesn't take a great deal of imagination to see the undesirable consequences when criminal justice "sequences" in so conspicuously a fragmented manner—*regardless of how well the particular specialist performs
his function.*

Indeed, it can be assumed that in addition to the severity concept discussed in the preceding chapter, still another major impediment exists to
institutional success—the fact that parole is organized systematically as
coming last in criminal justice. Parole occurs *after* families fail, after
schools fail, after social work fails, after police fail, after the community
itself fails, and after probation fails. Not surprisingly, parole often appears
to be a far less constructive process than the other criminal justice functions.

Therefore, since it is an extension of institutions that symbolize failure
by their very existence, it is amazing that parole administration can operate with *any* degree of optimism and positive orientation, particularly
in view of the systematic removal of control of the function assigned to
parole.

### Parole Control

Whereas the typical parole organization is structured under institutional administration, the control of parole is usually structured "outside,"
under some release-determining body, as well as the legal restrictions
already noted.

RELEASE-DETERMINING BODY.    Every state has placed the release decision from correctional institutions in the hands of either a parole board
or a commission, with a few states restricting the board's power to recommendations to the governor or state welfare department. Many jurisdictions turn over the responsibility for determining length of prison
terms to these same bodies. The quasi-judicial powers given many such
boards is intensive and impressive.[13]

Unlike the awesome power in the hands of **the individual** parole agent,
these quasi-judicial powers, however, are *indirect*—ever-present, but not
in a direct manner. The administrative problems in relating such power
to clearly defined plans is substantial, to say the least. Here is an example:

---

[13] Walter Hartinger, Edward Eldefonso, and Alan Coffey, *Corrections* (Pacific Palisades, Calif.: Goodyear Publishing Co., Inc., 1973), p. 191.

An inmate comes before the parole board and reviews the skills he has learned in shop, the team sports he participates in, along with a synopsis of what his counselor calls the "treatment program." The parole board informs him that everything is "fine" except the fact he has insufficient "insight"—to try for parole again next year.

Next year, the inmate presents an impressive array of psychiatric, sociological, and criminological jargon learned from his counselor, only to find he's now "manipulative" and cannot be granted parole.[14]

The very fact that parole is not granted establishes the power of the board to control parole. But how does the administrator relate his program to this indirect power?

Although correctional administration includes making correctional staff available for parole hearings, parole boards typically function to the exclusion of administrative influence—at least, *direct* influence upon their *indirect* powers.

This independence of the release-determining function in turn creates two methods of administering the parole function: (1) having parole responsible to the board directly, or (2) the parole board's permitting responsibility for parole to flow through the institutional administration *after* the release determination has been made. Either way, however, release *practice* has profound impact on the administration, and *practice* is the very consideration outside the scope of administrative control.

Because the practice of parole release occurs outside the administrative sphere of control, managerial concern focuses on accountability—or lack of accountability. To whatever degree accountability for specific functions is the key to administrative success, to that same degree is there an administrative problem when decisions regarding release on parole remain out of the control of parole administration.

Of course, the rationale for composing parole boards of members outside the sphere of administrative influence is sound: *The goal of community reintegration may not always be served if release is determined by those primarily responsible for the orderly continuity of institutional programs.*

The problem arises when these decisions about release are made without administrative accountability—that is, without a system of managerial accountability for decisions made, in terms of the outcome.

RELEASE ACCOUNTABILITY. Controlling parole through release-determining bodies that are not subject to direct, swift, and certain public ridicule for errors poses two administrative problems:

1. The appearance of administrative influence over what the board considers creates a subsequent impression that the administration is accountable for release-decision practices.

14 *Ibid.*

2. Inmate motivation is frequently a function of parole practice to a far greater degree than it is a function of administratively devised program decisions.

More often than not, accountability, in the managerial sense, rests with neither the release-determining body nor the administration of the institution. But because of the likelihood that unfortunate consequences will accrue to the administration when inappropriate release decisions are made, or when appropriate ones are *not* made, most institutional administrations abandon program plans that in any way violate parole practice. This is probably related to the fact that control of the inmate population while in the institution may depend on programs "fitting" parole practice.

Were it not for the current concern with the overall effectiveness of the correctional system, it might be possible to tolerate this goal-defeating situation. But in an era when demand increases for effectiveness, administratively substituting the practices of a parole board for clearly defined administrative goals and objectives is intolerable.

Many would argue that the goals of parole boards and institutional administrators are the same—both aspire to the goal of rehabilitated offenders. But as part of an overall American system of institutional corrections, parole practice employs far more personal judgment than program criteria—a fact that all but eliminates any semblance of systematic relationships between explicit administrative objectives and actual parole practices. In effect, this in many instances is the subtle reason that administrators seek to make programs "fit" parole practice.

Of course, there is no way to determine to what degree so subtle a process influences the administration of institutional programming, or to what degree the goal of long-range community reintegration is subverted rather than enhanced by it. However, the mere possibility that this process could in any way influence creative efforts to solve some of the dilemmas confronting institutions is reason enough to make note of it—*particularly in the context of growing concerns with institutional effectiveness.*

### Parole Innovations

From an administrative viewpoint, most of what might be considered innovative within the comparatively restrictive confines of parole operations has to do with the treatment methods used (to be presented in Chapter 9), since control of the parole process itself exists outside the sphere of parole operations, but determination of what constitutes parole rests clearly within the parole process.

Beyond treatment innovations, however, there have been some innovative efforts to improve the effectiveness of parole in recent years—the "halfway house" and the interstate reciprocity of supervision, for example.

HALFWAY HOUSES. Although correctional history is not directly related to correctional administration, the rate at which certain facets of corrections have developed has caused a corresponding modification in correctional methods. The "halfway house" is such an innovation, having evolved at almost the same rate as correctional awareness of the significance of the transition from institution to community. Not surprisingly, then, early halfway houses were used to ease inmates back into the community from which they were taken.

Innovations in recent years, however, have placed the halfway house not only halfway between institution and community, but also halfway between probation and institution—a kind of pre-institution, in many jurisdictions.

Such an innovation relates directly to the concept of community-based corrections, to be discussed in the next chapter. But it also has to do with the clear relationship between probation and parole, pre-institution and post-institution differences notwithstanding.

Typically, the halfway house is a large, older residence in an urban setting. It is not always staffed by parole agents as such; but the behavioral-science orientation and correctional philosophies of the staff in halfway houses nonetheless establishes the majority of them as performing a parole function in the broad post-institutional sense—at least, in those that are halfway between institution and community for the resident.

Some jurisdictions capitalize on the functional similarity of probation and parole, and combine offenders in both categories when establishing residence criteria. These criteria do not typically include court commitment in the same sense as commitment to a prison; consideration is typically given to the implications of the term "halfway." [15]

INTERSTATE COMPACT. Yet another parole innovation growing out of correctional history is the "interstate compact"—a mutual or reciprocal parole supervision between states.[16]

In an ever-increasing number of cases, offenders on parole are permitted, even encouraged, to "move to other states for the parole programming and removal from earlier influences upon the parolee." [17]

While such reciprocity creates mild increases in administrative responsibilities, the potential of this flexible concept in terms of alleviating

---

[15] F. McNeil, "A Half-Way House for Delinquents," *Crime and Delinquency*, Vol. 13, No. 4 (October 1967), 538–44. See also R. C. Meiners, "A Halfway House for Parolees," *Federal Probation*, Vol. 29, No. 2 (June 1965), 47–52.

[16] See, for example, *The Handbook on Interstate Crime Control* (Chicago: The Council of State Governments, 1966), pp. 3–31; and California Youth Authority, *Operations Manual: Interstate Compact For Juveniles* (Sacramento, Cal., 1968).

[17] Alan R. Coffey, *Administration of Criminal Justice: A Management Systems Approach* (Englewood Cliffs: N.J.: Prentice-Hall, Inc., 1974), p. 241.

jurisdictional restrictions is tremendous, particularly in the context of the major external restrictions imposed on the majority of parole operations.

## CONCEPTUAL RETOOLING

Perhaps the final consideration in examining the administration of parole is that of the parole function as a vital link between community and institution.

Evolving successful solutions to criticism of institutional effectiveness requires what may prove to be a "conceptual retooling" in corrections. The function of constantly relating solutions to the reality of the community may never be totally in the hands of parole, but certainly parole can and should be strongly influential in this conceptual retooling.

In fact, parole must *lead* the institution in the actual process of bringing new concepts to bear on the monumental problems confronting correctional administration. Rather than merely extending treatment programs undertaken within the institution, parole must create the "treatment atmosphere" to which institutional programs must relate. Those administering parole must recognize the implications of community-based corrections and of treatment, which will be presented in the next two chapters. In short, parole's influence must shift into a leadership rather than a follower context.

Situated as it is, operating externally but usually administered from within the institutional administration, the parole function is ideally suited to establish the link between institutional operations, tending to be totally removed from the social changes occurring in the community, and the community itself:

> Give me a system which will allow a parole officer to spend an hour in a bar with a parolee, developing rapport and a true counselor relationship, and which will require the officer to record only a line or two about it. Give me a system which permits him to do what the principles of parole suggest and which requires merely a summary statement after a long relationship. Our officers are overloaded not so much with cases as with self-defeating unused reports to their own agency.

> Our present accounting system promotes inefficiency, fabrication, and depersonalization of the consumers and the employees of the criminal justice system. Waste and ineffectiveness through bureaucratic techniques unrelated to the humanity of the offender or the officer are our present products.[18]

Cutting through the "waste and ineffectiveness through bureaucratic techniques unrelated to the humanity of the offender" remains a suffi-

---

[18] Marvin E. Wolfgang, "Making the Criminal Justice System Accountable," *Crime and Delinquency*, Vol. 18, No. 1 (January 1972), 17.

ciently difficult task to constitute a major challenge to institutional administration. The additional problem of keeping such an effort a community
reality must, of necessity, incorporate parole influence.

This conceptual retooling of the correctional field might also incorporate the implications of the following remarks:

> If we are seriously interested in doing something about our spiraling crime
> rate, does it not make sense to begin with the group of men who have dem-
> onstrated their ability to function lawfully and who, our statistics show,
> stand a better than 50 percent chance of failing in the future?

> We say we want law and order, protection from crime. If we mean it, we
> must do something constructive to reduce the chances that Collins and
> Barker will return to stealing. We must immeasurably improve the odds
> that Higgins will not return to selling hard narcotics to our children and
> that Hennigan will not again point a gun at motel clerks.

> Of course, there are those so twisted that no known treatment will avail to
> make them into people we would want on our streets. We have no choice
> but to keep them in custody until we do have some answers. Fortunately,
> they are the exceptions. The grist of our criminal mill can be redeemed, if
> only we will it and are wise enough to realize that if we seriously intend to
> do anything about the soaring crime rate, we have no alternative.[19]

The influence of the parole function on the conceptual retooling necessary to devise correctional solutions will, ideally, go beyond the implications of the remarks above, and combine such implications with this
reality:

> Leaders in the correctional field agree that *every person released from a
> correctional institution should be released under supervision.* The prisoner
> does not have a right to parole, but for the good of the prisoner and the
> community, all should be given the opportunity of a period of supervision
> after leaving the regimentation and confines of the institution. Any method
> of release which does not include the process of careful selection of those
> to be released and of optimum time for their release in addition to the
> necessary degree of supervision after release is not [an adequate approach
> to parole administration].[20]

The parole function, regardless of the particular approach to administering parole, bears the brunt of the frequently incongruous combination
of punishment and rehabilitation cited as posing a problem to probation
and institutions. Moreover, in doing so, it has far less latitude to minimize
the sometimes glaring paradox of such a combination. Indeed, because
all the institutional power is focused in the hands of the individual parole

---

[19] Gilbert Bettman, "Until Discharged by Law," *Crime and Delinquency,* Vol. 17,
No. 3 (July 1971), 280.
[20] *Manual of Correctional Standards* (New York: American Correctional Association,
1954), p. 532.

agent—power reaching every facet of the offender's life—this correctional paradox is emphasized rather than minimized in parole.

Parole, more than the other two major functions of the correctional field, symbolizes the combination of punitive sanction and constructive programming; probation tends to be freer of the punitive sanctions, and institutions freer of emphasis on treatment.

Because of this undiluted merger of the sometimes contradictory punishment and rehabilitation, administration of the parole function may well prove to be the key variable in bringing the entire correctional field to grips with the vast social changes that have engulfed the entire criminal justice system.

## SUMMARY

This chapter introduced the administration of the parole function in the context of five explicit parole objectives. The concept of reintegrating the offender back into the community was emphasized as the distinguishing characteristic of parole.

Parole operations were discussed in terms of limited administrative control over parole selection and length. This consideration was further elaborated on in terms of parole organization, emphasizing parole as an extension of the institution. Advantages and disadvantages of this extension concept were presented, stressing the rationale for institutional program continuity as the primary advantage, and the specialty isolation from probation field services as the primary disadvantage.

The specific concept of controlling parole was presented in the context of parole operations being under institutional administration, but without significant influence on that administration with regard to the release-determining process. The rationale for this structure and the managerial disadvantages were discussed. The rationale is primarily a matter of making release determinations independent of the responsibility to maintain institutional order, and retaining community-adjustment orientation to the exclusion of institutional concerns. Managerial disadvantages were discussed in the context of accountability, in the frame of reference presented in Chapters 2, 3, and 4.

Halfway houses and interstate supervision were presented as parole innovations corresponding to the general evolution of the current concept of parole. The role of parole in aiding the conceptual retooling needed for correctional solutions was presented, with emphasis on the strategic position of the parole function as a link between community and institution, and the fact that the sometimes contradictory punishment and rehabilitation are combined within parole operations.

## Discussion Topics

1. Discuss the five objectives of parole.
2. Elaborate on *reintegration*.
'3. Contrast probation and parole.
4. Describe the rationale for structuring parole as an extension of institutions.
5. Describe the administration of parole.
6. Distinguish between administrative influence over parole release and parole-board control of parole release.
7. Discuss accountability problems with parole-board control.
8. Elaborate on the rationale for parole-board control.
9. Discuss parole operations in terms of innovation.

## Annotated References

COFFEY, ALAN R., *Criminal Justice Administration: A Management Systems Approach.* Englewood Cliffs, N.J.: Prentice-Hall, Inc., 1974.

————, *Juvenile Justice as a System: Law Enforcement to Rehabilitation.* Englewood Cliffs, N.J.: Prentice-Hall, Inc., 1974. Both this and the book listed above contain chapters on parole affording a broad criminal justice context for what was discussed here under parole and corrections. See also Alan Coffey, Edward Eldefonso, and Walter Hartinger, *Introduction to the Criminal Justice System and Process,* Chap. 11. Englewood Cliffs, N.J.: Prentice-Hall, Inc., 1974.

DRESSLER, DAVID, *Practice and Theory of Probation and Parole.* New York: Columbia University Press, 1959. Good overview of the *practice* of parole as opposed to the *management* of parole—Chapters 1, 4, 5, and 6 in particular.

FOX, VERNON, *Introduction to Corrections.* Englewood Cliffs, N.J.: Prentice-Hall, Inc., 1972. A good comprehensive overview of the correctional system overall, including parole.

HARTINGER, WALTER, EDWARD ELDEFONSO, and ALAN COFFEY, *Corrections.* Pacific Palisades, Calif.: Goodyear Publishing Co., Inc., 1973. A broad-based, comprehensive examination of the correctional context in which parole functions.

O'LEARY, VINCENT, and JOAN NUFFIELD, *The Organization of the Parole System in the United States,* 2nd ed. Hackensack, N.J.: National Council on Crime and Delinquency, 1973. Excellent coverage of the title topic.

STUDT, ELLIOT, *People in the Parole Action System: Their Tasks and Dilemmas.* Los Angeles: University of California, Institute of Government and Public Affairs, 1971. 131 pages available in plastic ring binder. A perceptive analysis of the frustrating problems confronting parole officers in a paradoxical "action system."

# Community-Based Corrections

# Chapter 8

Correctional administrators, more often than not, interpret the term *community-based corrections* to mean either probation or parole, or both. Such a concept is accurate only if the intent is merely to distinguish between correctional institutions and field services. This limited distinction shows part of the reason for an expanded definition of community corrections.

Consider the following summary of "traditional" community corrections in terms of unfulfilled potential:

A person who is found guilty of a crime will often receive a suspended sentence, provided that he remain on good behavior and that he be placed under special supervision. Such a person is said to be on "probation."

A person who has served part of a given sentence in prison may be released under certain conditions, including special supervision. Such a person is termed to be on "parole."

Though the effectiveness of properly implemented parole and probation programs has been demonstrated many times, their full cost/benefit potential is yet to be achieved on a nationwide basis. A major weakness in probation and parole services is that they have never received adequate funds for the number of offenders under supervision. Two-thirds of all offenders are under probation or parole supervision, but these services receive less than one-third of the monies allocated for correctional efforts.

The President's Commission on Law Enforcement and the Administration of Justice notes that "probation and parole services are characteristically poorly staffed and often poorly administered." Of the 250 counties surveyed by the Commission, one-third provided no probation services at all. Average probation and parole caseloads vastly exceed the recommended standards of 35 cases per officer. Over 76% of all persons convicted of a minor offense and 67% of all those convicted of a major offense who are on probation are in caseloads of 100 or more. Less than 4% of the probation officers in the nation carry caseloads of 40 or less.

Despite the far-from-ideal conditions existing in the probation and parole fields, studies indicate that roughly 55–65% of parolees are not returned to prison during the period of their parole supervision. Of those that are, about two-thirds are returned for parole violations, not for new crimes. 60–90% of probationers complete their probation terms without revocations.[1]

This chapter will approach community-based corrections with a much broader scope—one that recognizes the major degree to which many "field services" are not really services provided in the field, and one that will acknowledge that:

> Instead of relying on the exercise of its own "expertise" in its own closed system of institutions and agencies, corrections must effect a greater inter-penetration with expanding community resources and services of education, vocational rehabilitation, health, and employment. Already stigmatized by his passage through the criminal justice system, the convicted offender must be reintegrated or assimilated into non-criminally oriented groups in the community. There are, as yet, no clearly defined guidelines for opening or creating new channels of communication between the offender and the groups with which he is expected to affiliate.[2]

Indeed, far beyond the customary restrictions placed upon correctional concepts, the basis on which this chapter approaches community corrections incorporates the concept of *prevention:*

> The majority of offenders come to the attention of the authorities or social agencies long before they have committed a major crime. To this day, however, no reliable treatment method has been developed for nipping a criminal career in the bud. Those in delinquency and correctional work, courts

---

[1] "Probation and Parole—Unfulfilled Promises," in *Marshaling Citizen Power to Modernize Corrections* (Washington, D.C.: Chamber of Commerce of the United States, 1972), pp. 2–3.

[2] Dr. Benjamin Frank, "Basic Issues in Corrections," *Perspectives on Correctional Manpower and Training* (Lebanon, Pa.: Sowers Printing, January 1970).

and supervisory agencies, and even law enforcement, can recall the many, many individuals who have passed through their hands, their rebellion against society unresolved and their drive towards destruction unabated.[3]

## PREVENTION LEVELS

Of course, it could be argued that prevention of crime and correction of crime are mutually exclusive; that once correction is necessary, it is by definition too late to prevent; that *prevention* means "preventing the need to correct."

This argument is consistent with logic, but it must nonetheless be noted that there is a *scale* of preventing crime and delinquency—a scale having tangible levels, regardless of how difficult these levels are to design:

1. The person who has never done anything that violates any law
2. The person who has never been suspected of violating a law
3. The person who has violated law and been suspected but not apprehended
4. The person who was apprehended
5. The person who was apprehended, then apprehended again, then apprehended again, then apprehended again, et cetera

Classically, the prevention of crime and delinquency deals with only category 4—prevention of recorded evidence that a crime or delinquent act has been committed. Clearly, however, preventing the second level from becoming the third level is actually no more preventive than preventing the third level from becoming the fourth, or the fourth from becoming the fifth, and so on.

Beyond our acknowledgment that the correctional treatment that prevents level 4 from becoming 5 is also "prevention," much of what will be discussed as community-based corrections in this chapter can readily include offenders from categories 4 and 5 in such a manner that the strategically important category 3 can also be involved—correctional treatment operated in such a manner that it becomes classical crime and delinquency prevention.

In other words, a community program for offenders already in the correctional system may prove useful to offenders on their way into the system, through preventing their ultimate involvement in the system. This is of singular significance in the context of the following:

[3] Clinical Services APTO, New York, "Offender Therapy in the Community," *International Journal of Offender Therapy*, Vol. 15, No. 1 (1971), 12–13.

An examination of the empirical data and experience of the last ten years indicates that there has been a failure to control the growth of crime and delinquency in the United States. To what degree this must be blamed on failures of the judicial process is a question relatively unanswerable in light of the complexities of causation and of the relation of lawless behavior to the entire institutional fabric. Nevertheless, the last several years raise questions as to the adequacy of the judicial process' performance of its functions in social control and, more fundamentally, of the assumptions that underlie those functions.[4]

Based upon this broad conception of community-based corrections, this chapter will approach administration of the programming involved as though *all* the influences on crime and delinquency can be considered—including some not typically associated with the correction of crime and delinquency:

> I would like to conclude these comments concerning explanations of delinquency by noting the key importance which I attribute to systems of opportunity and unrealized expectations as especially potent contributory factors in generating delinquency-producing situations. The concept of opportunity itself is a very vague term that gains specificity only as it is related to particular ends which people may seek, such as economic rewards, prestige, fame, power, or affectional gratification. Opportunities for realizing such goals become institutionalized and controlled by organizations such as the family, school, employment office, and labor union.[5]

With this broader-based approach to the correctional process, community corrections may well be able to profoundly influence even those trends toward law violations that are not customarily thought of as crime:

> As observed by a legal scholar . . . it is necessary to persuade those bent on civil disobedience that their conduct is fraught with danger, that violation of one law leads to violation of other laws, and eventually to a climate of lawlessness that by easy stages leads to violence.[6]

But whether or not community corrections proves influential on even the peripheral crime problems, giving corrections a real community orientation should certainly enhance its effectiveness in coping with the primary responsibility of the correctional field—the recidivous adult and juvenile law violators.

---

[4] Gary Bellow, "Prevention Through the Judicial Process," in *Delinquency Prevention*, eds. William Amos and Charles Wellford (Englewood Cliffs, N.J.: Prentice-Hall, Inc., 1967), p. 212.
[5] Lloyd E. Ohlin, "Opportunity Systems," *A Situational Approach to Delinquency Prevention* (Washington, D.C.: Dept. of Health, Education and Welfare) 1970, p. 10.
[6] Abe Fortas, *Concerning Dissent and Civil Disobedience* (New York: New American Library, Signet Books, 1968), p. 59.

## COMMUNITY ORIENTATION

From an administrative perspective, the idea of orienting correctional programs to the community immediately raises the question, Who actually constitute the "community"? There are many articulate groups each claiming to be "the community," and each such claim must be evaluated by correctional administrators seeking to develop a community orientation. Moreover, many groups that are neither articulate nor claiming to be "the community" must be evaluated in the same manner as those making the position clear.

For example, many times the perspective of the classroom teacher is not precisely the same as that of "parent–teacher" groups. The latter tend to be more articulate, but this does not eliminate the need to seek out the voice of the classroom teacher when educational problems are considered. Indeed, *meaningful* administrative evaluation may in some instances depend more upon the unarticulated views of certain community influences.

Such evaluation is extremely difficult. One author recently presented the following comments:

> Among the soothsayers of River City were several who held that alienation —and hence delinquency—grows out of class conflict; that to eliminate delinquency we must first eliminate poverty and inequality. But the committee early shelved this suggestion. There were too many evidences that delinquency increased as affluence increased; that delinquency was as prevalent in the middle class as in the lower class; and that much alienation was not conflict *between* classes, but within: rebellion of middle-class youth against middle-class norms. The committee held that while reduction of poverty was a justifiable pursuit per se, it was not expected to have any significant effect on crime and delinquency rates.
>
> The same ultimate conclusion was forced concerning health: Pursuit of better health was in itself a justifiable end, but if all the River City youth were in top physical shape, the drop in delinquency would likely not exceed 1 percent. Among the remaining 99 percent we would merely have healthier hoods.
>
> The same held true of mental health. The committee found several hundred social workers willing to testify that all delinquents are emotionally disturbed; but for every kid who fits this stereotype the committee found a half dozen kids who seemed at least as well adjusted as the social workers.[7]

The specific implications of these remarks for correctional administrators is that many "authorities" on what the community must do about crime and delinquency may, when forced to examine their expert opin-

[7] Dale G. Hardman, "Corrections and the Community: A View Through a Crystal Ball," *Federal Probation*, Vol. XXXIV, No. 1 (March 1970), 21.

ions, find they are coping with problems that have virtually nothing to do with reducing crime and delinquency.

A community orientation for correctional programming, then, may or may not include many of the influences of any group or any "expert." The key consideration is the potential to achieve administrative results, as discussed in Chapter 2. But even though relating all evaluations of groups and expert opinion to results orientation is useful, perhaps a definition of *community* would also clarify the administrative task in establishing community orientation.

### Community Defined

For purposes of community-based correctional programming, *community* is defined as *those groups and authorities having major influence, direct and indirect, upon the reduction of crime and delinquency.*

Such a definition is likely to include such groups and authorities as these:

Police

Courts

Schools

Churches

Minority groups

Service clubs

Majority groups

Labor unions

Militant factions

Women's groups

Employment agencies

Psychiatrists and psychologists

Social workers

Youth groups

Government leaders

Politicians

Industrialists

Home owners

Merchants

Public health organizations

Recreation authorities

The combination of these diversified groups that is chosen by correctional administration as "the community" establishes the basis of community orientation. Determining the best combination, however, is administratively difficult, to say the least; but in light of its importance, further exploration of the approach needed in combining groups is worthwhile.

The "sensor-matrix approach" is one method by which correctional administrators can continually focus upon this combination of groups in terms of influence on crime and delinquency.

### Sensor Matrix

The term *sensor matrix* is intended to suggest a *systematic method of assessing all significant community variables in an ongoing manner.*

In other words, a sensor matrix is the correctional administrator's method of gathering and evaluating the information he needs to determine which combination of groups best forms the community to which corrections will be oriented.

By the inclusion of "in an ongoing manner" in the definition, explicit acknowledgment is made that the community is constantly changing. As updating and other modifications in the particular program occur, correctional programming itself is also constantly changing. Change is of considerable significance, then:

> Perhaps the greatest clarity of the concept of *change* can be gained by first noting that change is *not optional*. The Grand Canyon is becoming deeper at the rate of one inch a year, whether people approve of such change or not. Scotland moves toward Ireland about eight feet annually, and Europe and the United States are moving about one foot apart each year. London sinks a fraction of an inch annually, while the North Pole moves southward one-half foot.
>
> When you note such changes in the tangible physical world, then changes in the social world should be no surprise. Any difference in human behavior over a period of time is *change*, and differences in human behavior are constantly observable. But *change* may not always be of a positive nature. . . .[8]

This ongoing change concept tends in effect to redefine the community to which corrections must remain oriented during such change if *effective* corrections is to be achieved.

Two considerations are therefore crucial in sensor matrix: (1) administrative information about all community influences; and (2) a system of continuously updating this information—of continuously receiving "community input."

COMMUNITY-INFORMATION INPUT. In view of the discussion in Chapter 3 of management information and the MIS, it should be clear that correctional administrators suffer not from a *lack* of information, but from an *excess* of it. The MIS, to be useful, must reduce information to relevance first, and then to decision-aiding data.

This same principle holds true for the community-information input from the sensor matrix. Vast amounts of information must be reduced *by specific criteria* to decision-aiding data. To all intents and purposes, this makes a sensor matrix a subsystem of the MIS—but a strategically important subsystem.

Of course, the nature of the correctional organization itself tends to influence the variety of sources of community-information input, and

---

[8] Alan Coffey, Edward Eldefonso, and Walter Hartinger, *Human Relations: Law Enforcement in a Changing Community* (Englewood Cliffs, N.J.: Prentice-Hall, Inc., 1971), p. 146.

therefore also the variety of information that is to be reduced to managerially decision-aiding data. A probation department, for example, with a variety of adult and juvenile programs has many more sources of community information than, say, an adult prison that depends totally upon the input of adult parole agents. In other words, some correctional administrators will probably be confronted with the need to develop community-information input, while others find a virtual excess of information, owing to the nature of the organization.

Developing sources, however, is a lesser problem than that of devising methods of systematically reducing the information to relevant decision-aiding data. Perhaps one reason has to do with developing the crucial criteria by which information is reduced.

The problem with reducing information to relevance is the profound question, What gets thrown out? In other words, some information must be discarded systematically; *which* information? Each correctional organization must develop methods to reduce information, if correctional effectiveness is the goal.

There is no set formula for devising such methods. However, the guidelines for establishing an MIS, discussed in Chapter 3, are singularly relevant in developing community-information input. Even more important, correctional administrators should bear in mind what the sensor matrix is *not: Sensor matrix is not an intelligence system.* Indeed, if specific time is set aside to gather community information, the process may be "survey," it may be "investigation," it may even qualify as "research," but it is *not* sensor matrix in the context of community orientation. Regardless of the design of the MIS, and regardless of the number of sources of community-information input, the sensor matrix gathers *only* information that flows through the correctional process being administered.

This, of course, is to the administrative advantage in keeping correctional programming *relevant* to the realities of the community—forcing the information flow to simultaneously determine how relevant the program is in community realities. In other words, if programming is the only source of information, and the information proves irrelevant, it can be assumed that the program is somewhat irrelevant—a kind of "checks-and-balance" systematized.

But beyond these managerial implications of structuring informational input through correctional operations, there is the tremendous advantage of avoiding the typical "Ping-Pong game" that customarily follows when an outside study group tells correctional administrators what the "real" community is all about. Avoiding the problems surrounding this difficulty constitutes a major administrative advantage, particularly if the informational approach to avoiding such problems is continually updated.

UPDATING COMMUNITY INFORMATION.    To qualify as a sensor matrix, information reduced to decision-aiding data must also be updated—systematically reduced over and over on each "cycle" of input. The cycle can vary, but most correctional organizations already have "rhythming cycles" available. Monthly division reports, bimonthly section reports, and weekly unit reports afford not only the needed systematic rhythm of updating, but also fit the functional management system model presented in Chapters 2, 3, and 4.

The key, of course, is to assign specific responsibilities regarding community-information input to each of these reporting cycles. Accountability should be assigned by function for specific categories of community information relating to the particular operation. Of course, this information must be reduced by specific criteria and in the context of the immediate month—a systematic updating, by definition.

Community orientation, then, is complex if approached correctly, and even more complex when one is constantly redefining the community to which corrections must be oriented to be effective. The problems in developing a sensor matrix to cope with this complex administrative process are many. But the problems are far outweighed by the ultimate advantages, which have the potential to produce effective community corrections.

Against this background of complexities involved in orienting correctional programs to an ever-changing community, attention is now directed to some approaches to community-based corrections.

## COMMUNITY OPERATIONS

As we will see in the next chapter, treatment methods are essentially the same regardless of the correctional function—probation, institution, parole, or some community-based variation. The many seeming distinctions between methods of treatment that appear to be necessitated by function or by geography are simply expressions of administrative preference or local circumstance, or both.

Nevertheless, there *are* differences in the situations in which treatments occur—very real differences in correctional programming. A few examples of differing community programs may serve to clarify this in terms of the overall concept of community-based corrections.

### Community Residence Programs

Programs in which the concept of "living-in" are applied have become a significant segment of community-based corrections:

An outstanding development in the correctional field in recent years has been the great new interest and wide experimentation in residential programs that might serve in one way or another to help the offender avoid going to or staying longer in a penal institution. The trend provides a distinctly new dimension in the correctional field, which had always before offered just two housing choices—the custodial institution or home (probation or parole). It includes an element that has been familiar in other countries but not so well known in the United States: the use of a private agency in the service of the correctional field, often with some kind of subsidy from the state. The best-known form of this new correctional facility is the halfway house, often run by private eleemosynary organizations but serving and working closely with governmental agencies. . . .

. . . At present the function characteristics that seem to be common to most halfway houses for adults are the following: (1) to provide permissive but supportive housing to the person who must leave a correctional institution without a suitable job or home, or both; and (2) to give some degree of personal help to the resident in getting him properly adjusted to free society again.[9]

Recalling the discussion of the halfway house in the preceding chapter on parole, we can see more clearly why the position was taken that there can be a great similarity between the practice and the treatment methods of probation and parole.

Of course, the distinction between probation and parole remains discernible if their functional differences are considered in terms of community operations. Bearing probation and parole differences in mind, consider the following:

Community treatment programs for offenders due to be released from prison are still in a relatively early stage of development. Before any firm conclusions can be drawn regarding their effect on reducing recidivism, or other criteria of success, considerably more research will be required. However, there is no question but that programs of this type do help facilitate the offender's inevitable reentry into the community by: (1) providing some continuity with education and training programs begun in the correctional institutions; (2) assisting the offender in obtaining adequate employment; (3) increasing utilization of community resources; and (4) providing needed support during this difficult initial period of adjustment. On this basis alone, the question is not one of whether a correctional agency should become involved in community treatment programs, but rather how and to what extent.[10]

Even though differences can readily be discerned, the similarities outnumber the differences between probation and parole when the broader

[9] Paul W. Keve, *Imaginative Programming in Probation and Parole* (Minneapolis: Minn.: University of Minnesota Press, 1967), pp. 222–23.
[10] Bertram S. Griggs and Gary R. McCune, "Community-Based Correctional Programs: A Survey and Analysis," *Federal Probation*, Vol. XXXVI, No. 2 (June 1972), 12.

correctional objectives are recalled—objectives relating to reducing crime and delinquency in the community:

> Many correctional systems currently are using community-based programs as part of their array of services in pursuit of reintegration. But few, if any, provide a full range of alternatives, and there is little evidence of systematic planning for development of the most appropriate and most needed programs at local and State levels. Rather, programs have sprung up as grant funds have been available or as a result of the specialized interest of a staff member or administrator. There is a clear need to systematize on a State level the orderly development of community corrections, with full consideration of specific local needs.
>
> The purpose of such effort is to insure that: (1) no individual who does not absolutely require institutionalization for the protection of others is confined; and (2) no individual should be subjected to more supervision or control than he requires. Overrestriction of offenders has been practiced because alternative programs and understanding of offender needs have been lacking or inadequate. This situation should be changed by development of a systematic plan for creation of varied community-based programs that will best respond to the range of offender needs and community interests.[11]

Shifting from this broad correctional context back to administrative pragmatics, let us consider the staffing of a residence program. Of necessity, staffing residence programs must be guided more by sensor matrix than by tradition. Probation and parole agents may not even be involved in some jurisdictions; in others, residence programs may involve direct participation of both probation and parole staff.

An example of staffing concepts used in one residence program is shown in excerpts from an article by a Youth Authority parole agent:

> Parolee House . . . provided an opportunity for a line parole agent to function as a correctional *professional*, utilizing community resources and known social-psychological techniques to effectively curb delinquent behavior in one segment of his caseload. . . .
>
> . . . The program elements at Hillcrest and Parolee House were designed to therapeutically modify the ward's self-image. This modification of self-image, it was felt, could best insulate the ward from further delinquency, provide a more constructive value system, and impart a sense of direction and purpose to his life. . . .
>
> The role of the parole agent was seen as being of fundamental importance. Most wards possess such distrust and hostility toward authority that the correctional worker, burdened with a high caseload, finds it difficult, if not impossible, to establish communication. Hence, he functions with decreased

11 Working Papers for the National Conference on Criminal Justice, Law Enforcement Assistance Administration, Washington, D.C., January 23–26, 1973, p. c–141.

effectiveness because of his identification with the establishment and his lack of time.

The posture of the parole agent, then, was to present a new view of authority. . . . Emphasis was placed on relating to each ward on a person-to-person basis, avoiding superior or subordinate relationships. Little or no emphasis was placed on structuring, advice giving, implied threats, or surveillance. The first priority was to establish a trustful relationship as quickly as possible. . . .

It is a truism that most adolescents in present-day society are influenced more by their peer subculture than parents, school, or church. At Parolee House, every program element, every move, therefore, was structured around and within the peer group subculture. Major emphasis was placed on minimizing Parolee House affiliation with the parent agency. There was a purposeful lack of structure. The parole agent exercised no formal supervision within the house and rules came from the peer group and/or house manager. In a real sense, the house belonged to the wards, who were almost totally responsible for the overall operation. The parole agent shared his authority with the group. Screening of new candidates, as well as disciplinary actions and removals, involved decisions made by the peer group. . . .

House group meetings were utilized within the program for the residents, house manager, and parole agent to discuss overall house operations. Attendance was voluntary. This weekly meeting was initially structured to avoid any semblance of group counseling in order to provide a non-threatening opportunity to ventilate gripes and encourage attendance. Here, new candidates were screened, assessment made of individual progress, and certain routine business handled. Outside visitors were welcomed during these meetings, and included police officers, employment counselors, local businessmen, and students. In the absence of pressing house business, current topics of interest were discussed, such as love-ins, narcotics use, and "sex and the single parolee." . . .

The very nature of this project dictated that volunteers would have to be utilized in every area of programming. A startling result was the abundance of interested, competent individuals who volunteered their services. These volunteers came from all walks of life and included professionals, students, ministers, parents, ex-wards, adult felons, and others.

Again, subjectively, it is felt that "untrained" volunteers proved to be more effective in relating to the wards than their paid, professionally trained counterparts. It was apparent that by reason of their wanting to volunteer, these individuals gave more of themselves and were able to drop their occupational roles more easily and relate on a person-to-person, friend-to-friend basis. Wards appeared to view them with less suspicion and hostility. . . .

The writer feels that the Parolee House concept does offer a realistic alternative to incarceration for the majority of offenders. . . .

It is conceivable that local courts and correctional agencies could subsidize elements within the community to provide treatment and rehabilitative services. In lieu of detention and incarceration, offenders could be placed in a series of Parolee House type facilities scattered throughout the city and county. Here, the offender would stay until pronounced ready to leave by a panel composed of his peers, volunteers, and professional correctional workers. Within this setting, the broad range of community resources could be brought to bear upon both the offender and his family. . . .[12]

## Youth Service Bureaus

Another example of community-based corrections is the Youth Service Bureau. Not all agree that the YSB is a part of corrections; indeed, many contend that it should not be administered by corrections:

> The Youth Service Bureau is *not* a part of the justice system, although it may accept referrals from it. Its immediate goal is to keep children from becoming involved with the justice system. Its long-range goal is to reduce home, school, and community pressures to which children react with anti-social behavior.[13]

But despite his opinion that the YSB should not be part of corrections, the same author concludes that the nature of the YSB fits correctional goals and objectives:

> *The Youth Service Bureau is a noncoercive, independent public agency established to divert children and youth from the justice system by (1) mobilizing community resources to solve youth problems, (2) strengthening existing youth resources and developing new ones, and (3) promoting positive programs to remedy delinquency-breeding conditions.*
>
> The YSB should preferably be organized on a town-, city-, or county-wide basis with neighborhood-based branches in high-delinquency areas. It should be independent of other agencies and systems.
>
> The YSB should make its services available to children seven to eighteen years old (a) who have been referred to the justice system but for whom the authoritative intervention of the court is not needed, or (b) who have problems that might eventually bring them within the jurisdiction of the court. Although this is the primary target group, neither older nor younger children need be excluded.[14]

In effect, the only disagreement Norman displays is on who should administer the program. Agreement on the *nature* of YSB permits the question of who runs it to be separated temporarily as a consideration in order to focus upon the *results* it is intended to achieve. One such result is, of course, prevention.

[12] Kenneth R. Cilch, "Parolee House," *Youth Authority Quarterly*, Vol. 24, No. 4 (Winter 1972), 3–12.
[13] Sherwood Norman, *The Youth Service Bureau: A Key to Delinquency Prevention*, (San Francisco: National Council on Crime and Delinquency, 1972), pp. 8–9.
[14] *Ibid.*

It is noteworthy that the argument against correctionally operated YSB's nevertheless indicates support for including as part of their operations juveniles "referred to the justice system," who are in both category 4 and category 5 of the prevention levels we discussed earlier. Of course, the YSB, if effectively operated, would include noncriminal cases as well:

> . . . A Youth Services Bureau will get most noncriminal cases out of the juvenile court; it frees probation officers for work with more serious offenders, helps kids stay out of trouble when they first get into it, and provides a reliable basis for planning priorities in social services. . . .[15]

But in addition to the noncriminals involved, categories 4 and 5 are definitely included—juveniles apprehended, and juveniles apprehended over and over. To whatever degree corrections is responsible for preventing further repetition in level 5, to that same degree it is appropriately involved in YSB—even though noncriminals are also involved.

The fortunate reality is that correctional programs geared to preventing repetition of level 5 can be operated in such a manner that juveniles in levels 3 and 4 also avoid deeper penetration into the system. Operating the program in this manner necessarily increases the likelihood that the noncriminals involved in YSB programming also profit tremendously.

The administrative context in which such operations can occur may be clarified by the following:

> Basically, there are four program approaches which can be chosen for emphasis in planning a strategy for preventing juvenile delinquency: (1) programs based on behavior modifications; (2) programs based on improving institutional services to delinquents; (3) programs based on developing new services and delivery systems to predelinquents and delinquents; (4) programs that address themselves to the processes in communities that propel children into the juvenile justice system.

> The first, which deals with modification of behavior, is extremely limited. It presupposes early identification and is a highly individualized and expensive process. The state of the art is developing rapidly, however, and the approach might be used to work with youth already identified as being alienated from the social system.

> The second and third are approaches that have been and are currently being utilized. They both deal with previous efforts at reform and frequently address themselves to narrow issues like training of institutional staff, reducing caseloads, and innovative treatment programs. Efforts in these areas would have a minimal impact because they tend to oversimplify the problem and do not deal with those community processes that are responsible for most delinquency.

> The fourth is the strategy discussed in this article. It is advocated for na-

[15] NCCD, "Corrections: A Public Youth Services and Planning Bureau," Citizen Action to Control Crime and Delinquency, April 1969, p. 51.

tionwide adoption because it offers two avenues for diverting young people from the juvenile justice system: first, by providing prevention programs; and second, by offering community-based rehabilitation programs as alternatives to placement of delinquent youths in traditional correctional facilities.[16]

Staffing YSB's, just like staffing community residence programs, varies in terms of sensor-matrix-verified "needs." The *team approach*, however, with a staff made up of representatives of many organizations, is administratively desirable for a number of reasons. Staffing a YSB with a policeman, a social worker, a probation or parole officer, and an institutional group counselor immediately establishes a variety of expertise felt by many to be correctionally useful. But from the specific reference of administrative advantage, borrowing each team member from another agency customarily increases the program commitment of the lending agency. The project director can increase this commitment even more when his advisory board is composed of citizens and representatives of participating agencies.

This somewhat uniform concept is applicable to YSB's in general, but there is great variety in the structure of YSB's:

The Study identified a significant number of Youth Service Bureau programs throughout the United States which have funding from Federal sources. In addition, a number of other programs which existed before the availability of Federal funding or do not rely on Federal funding were located and described. As a result, it is estimated that there are less than 170 Federally funded programs nationally that are significant to the Youth Service Bureau concept. Further, the total amount of Federal funding for these programs appears to be less than 15 million dollars.

In addition to the "recognized" programs, there are many others, federally supported, locally supported, and privately supported, that are equivalent in program to those reported in this study. Some of these programs operate from a traditional framework, and others are "street programs" which offer similar services and have similar objectives to recognized Youth Service Bureaus. In one sense, the National Study has explored only the tip of the iceberg. It falls to those who follow to explore that which was not visible nor clearly identifiable.

The term "Youth Service Bureau" covers a vast and varied range of programs. Where a program is viewed as a Youth Service Bureau in one part of the United States, it is not recognized as a bureau in another area of the Nation. Youth Service Bureaus are a relatively new and experimental phenomenon, and several came into existence, and went out of existence, during the course of the study. Without a doubt, several programs that were

[16] Robert J. Gemignani, "Youth Services Systems," *Federal Probation*, Vol. XXXVI, No. 4 (December 1972), 49.

visited will not be in operation at the time this report is published while other new programs will have just opened.[17]

## Diversion Programs

The practice of diverting offenders from the justice system, like the YSB's, is thought by some to be outside the scope of correctional responsibilities. But just as YSB's are compatible, even appropriate, for corrections in terms of preventing "level 4's" from becoming "level 5's," so also is diversion an appropriate correctional operation, although it is a somewhat more coordinative function to administer than the relatively direct administrative links in the residence programs and YSB's.

In its simplest terms, *diversion* is the *systematic development of alternatives for selected offenders;* the alternatives consist of dispositions of cases outside the justice system, and handled by non-justice-system programming.

The point at which diversion can occur is not nearly as significant as the philosophy of diversion. Once the philosophy is accepted that "the system" may not be best for every offender, the point at which the actual diversion occurs in the system can be any of the following:

School (choosing an alternative other than police)
Police (choosing an alternative other than juvenile probation)
Police (choosing an alternative other than the prosecutor)
Juvenile probation (choosing an alternative other than juvenile court)

Alternatives range from family counseling to volunteer foster homes, and from Alcoholics Anonymous to suicide prevention. The key is preventing deeper penetration into the system when alternatives are appropriate—when the danger to the offender and to the community is such that the potential value of some alternative exceeds that of the justice system.

As in the case of virtually all community programs, the sensor-matrix-verified information should be more influential than tradition when staffing diversion projects. The administrative trouble involved may, at times, be substantial, but it is readily compensated for:

. . . The results to date, however, are a powerful demonstration of the value of the diversion concept in combination with the use of family crisis counseling at the point of probation intake. Because the approach makes

[17] Prepared by Department of California Youth Authority, *National Study of Youth Service Bureau*, Youth Development and Delinquency Prevention Administration, Washington, D.C., 1972, pp. 3–4.

use of existing personnel, it can be created without the addition of major new resources. Because it is both specialized and reasonably self-sufficient, it has the ability to make more effective use of other community resources while at the same time not becoming dependent upon them. For jurisdictions with reasonably strong probation services, it can do in fact what so many programs claim, that is, pay for itself. . . .[18]

## ADMINISTRATIVE FORTITUDE

There are few if any seasoned correctional administrators unaware of the public interest in crime and delinquency that seems to be increasing in direct proportion to three specific factors:

1. Criticism of correctional effectiveness
2. Evidence of fragmentation in criminal justice
3. Increased difficulty in funding mental health, social work, recreational, and community service programs.

This entire volume is geared to the first two factors: to attempt to cope *managerially* with the reality that correctional effectiveness has indeed lagged, and that criminal justice is indeed fragmented at present.

The third consideration, however, relates only to community-based corrections, and is therefore considered only in this context. The problem is related to the following:

Corrections, as an agency of state and local governments, greatly needs the cooperation of the other public and private agencies, for it too is responsible for the well-being of society. In many instances it deals with the same population that requires and uses services of other public agencies. Nevertheless, to date it has had few working relations with, and has not been accepted as a member of, the family of community agencies. Leaders in the field of correction have repeatedly pointed out that the correctional institutions are one segment of the health and welfare services of a community. They insist that correctional agencies cannot be effective in their mission if other social agencies do not cooperate in an integrated rehabilitation program extending beyond the prison walls.[19]

### Competition

Correctional programs are frequently originated and operated by people who are far more concerned with how offenders "feel about themselves"

[18] Robert Baron, Floyd Feeney, and Warren Thornton, "Preventing Delinquency Through Diversion: The Sacramento County 601 Diversion Project," *Federal Probation*, Vol. XXXVII, No. 1 (March 1973), 18.
[19] Wallace Mandell, "Making Correction a Community Agency," *Crime and Delinquency*, Vol. 17, No. 3 (July 1971), 281.

than with whether the offenders stop offending. It may be true that corrections has failed to establish a track record of impressive proportions, but serious damage can be done to the society by this "distortion."

But as correctional administrators come to grips with the need to achieve results that can be measured in reduced recidivistic crime, the severity of this distortion increases in direct proportion. This fact may—perhaps *should*—generate competition for correctional programming.

It is unlikely, of course, that anyone would seriously compete with corrections for the functions of probation, institutions, and parole programming; however, the increasing difficulty in funding social programs in general appears destined to increase the interest in the one problem that cannot be ignored in a society—crime and delinquency.

Nonproductive encounters relating to the size of the budget are not the administrative consideration being isolated here. Instead, the question is being raised, Does the administration of corrections have the fortitude to cut through proposals presented in the name of corrections but serving other purposes?

Emphasis must of necessity remain on the development of an effective, nonfragmented *system* of corrections. But as such a system emerges, the question of who administers community programs becomes crucial. Of course, the absence of such a system removes the significance of who administers anything; it matters little who is involved in spending correctional money if it becomes clear that no one achieves correctional results.

As we have seen, reducing poverty, improving mental and physical health, or in fact alleviating *any* social problem cannot in itself reduce crime.[20] Community-based corrections is likely to prove the determining factor in whether those who are attracted to competing with corrections for funding realize this.

More simply stated, correctional administrators may find out through community programming whether corrections is in the corrections business totally or partially. If partially, it does not really matter. If it is totally involved, however, they must acknowledge the necessity to repair fragmentation in the American system of coping with crime:

> . . . The reality is that the community, the police, the courts, and the correctional agencies *do* combine to attack the problem of crime and process the criminal offender. The fantasy lies in the speculation that the various agencies approach these processes in a coordinated and rational fashion. To make the fantasy a reality requires planning comprehensively for the goals, the procedures, and the assessment of the impact of the various components of the criminal justice system. A comprehensive plan for the criminal justice system requires, *ipso facto*, some form of "systems analysis," the newest

[20] Hardman, "Corrections and the Community."

popular application of behavioral science thinking to complex social problems.[21]

The task, the challenge is at hand.

## SUMMARY

This chapter introduced the concept of community corrections in the broad context of reducing crime and delinquency, rather than within the traditional limitations of probation and parole functions.

The concept of prevention was related to corrections in terms of levels or degrees of prevention—with emphasis on preventing further involvement once an offender is apprehended.

Community orientation for programming was discussed in the context of constant change; the administrative need is to develop an ongoing system of updating the correctional orientation to a changing configuration of community influences. The sensor-matrix approach to this was discussed as paralleling managerial information systems.

Community operations discussed were residential programming, Youth Service Bureaus, and diversion projects. Varying diversion points were compared to various levels of prevention in relating the correctional field to this prevention function.

The position was taken that development of an effective system of corrections may include the obligation to deny administrative access to correctional programs to those concerned with improving social problems other than the reduction of recidivistic crime and delinquency.

### Discussion Topics

1. Explain the distinction between defining probation and parole as community-based corrections, and the broad definition used in this chapter.
2. Relate levels of prevention to this broad definition.
3. Discuss community orientation.
4. Elaborate on the influence of change on community orientation.
5. Relate *sensor matrix* to this chapter.
6. Contrast the residence program and the YSB.
7. Discuss the various points of diversion in terms of correctional involvement.
8. Relate administrative fortitude to this chapter.

[21] Malcolm W. Klein, Solomon Kobrin, A. W. McEachern, and Herbert R. Sigurdson, "System Rates: An Approach to Comprehensive Criminal Justice Planning," *Crime and Delinquency*, Vol. 17, No. 4 (October 1971), 357.

## Annotated References

BARON, ROBERT, FLOYD FEENEY, and WARREN THORNTON, "Preventing Delinquency Through Diversion," *Federal Probation*, Vol. XXXVII, No. 1 (March 1973) 14–18. Excellent context material for conceiving of the correctional role in diversion.

COFFEY, ALAN R., *Correctional Administration: A Management System Approach*. Englewood Cliffs, N.J.: Prentice-Hall, Inc., 1974. Chapters 5 and 6 elaborate on the context in which information systems that would include "community sensor matrix" are developed.

———, *Juvenile Justice as a System: Law Enforcement to Rehabilitation*. Englewood Cliffs, N.J.: Prentice-Hall, Inc., 1974. Describes the YSB in greater depth in several related contexts, emphasizing the police-probation interface.

COFFEY, ALAN R., EDWARD ELDEFONSO, and WALTER HARTINGER, *Human Relations: Law Enforcement in a Changing Community*. Englewood Cliffs, N.J.: Prentice-Hall, Inc., 1971. Comprehensive coverage of what this chapter presented as "community change."

———, *Introduction to the Criminal Justice System and Process*. Englewood Cliffs, N.J.: Prentice-Hall, Inc., 1974. Comprehensive elaboration of the overall system of criminal justice within which effective programming as presented in this chapter must occur.

———, *Police-Community Relations*. Englewood Cliffs, N.J.: Prentice-Hall, Inc., 1971. A succinct commentary on the similar and relevant law-enforcement approaches to a changing community.

COFFEY, ALAN R., and VERNON RENNER, eds., *Criminal Justice: Readings*. Englewood Cliffs, N.J.: Prentice-Hall, Inc., 1974. Full range of supplemental readings in the context of correctional programming in general.

GEMIGNANI, ROBERT J., "Youth Services Systems," *Federal Probation*, Vol. XXXVI, No. 4 (December 1972), 28–52. Good elaboration of the title subject in the context of this chapter.

HARDMAN, DALE G., "Corrections and the Community," *Federal Probation*, Vol. XXXIV, No. 1 (March 1970), 20–24. Excellent community context for many segments of this chapter.

NORMAN, SHERWOOD, *The Youth Service Bureau: A Key to Delinquency Prevention*. San Francisco: NCCD, 1972. An excellent elaboration of YSB from the opposing view, that such services should not be administered by corrections.

# STAFFING THE
# FIELD OF
# CORRECTIONS

# THREE

# Correctional
# Treatment and
# Staff Training

# Chapter 9

In presenting the operations of the correctional field in the four preceding chapters, consideration of correctional treatment was deferred until now for several reasons. First, and perhaps foremost, treatment geared to preventing offenders from committing further law violation is (or could be) the same whether offered by a probation officer in an offender's home, an institutional counselor conducting group counseling in a prison, or a parole officer at the site of an offender's employment. Moreover, when isolated in terms of program and administration of program, treatment emerges as virtually the same for both adult and juvenile.

Perhaps it is at this point that emphasis should be placed upon "continuing education" for correctional administrators. Education for administrators differs substantially from the staff training that will be discussed in this chapter. Consider, for example, the continually changing administrative skills required to distinguish between "treatment" and "treatment programs" in the following context:

> Interest in continuing adult education for public administrators represents one contemporary response to the age-old concern of our field. That con-

cern is best expressed by the question, 'What do administrators need to be more effective?' It is asserted (assumed) that what administrators need in order to be more effective is more education. Administrators need education that is remedial, relevant, and/or renewing, education that continues beyond their formal academic preparation for their administrative roles.

Continuing education may be *remedial* in the sense that it provides administrators with needed knowledge or skills which were erroneously excluded from their formal schooling. As an example, not all administrative curricula include coursework in organizational change, although the more progressive schools have long recognized this as a critical arena of administrative expertise. Continuing education may be *relevant* in the sense that it meets those educational needs of administrators which they saw as meaningful only after assuming their administrative duties. The knowledge and skills of grantsmanship are illustrative of continuing education responding to the administrative need for relevancy. Finally, continuing education responds to the *renewal* needs of public administrators, offering knowledge and skills which have been discovered/developed since the completion of an administrator's education. Environmental management, PPBS, new legislation all represent content of continuing education as renewal.[1]

While the administrative skills required to isolate correctional treatment segments of treatment programs are skills that are assumed in this chapter, it remains important to emphasize the continually changing nature of such skills—the continuous demand for updated administrative training.

Against the background of this consideration, attention is returned to isolating treatment as opposed to administration of treatment program—a distinction that usually places the treatment in the same context for both adult and juvenile. The treatment selected, in other words, is a function of administrative preference and ability to pursue preferences that are based upon *needs*, which in turn establish an administrative program-priority.

Of course situation dictates a great deal in terms of administrative ability to pursue preference in meeting needs through program-priority. For example, the prison counselor cannot pursue family counseling in the home. Nevertheless, if prison administration prefers family treatment meeting counseling needs, family members *can* participate in the prison—members can join the offender for such sessions.

The situational restrictions on traditional probation and parole can similarly be modified, if a particular approach to treatment is preferred administratively. And, of course, the community correctional programs discussed in the preceding chapter are even more flexible in terms of modifying various treatment approaches.

Another reason for deferring the subject of treatment until the present

[1] Michael E. McGill, "Learning From Administrative Experience," *Public Administration Review*, Vol. 33, No. 6, November/December 1973, p. 499.

chapter involves the need for emphasis upon the administrative distinctions between elements of correctional programs. From an administrative point of view, an effective program requires a great deal more than the treatment for which it becomes known, regardless of the significance of that treatment. No matter how innovative or creative the treatment in a correctional program becomes, *treatment is only one of many administrative concerns.*

Still another reason for deferring treatment considerations has to do with reinforcing the distinction between the *practice* and the *management* of corrections. By isolating the factors that cause many administrators to "think casework rather than management," we have tried to remove a major impediment to unifying the correctional field—no small accomplishment, in view of the frequency with which this particular impediment presents itself. Chief probation officers, for example, all too frequently function more like line workers than some of the line workers do.

The final consideration in postponing consideration of treatment until this chapter has to do with the clear administrative responsibility for staff training. While this responsibility encompasses all facets of corrections, the most significant of training responsibilities is in the area of correctional treatment. This treatment is one of the most significant variables in achieving or failing to achieve the results defined in Chapter 2, and it depends in large measure on the training that correctional staff receive:

> The correctional field is now working to substitute specific program goals for general statements of purpose. It is, for example, developing different styles of treatment most appropriate for particular types of offenders. As this movement progresses, it will be possible to communicate more effectively with decision-makers and to work out more satisfactory educational programs related to the tasks and skills actually required of correctional workers.[2]

In specific managerial terms, administrative concern with the training —or lack of it—of correctional staff is significant because results depend on treatment skills of staff, even though many organizations set up a virtual system of countering training—a type of "disincentive process," in which:

1. The benefits of training and development are not clear to top management.

2. Top management rarely evaluates and rewards managers and supervisors for carrying out effective training and development.

---

[2] E. K. Nelson, "Strategies for Action in Meeting Correctional Manpower and Program Needs," *Crime and Delinquency*, Vol. 12, No. 3 (July 1966), 221.

3. Top management rarely plans and budgets systematically for training and development.

4. Managers usually do not account for training and development in production planning.

5. Supervisors have difficulty meeting production norms with employees in training and development.

6. *Therefore*, supervisors and managers train and develop employees unsystematically and mostly for short-term objectives. . . .[3]

Consider this "disincentive process" in terms of the following, and the administrative significance in terms of achieving results:

Today corrections is undergoing change throughout the country. Current trends call for increased efforts to change the offender's basic attitudes rather than simply contain him. This has created a need. Part of that need is for more training. This problem is present not only in corrections but in virtually every occupation and profession. Industry is calling for a higher level of education and skill among its workers. A great need exists for more professionals and technicians in education, health, and other community services. The need is far greater than the rate at which the educational system can produce them. The manpower problem is becoming critical; in fact, for present day needs, it is already critical. In no area is this more true than in the field of corrections.

Training, particularly in-service training, focuses on present problems, although it is also concerned with the future. Together with this concern for present and future goes the task of facing daily "built-in" problems. If change is involved, these problems are magnified. Change is difficult in most walks of life, but in corrections it seems to be the most painful problem of all.[4]

Painful or not, change is inevitable. The only question is, Will the change in corrections be influenced by correctional administration? If so, training is vitally important:

General acceptance of the idea that competent staff is needed in order to promote the rehabilitation of offenders has meant that correctional administrators are giving more attention to training. The aim of staff development, through orientation and in-service training, is to improve services by improving staff performance.[5]

Beyond this important goal of improving staff performance, training relates, in a high-priority manner, to improving the criminal justice system overall:

[3] U.S. Civil Service Commission Bureau of Training, "Study Shows Obstacles to Effective Training," *Federal Trainer*, No. 16 (June 1973), 1.

[4] Henry Burns, Jr., "Training the Correctional Staff Trainer," *Public Personnel Review*, Vol. XXXII, No. 1 (January 1971), 16.

[5] Merritt Gilman, "Problems and Progress in Staff Training," *Crime and Delinquency*, Vol. 12, No. 3 (July 1966), 254.

Better and more training and education of personnel in the criminal justice agencies of this nation has long been on the list of priority tasks for improving the system of justice.[6]

Inasmuch as training in the treatment techniques is probably the most significant of all administrative training responsibilities, let us consider first the *nature* of correctional treatment.

## CORRECTIONAL TREATMENT

Many administrators mistakenly distinguish between adult training and juvenile training, as though treatment training for adult programs and for juvenile programs should be approached differently. However, although there are a number of procedural differences between treating adult and juvenile offenders, the concepts are essentially the same, particularly in the administrative context, where program rather than procedure is being considered.

A further justification for dealing with treatment as interchangeable between adult and juvenile corrections has to do with separating treatment from the programs that were presented in the four preceding chapters. This suggests a clear definition for *treatment*.

For purposes of this chapter, *correctional treatment* is defined as *any activity other than investigation, surveillance, or supervision in which the probation officer, counselor, or parole agent engages with the client for the sole purpose of rehabilitation.*[7]

Of course, investigation, surveillance, and supervision are integral segments of the *practice* of corrections; consideration here is directed specifically to *treatment*. Even restricted in this manner, treatment has a very wide scope:

> The involvement of many disciplines in corrections and criminal justice—social work, clinical psychology, psychiatry, law, and education—without a meaningful relationship to criminology and criminal justice is a most undesirable situation. . . . These disciplines have little or no contact with criminology, behavioral psychology, and sociology. An interdisciplinary program in criminology is needed at this time if we are to make any progress in the control of the crime problem.[8]

[6] Stanley Vanagunas, "A Role for the States, A Model Interstate Compact for the Training and Education of Criminal Justice Personnel," *Crime and Delinquency*, Vol. 19, No. 1 (January 1973), 49.

[7] An extensive list of annotated references is presented at the conclusion of this chapter covering the entire range of causation theory, correctional treatment, and offender classification.

[8] C. Ray Jeffery, *Crime Prevention Through Environmental Design* (Beverly Hills, Calif.: Sage Publications, Inc., 1971), p. 261.

In other words, since the treatment practices of corrections can and often do range through "social work, clinical psychology, psychiatry, law, and education" somewhat independent of "criminology, behavior psychology, and sociology," there is no uniform conceptual frame for correctional treatment, nor any uniform application of treatment in correctional practices. Treatment is indeed an unrestricted concept in the correctional field, an increasing cause of administrative concern and administrative responsibility to remedy.

There are a number of reasons that treatment is so diversified. One such reason is the breakthrough that has permeated the literature since it has become fashionable to include "psychology, psychiatry, social work, law, education, criminology, behavioral psychology, and sociology" in definitions of treatment. The following is typical of this variety of literature:

> In several senses, corrections today may stand at the threshold of a new era, promising resolution of a significant number of the problems that have vexed it throughout its development. At the very least, it is developing the theory and practical groundwork for a new approach to rehabilitation of the most important group of offenders—those, predominantly young and lower-class, who are not committed to crime as a way of life and do not pose serious dangers to the community.[9]

Another possible reason for the virtually unrestricted concept of correctional treatment is the cumulative pressure to develop something "new" because of mounting evidence that corrections does not often correct in the more severe cases. This awareness, occurring coincidentally with a cultural transition to greatly increased leisure time, may well have been excessively influenced by ideas such as the following:

> The transition from agriculture to industry, known as the Industrial Revolution, tended to displace both the Northern children and the newly freed Southern slaves toward cities—cities busily replacing human labor with machinery at an even faster pace than the mechanization that was occurring on rural farms.

> One immediate result of the Industrial Revolution was increased leisure time for many. In the case of those who worked, the mechanization of labor reduced the amount of time needed to achieve desired production levels. For those unable to gain employment in urban factories, leisure time also increased dramatically, if not desirably—at least the "leisure" that was available during periods when employment was being sought. In either event, the dawn-till-dusk workday began to fade from the urban scene. With it also faded the security of the dreary but certain continuation of living out a predictable life on the farm or plantation. Several major wars and a never-

9 President's Commission on Law Enforcement and Administration of Justice, *Task Force Report: Corrections* (Washington, D.C.: U.S. Government Printing Office, 1967), p. 6.

ending elimination of jobs by machinery have done little to ensure the
security of the modern urban worker—in spite of, and perhaps because of,
ever-increasing leisure time.[10]

The emergence of culturally accepted leisure doubtlessly influenced
those who conceived of criminal behavior as simply "laziness," which in
turn supported another motive to try something new, since corrections
were based on the "work ethic," discredited somewhat now by the
"leisure ethic." Compounding the confusion of such a transition was the
emergence of guilt with respect to treating offenders:

> Included among the crimes that make up the total are those which *we* com-
> mit, we noncriminals. These are not in the tabulations. They are not listed
> in the statistics and are not described in the President's Crime Commission
> studies. But *our* crimes help to make the recorded crimes possible, even
> necessary; and the worst of it is we do not even know we are guilty.
>
> Perhaps our *worst* crime is our ignorance about crime; our easy satisfaction
> with headlines and the accounts of lurid cases; and our smug assumption
> that it is all a matter of some tough "bad guys" whom the tough "good
> guys" will soon capture. And even the assassination of one of our most be-
> loved Presidents has not really changed public thinking—or nonthinking—
> about crime.[11]

In addition to this pressure to try something new was the national recognition given the influence of "cultural deprivation." For a number of
years, this consideration has focused increasingly upon the field of corrections and, not surprisingly, in a manner that includes implications for
correctional treatment:

> Corrections has a special interest in people who are culturally different from
> the majority because many of the minority groups are overrepresented in
> the offender population or are moving toward overrepresentation. If correc-
> tions is to become truly corrective, its staff must know well the people with
> whom they work. It is not enough, for example, to provide the usual type
> of correctional program for a youth or adult whose native language is not
> English, whose view of life is quite different from that of the white middle
> class. To ignore these basic facts is almost inevitably to fail to rehabilitate
> him. He is released from custody bewildered or embittered, unable or un-
> willing to conform to ways of living which are acceptable to the majority
> of his fellow Americans. By following such a course, corrections is ignor-
> ing differences that can make the difference between a rehabilitation and
> recidivism.[12]

[10] Alan R. Coffey, Edward Eldefonso, and Walter Hartinger, *Police–Community
Relations* (Englewood Cliffs, N.J.: Prentice-Hall, Inc., 1971), p. 49.
[11] Karl Menninger, M.D., *The Crime of Punishment* (New York: The Viking Press,
Inc., 1968), p. 3.
[12] Alice Maxwell and William F. Meredith, "Introduction," *Differences That Make
the Difference*, ed. Roma K. McNickle (Washington, D.C.: Joint Commission on
Correctional Manpower and Training, August 1967), p. 1.

When these and many other influences are considered, we can see why correctional treatment is not only complex in many instances, but very diversified as well, and virtually without uniformity. Let us consider the range of this diversification.

### Causation Theories

The theoretical concept of the causes of crime and delinquency may or may not bear directly upon correctional treatment. But there is an indirect relationship, through the influence of various disciplines that are used to educate correctional personnel, as opposed to training them.

Therefore, there is *some* theoretical basis for every correctional treatment method. Some methods are directly influenced by a specific theory; some reflect a combination of various theories. Moreover, some theories are scientific, some are philosophical, and some are both. Some theories are largely folklore or tradition, but most flow from one particular academic discipline out of a rather expansive array of them.

Regardless of the academic discipline involved, however, these theories of causation can be administratively considered as in three broad categories. Without abandoning our administrative orientation, we can say that this classification might also prove *managerially* useful.[13]

1. Deterministic deviance
2. Self-deterministic deviance
3. A combination of self-determined and determined deviance

The semantics of each term suggests the theory involved: *Determined* implies that the deviant behavior is determined by outside forces, beyond the control of the offender; *self-determined* means that the offender himself determined the offense. The combination of the two expresses the theory that crime is caused by a little of both.

Not much theoretical explanation is needed for the self-determination concept of crime causation; the offender simply chose to offend. It is noteworthy that *corrections depends totally on at least some degree of this philosophy:* The offender cannot be corrected if he has no control over his offenses.

While the self-determination theory is relatively simple, the deterministic category tends to proliferate. Major families of theory in this regard are as follows:

---

[13] For a fuller elaboration of these theories, see Chapter 2 of Alan R. Coffey, *Juvenile Justice as a System: Law Enforcement to Rehabilitation* (Englewood Cliffs, N.J.: Prentice-Hall, Inc., 1974).

I    Sociological theory
    A.  Cultural
    B.  Social
    C.  Ecological
II   Psychological theory
    A.  Personality disorder
    B.  Psychoanalytic
    C.  Behavioral
III  Physiological theory
    A.  Anthropological
    B.  Biochemical
    C.  Heredity

For the sake of brevity, these theories can be grossly oversimplified by stating that the cause of crime is a reflection of the particular academic discipline associated with theory. Although this by no means diminishes the significance of any one theory, a truly administrative perspective demands recognition of the overwhelming evidence that when crime is caused by sociological—or psychological, or physiological—problems, not everyone subjected to the same problems will become criminal.

Nevertheless, approaching an administrative understanding of correctional treatment requires a knowledge of the general theoretical influences upon any given treatment—or, at least, the potential influences. At a minimum, it requires a general understanding of the restrictions imposed by the particular academic discipline involved.

### Treatment Methods and Techniques

Before moving into correctional treatment methods, let us review what is *not* meant by treatment methods and techniques. As we have already noted, treatment is *not* the investigation, the surveillance, or the supervision involved in correctional practice. But more to the point, treatment is *not* the activities typified by the following:

> For the parolee, the parole agent is God. Parole has been revoked without hearings, and parolees have been denied the right to appear in their own behalf and confront their accusers. In one instance, the wife of an ex-convict incurred $1,000 in medical bills. When her husband sought bank credit, the parole officer blocked the loan. Hiring a friend to drive him to a different town, the parolee earned about $1,000 on a legitimate lumber sale. The parole officer then jailed the offender for "leaving the jurisdiction without permission." A court, after reviewing the evidence, fortunately freed the ex-convict. And a landmark 1972 Supreme Court decision has held

that parole boards must observe due process of law, at least in revoking paroles.[14]

Correctional activities of this variety that pass for treatment techniques are definitely *not* correctional treatment in the context of this chapter. Such methods are simply what the court found: correctional abuse.

CASEWORK. Casework involves a wide variety of activities, but a relatively simple definition of it exists. There are three considerations in establishing this definition.

According to the Council on Social Work, correctional casework is what the appropriate agency conducts with officially designated law violators. This generalized definition is tightened up somewhat when we add that corrective action must be taken with the designated law violator.[15] Finally, the definition is complete with the addition of the element of services that relate to the offender's difficulties.[16] *Correctional casework means services by the appropriate agency to a designated offender for the purpose of corrections.*

The key to understanding casework techniques has to do with these "services by the appropriate agency." In effect, these services are frequently coordinative, involving further referrals in many instances. The services have to do with assisting the offender or his family with problems related to employment, education, medical and dental troubles, marriage, family counseling, and a host of other matters with which the offender is unprepared to cope—theoretically for any or all of the sociological, psychological, and physiological reasons suggested in causal theory.

The distinguishing characteristic of casework techniques is the *indirect* involvement of the probation or parole agent, as contrasted with some of the more direct techniques that we shall now consider.

COUNSELING. For purposes of this discussion, the difference between counseling and therapy is a matter of *dependence*. In the case of counseling, the offender depends upon what amounts to the advice of the correctional specialist. Therapy, on the other hand, guides the offender toward depending upon his own advice, toward self-dependence.

Of course, the intent of counseling is exactly the same as that of therapy—to develop a self-reliant individual. But at the time the two techniques are employed, counseling is more in the form of directive ad-

---

[14] Herman Schwartz, "Let's Abolish Parole," *Reader's Digest*, August 1973, p. 190.
[15] H. D. Laswell and A. Kaplan, *Power and Authority* (New Haven, Conn.: Yale University Press, 1950), p. 133.
[16] E. Nicholds, *A Primer of Social Casework* (New York: Columbia University Press, 1960), p. 78.

vice, and therapy is customarily nondirective in nature, significant exceptions in both cases notwithstanding.

The directive advice reflected in the counseling techniques covers a broad spectrum, ranging from personal problems through education to offender attitudes. In many instances, counseling is structured in terms of two influences: (1) the philosophy and policy of the particular organization, combined with (2) the theoretical preference of the counselor in terms of sociological, psychological, or physiological causes of crime.

THERAPY. Therapy as a correctional technique reduces to a relatively simple division between emotions and behavior—a distinction that also suggests in many instances the further distinction between nondirective (emotion) and directive (behavior). Not surprisingly, a great deal of what is called correctional therapy attempts to combine emotions ("insight," "feelings," etc.) with behavior, and the implications of such effort are worth exploring.

As we have seen, asking an offender not to hit his wife but then asking him how he feels about hitting her is contradictory, to say the least. However, many correctional practitioners call upon the paradox of punishment and rehabilitation to justify this contradictory combination, one that brings authoritative relationships enforced by law into emotional therapy.

There is a vast array of thinking on how emotions and insight can be integrated with behavior and how efforts to do it are justified. Such thinking often bears terms like "treating the whole person."

In spite of overwhelming evidence that behavior, not emotion, is the basis for conviction of law violators, emotional therapy is in many instances given greater priority than behavioral concerns. For this reason, some consideration of the broader categories of emotional therapy should be noted. The following are some of the names of certain methods and techniques emphasizing the emotional factors in therapy. Details on them can be found in the literature listed in the annotated references at the conclusion of this chapter.

Psychoanalysis
Transactional analysis
Gestalt therapy
Encounter groups
Psychodrama and sociodrama
Transcendental meditation
Marathon groups
Self-enhancement groups
Conjoint family therapy

Insight encounter
Bioenergetics

These techniques can be either directive (a "leader") or nondirective (a "facilitator"), with or without "transference/countertransference" and with or without "rapport" between the correctional specialist and client. This last consideration, rapport, is related to the constant reality that the client is not a volunteer, even when he is asking for therapy—the law volunteers him.

The desired outcome of therapy geared to emotions includes such things as "insight" into motives, "self-other resolution," "self-awareness," "self-acceptance," "interpersonal stability," "awareness of human needs," and many other terms in a virtual lexicon of treatment results. Implicit in such goals, of course, is the idea that emotion and feeling are subject to direct manipulation, a premise underlying considerable disappointment for those entering treatment with such hope.

In contrast, therapy geared explicitly to behavior is less subject to disappointment, because behavior, unlike emotions, is optional. Moreover, *it is behavior that violates the law—not emotions.*

The current applications of behavior therapy as a correctional technique are, in one way or another, related to what has become known as behavior modification, or behavior management. Drawing heavily upon a learning theory known as operant conditioning, behavior modification is a kind of hedonistic technique operating on the premise that human behavior is a function of "positive and negative reinforcers"—that is, that humans repeat satisfying experiences and abandon unpleasant experiences. The literature noted in the extensive annotated references at the conclusion of this chapter affords information on the complexities that accompany this relatively simple principle; but from an administrative viewpoint, behaviorally oriented treatment remains essentially just as simple as indicated.

As a correctional technique, behavior modification requires clarification of the control that the offender has over consequences. The idea that misery is optional is communicated via clearly defined choices, with equal clarification of clearly defined consequences, including "rewards" for appropriate behavior (earlier release, privilege use, etc.), and "punishment" for inappropriate behavior—*rewards and punishment on a clearly defined, systematically predictable basis.*

Recognition of the validity of many influential factors dealt with directly in emotional therapy requires a somewhat more sophisticated approach to behavior modification than is suggested by this administrative overview. Nevertheless, *responsibility for behavior* remains the key; at no time does emotion justify poor behavior. As one training director puts it, "You're always in charge of your own fists, no matter how big your id may be."

An administrative advantage often overlooked in considering behavioral approaches to correctional treatment is that once therapy is anchored to behavior, a uniform continuity can be established: individual correctional treatment in court, followed by institution, followed by outside treatment, with authority not contradicting itself as one subsystem of criminal justice focuses on behavior and another on feeling. Moreover, the relevance of behavior permits a wide range of behavioral understanding to emerging realization—family systems, for example.

But the main advantage remains the consistency of correctional treatment for offense that is by definition based on misbehavior—treatment geared to the nature of the problem presented.

Even while sensitive to the emotional pain involved in the need to change behavior, the behavior-modification variety of therapy permits the client to experience for himself that his self-determinism can overcome his determinism—*misery is optional.*

CLASSIFICATION. Although not a treatment technique as such, offender classification is conspicuously relevant to appropriate correctional treatment. A brief review of correctional classification is therefore indicated.

As in the case of the actual correctional treatment, classification of offenders is more relevant to the nature of corrections when approached in terms of behavior—or perhaps behavior severity. The current trends in classification, however, tend to encompass a wider range of emotional variables than did earlier efforts to establish "typologies." The latter were geared to a specific offense, which at least suggested behavior that needs modification.

Classification, then, includes a very wide range of approaches, behavioral and otherwise. A mere sampling would include the following typologies: Warren (Interpersonal Maturity—I-Level), Hunt, Hurwitz, MacGregor, Mackey, Quay, Reiss, A.P.A., Argyle, Gibbons, Jenkins and Hewitt, McCord, Rickles, Schray, and Studt. More detail on these typologies is available in the literature suggested in the extensive annotated references at the conclusion of this chapter.

Administratively, it is noteworthy that considerable time and effort have been committed to each of the typological approaches associated with the names above. In attempting to assess the potential of any or all of these classification concepts, consideration must be given the diagnostic influences borrowed from psychiatry and psychometrics, such as Rorschach, FIRO-B, C, F and MATE, TAT, Intelligence tests, Aptitude tests, and so on.

Administratively, classification (or "diagnosis") is extremely significant, in that treatment is often guided by classification, so that treatment training and policy may well be far less influential than classification in some instances.

For this reason, once an administrative position is adopted on staff training in treatment methods, equal concern should accrue to a position on classification and subsequent training.

## CORRECTIONAL STAFF TRAINING

Just as correctional treatment is essentially the same for adult and juvenile (from the administrative perspective rather than that of practice), staff training in treatment techniques can be approached in the same manner.

### Training vs. Education

The personnel requirements of the correctional field include, of course, certain educational requirements. In addition, a person who fills a position in this field must be trained for it. *Education and training are not the same thing, and both are needed.*

> . . . *Education* is broadly inclusive of academic and theoretical principles
> . . . training is restricted in nature and scope to methods, strategies, techniques. . . .[17]

The significance of this distinction between training and education is that administrative programs depend upon training, and training often succeeds or fails on the basis of the education of the personnel being trained.

One incidental distinction has to do with motivation. At least on a comparative basis, those pursuing education are customarily more motivated than those subjected to training:

> Motivation for training appears to be a serious problem. How can we motivate people so that the training effort is not nullified? One of the ways is through the use of training techniques that involve them in the training. Present pessimism about training is based on the non-involved methods such as lectures and films. . . .
>
> . . . Training of correctional officers in group counseling is a familiar fad these days. Too often, the organizational change that must precede this training does not take place. Although it can be rationalized that the training will sensitize the trainees, the lack of structure within which this new training can be used negates the training effort.

[17] Alan R. Coffey, *Criminal Justice Administration: A Management Systems Approach* (Englewood Cliffs, N.J.: Prentice-Hall, Inc., 1974), p. 158.

Too often trainees are aware that change will not take place to accommodate the new training. This is especially true when the trainees, having evaluated their superiors, realize that new behaviors will not be accepted and new methods of doing the job will not be tolerated. It is difficult for the trainer to be effective in the face of opposition to new ideas revealed by evaluation of a superior's response.

To what extent must training reach the superior? How high up the administrative hierarchy must training begin in order to prepare the groundwork for effective training in the lower ranks? Obviously, we cannot expect to take busy administrators away from their work in order to train them. Yet it is necessary to involve them in training somehow. We make a mistake, however, in thinking that the top administrator should actually be put through a training program. By the time a person becomes a top administrator, it is too late to give him training. The only realistic concern here should be to get a training commitment from him. We want him to support the training program and back it when the going gets rough.[18]

In the specific context of correctional administration, consider the educational implications of the following:

There has been extensive discussion regarding the utility of advanced formal education (beyond high school) for persons working in the criminal justice system (courts, police, social work agencies, correctional institutions). Depending on the particular professional orientation of the agency, the debate has taken assorted avenues and manifests itself with varying degrees of intensity. There are convincing arguments, both pro and con, concerning the relative merits of both formal education and experience.

Whether the criminal justice organization is a social work agency or a police agency, it is usually acknowledged that a college education is not, in itself, necessarily a guarantee for effective performance. This, however, is not sufficient rationale to discount or degrade the educational process.

One of the most important functions of advanced education is to provide the individual with the abstract experience that will assist him in becoming an astute decision maker. Organizational goals are not achieved without decisions being made and decisions are made by decision makers.[19]

Of course, the implications of this higher education for decision makers has another dimension—that of research:

For many years we have known that a gulf exists between knowledge derived from systematic research and the utilization of that knowledge in correctional decisions and programming. Observers of correction in America today are concerned with the failure of research findings to influence

[18] Marshall Fels, "Discussion," *Targets for In-Service Training* (Washington, D.C.: Joint Commission on Correctional Manpower and Training, May 4–5, 1967), pp. 26–27.
[19] John M. Trojanowicz and Robert C. Trojanowicz, "The Role of a College Education in Decision-Making," *Public Personnel Review*, Vol. XXXIII, No. 1 (January 1972), 29.

the policies and programs of correctional agencies. There are striking and disconcerting similarities between the prison of 1871 and that of 1971. Perhaps more significant, inmates' perceptions of prisons are the same today as they were one hundred years ago. The inmate continues to perceive imprisonment as a deprivation. Although the ideology of punishment has been pronounced dead, it is by no means buried. Despite the great emphasis today on rationality in society, the bulk of correctional decisions are nonrational and are based on vague subjective impressions, untested rules of thumb, and an appeal to morality, tradition, and authority.[20]

Leaving educational considerations to discuss training, let us nevertheless acknowledge that higher education is the general source of learning research concepts.

### Significance of Staff Training

Accepting administrative responsibility for staff training as a "generic management function" may or may not incorporate the significance of training in the correctional field. In this regard, closer examination of the role of training in the correctional organization may prove useful:

Training is not a method with which to solve otherwise insoluble organizational problems; it is rather a ubiquitous something without which organizations do not long survive. Training is more than method, more inclusive than program, more than personnel development, and is more than an aid to problem solving. As a ubiquitous something it can be likened to a religion. In its ultimate form training is a process through which the attempt is made to maximize human effort toward the more effective interdependence necessary for effective group effort. The supervisor, at all organizational levels, must understand and facilitate the process.[21]

The clear implications of the role of training in terms of this commentary are the *managerial* responsibilities it involves, which are often "dropped" on a training officer, staff development director, or training coordinator.

Centralizing training, of course, is desirable, particularly in the context of educational influence on training:

. . . Ideally, responsibility for training should be lodged within some specific academic field or discipline in order to insure comparability of training. Training should include the detailed study of causal theory and research data, diagnostic models, and principles of treatment. In effect, this educational program would be analogous to that in medical schools and

[20] Peter G. Garabedian, "Research and Practice in Planning Correctional Change," *Crime and Delinquency*, Vol. 17, No. 1 (January 1971), 41.
[21] John M. Pfiffner and Marshall Fels, *The Supervision of Personnel: Human Relations in the Management of Men* (Englewood Cliffs, N.J.: Prentice-Hall, Inc., 1964), p. 204.

other professional schools, where the basic curriculum content remains constant from one specific training institution to another.

It is certainly not the case that correctional education has this character at present. Instead, the heterogeneous mixture of backgrounds now represented among treatment workers vitiates any claim that there is a profession of correctional work in existence. Persons with backgrounds of social work, sociology, correctional administration, criminology, psychology, and other undergraduate majors all find their way into correctional employment.[22]

Moreover, there is considerable administrative advantage to isolating accountability for such a vital function, since it is required in the same context as the functional accountability described in Chapters 2, 3, and 4.

Nevertheless, training is an administrative responsibility regardless of who is held accountable for this function. Administrative responsibilities in this area even incorporate the isolation of training needs:

> Finding and fixing such non-training-related reasons for poor performance is part of management's job. The answers lie beyond training. The air-conditioning salesman needs new sales techniques and tools (i.e., a method for qualifying prospects by phone so he won't waste time on nonproductive house calls). The room clerk needs an incentive deal that makes the extra effort to sell a high-priced room worthwhile. The technician will work effectively if the sampling system makes every tape collected meaningful.[23]

The significance of this managerial responsibility to find and fix training answers that "lie beyond training" is increased by the organizational implications of training, which are of profound administrative significance:

> The central evaluation question remains: "Does the training assist in producing the desired organizational change?" and not: "Does the training accomplish it by itself?" Does the training provide a bridge to organizational change? In view of the resistance to change and institutional lag generally associated with organizations, this type of follow-up evaluation research seems to have merit. This is especially true when one considers that organizations change primarily to optimize their survival and not because training has or has not been held.[24]

### Program Staffing

Finally, in clarifying the administrative significance of staff training, we take up what the preceding chapter discussed as "program staffing."

---

[22] Don C. Gibbons, *Changing the Lawbreaker, The Treatment of Delinquents and Criminals* (Englewood Cliffs, N.J.: Prentice-Hall, Inc., 1965), pp. 16–17.
[23] David Sage, "What to Do Before the Trainer Comes," *Training and Development Journal*, Vol. 27, No. 6 (June 1973), 30.
[24] E. J. Karras, "Training—A Link to Organizational Change," *Training and Development Journal*, Vol. 27, No. 5 (May 1973), 14.

Staffing is not merely a consideration of the number of personnel; staffing is also a concern with the *competence* of personnel:

> The need for trained staff has greatly increased in the past decade because of the general population growth, a continuing rise in delinquency and crime, and an increasing demand on the part of the public that the problem be dealt with effectively. At the same time, the existing manpower supply in correction is being tapped for antipoverty programs and training centers, mental health programs, mental retardation services, and social problem prevention campaigns. Personnel essential to correctional rehabilitation include teachers, social workers, psychologists, psychiatrists, lawyers, sociologists, management and training specialists, and thousands of nonprofessional but equally important persons with special skills in designing prevention programs. The situation has become so acute that it is impossible to staff new or existing programs adequately in most jurisdictions.[25]

The actual process of training takes many forms. In developing the appropriate form for a particular correctional organization, administrators sometimes find consultants useful.[26] There is no formula for either devising pertinent training or engaging consultants; both require considerable administrative thought. The consequence of failing to give this thought may well be an increase in the general concern currently focused upon the effectiveness of the correctional field overall.


## SUMMARY

This chapter introduced the concept of correctional treatment in the context of administrative responsibility for training correctional staff. Specifically, it focused on training and treatment methods, holding treatment the most significant variable in correctional programming.

Treatment was isolated from other program considerations in order to provide an administrative perspective, since treatment is administratively the same for probation, institution, parole, community, adult, and juvenile once the administrative context is isolated. The variations in situation and practice were acknowledged.

Theoretical approaches to crime causes were reviewed in terms of influences upon treatment methods.

Methods of treatment were classified behavioral or emotional, with recognition of certain values in emotional therapy, but emphasis on the administrative advantages of behavioral treatment.

Distinctions were made between education and training in emphasizing

---

[25] Milton G. Rector, in *Manpower and Training for Corrections* (New York: Council on Social Work Education, 1966), p. viii.

[26] See Coffey, *Administration of Criminal Justice*, Chapter 14, on use of consultants.

the significance of both, as well as of administrative responsibility for training.

## Discussion Topics

1. Discuss the concept that correctional treatment as defined in this chapter is the same for probation, institution, and parole from an administrative viewpoint.
2. Discuss the same concept in terms of juveniles and adults.
3. Relate causal theories to administrative responsibilities for treatment.
4. Discuss the distinction between emotional and behavioral treatment.
5. Relate each to corrections.
6. Elaborate on administrative training responsibilities.
7. Distinguish between training and education.

## Annotated References

ANDRY, R. G., *Delinquency and Parental Pathology*. London: Methuen, 1960. Good elaboration of the title subject in general context of this chapter.

BANDURA, A., *Principles of Behavior Modification*. New York: Holt, Rinehart & Winston, Inc., 1969. An encyclopedic volume covering what this chapter presented as a useful treatment method. See also Thorne, W., Tharp, T., and Wetzel, H., "Behavior Modification Techniques: New Tools for Probation Officers," *Federal Probation*, Vol. 31, No. 2 (June 1967).

BARNES, H. E., and N. K. TEETERS, *New Horizons in Criminology*. Englewood Cliffs, N.J.: Prentice-Hall, Inc., 1960. An excellent survey of the causative theories in crime and delinquency.

BERNE, E., *Group Treatment*. New York: Grove Press, Inc., 1966. An excellent technical elaboration of transactional analysis. See also Berne, *Games People Play; What Do You Say After You Say Hello?;* and *The Structure and Dynamics of Organizations and Groups* (Garden City, 1966). Also, for those interested in the technical application of this method, P. Mc-Cormick, "Transactional Analysis: A Promising Treatment Method for Corrections," *Journal of the California Probation, Parole and Correctional Association*, Vol. 1, No. 2 (Fall 1964).

COFFEY, ALAN R., *Criminal Justice Administration: A Management Systems Approach*. Englewood Cliffs, N.J.: Prentice-Hall, Inc., 1974. Chapter 8 elaborates on training and education in the managerial context.

FERDINAND, T. N., *Typologies of Delinquency*. New York: Random House, Inc., 1966. Comprehensive coverage of the "typological approach" to delinquency classifications not dealt with in this chapter directly, but handled implicitly in the discussion of causes.

GIBBONS, D. C., "Differential Treatment of a Delinquent and Interpersonal Maturity Level Theory: A Critique," *The Social Service Review*, Vol. 44, No. 1 (March 1970). An outstanding synoptic review of what this chapter presented as an example of a classification system.

————, "Observations on the Study of Crime Causation," *American Journal of Sociology*, Vol. 77, No. 2 (September 1971), 262–78. A meaningful critique of causation theoretical approaches.

KENNEDY, D. B., and B. KENNEDY, *Applied Sociology for Police*. Springfield, Ill.: Charles C. Thomas, Publisher, 1972. Excellent elaboration of sociological concepts referred to in this chapter.

PHILLIPSON, M., *Sociological Aspects of Crime and Delinquency*. London: Routledge & Kegan Paul, 1971. A comprehensive criminological context for this chapter.

POVEDA, T. G., "The Image of the Criminal: A Critique of Crime and Delinquency Theories," *Issues in Criminology*, Vol. 5, No. 1 (Winter 1970), 59–83. Combines a critique with a survey of delinquency theories overall.

ROEBUCK, J. B., *Criminal Typology*. Springfield, Ill.: Charles C. Thomas, Publisher, 1971. While focused on adult criminality, the text affords an innovative conceptual reference point for this chapter.

SATIR, V., *Peoplemaking*. Palo Alto, Calif.: Behavior and Science Books, 1972. An excellent context for the example of family therapy given in this chapter. See also Satir, *Conjoint Family Therapy*. Behavior and Science Books, 1966.

TAPPAN, P. W., *Crime, Justice and Correction*. New York: McGraw-Hill Book Company, 1960. A virtual encyclopedia of both causative theories and their criminological context in general. See also Tappan, *Juvenile Delinquency*. New York: McGraw-Hill, 1959.

WARREN, M. Q., "Classification of Offenders as an Aid to Efficient Management and Effective Treatment," *Journal of Criminal Law, Criminology and Police Science*, Vol. 62, No. 2 (June 1971). An extremely comprehensive analysis of the classification concept presented in this chapter, valuable because of the increasing significance of classification to probation, correctional institutions, and parole.

WOLFGANG, M. E., ed., *Crime and Culture: Essay in Honor of Thorsten Sellin*. New York: John Wiley & Sons, Inc., 1968. An outstanding collection of contributions from many of the most prominent theoreticians in criminology, dealing in great depth with delinquency as the conflict between "social norms" and "legal norms."

### Further References

BUTLER, EDGAR W., and S. N. ADAMS, "Typologies of Delinquent Girls: Some Alternative Approaches," *Social Forces*, 44 (March 1966), 401–7.

California Youth Authority, *The Community Treatment Project After Five Years*. Sacramento, Calif.: Department of the Youth Authority, 1971.

———, *The Status of Current Research in the California Youth Authority*. Sacramento, Calif.: Department of the Youth Authority, 1968.

FERDINAND, T. N., *Delinquent Behavior*. Englewood Cliffs, N.J.: Prentice-Hall, Inc., 1970.

———, "Problems of Causal Analysis in Criminology: A Case Illustration," *Journal of Research in Crime and Delinquency*, 3 (January 1966), 301–8.

GOUGH, HARRISON, "Theory and Measurement of Socialization," *Journal of Consulting Psychology*, 24 (February 1960), 23–30.

HARTJEN, C. A., and D. C. GIBBONS, "An Empirical Investigation on a Criminal Typology," *Sociology and Social Research*, 54 (October 1969), 56–62.

JESNESS, C., "Typology and Treatment," *California Youth Authority Quarterly*, 19 (Summer 1966), 17–29.

JOHNS, D. A., J. K. TURNER, and J. W. PEARSON, *Community Treatment Project, An Evaluation of Community Treatment for Delinquents: Seventh Progress Report, Part 1, The Sacramento-Stockton and the San Francisco Experiments*. Sacramento, Calif.: Department of the Youth Authority, 1968.

LERMAN, P., "Evaluative Studies of Institutions for Delinquents: Implications for Research and Social Police," *Social Work*, 13 (July 1968), 55–64.

SULLIVAN, C., M. Q. GRANT, and J. D. GRANT, "The Development of Interpersonal Maturity: Applications to Delinquency," *Psychiatry*, 20 (November 1957), 373–85.

United States Department of Health, Education and Welfare, National Clearinghouse for Mental Health Information, *Typological Approaches and Delinquency Control: A Status Report*. Washington, D.C.: U.S. Government Printing Office, 1967.

———, President's Commission on Law Enforcement and Administration of Justice, *Task Force Report: Corrections*. Washington, D.C.: U.S. Government Printing Office, 1967.

# Personnel Requirements and Correctional Careers

# Chapter 10

It is the responsibility of correctional administration to determine what personnel are needed and what will be required of them:

> Systematic, intelligent administration must be based on facts. Since management depends on people to implement the program of an organization, fact-finding about their jobs is vital. Put another way, management must determine (1) what work must be done to accomplish various goals; (2) what skills are necessary for this work; and (3) how much work can be assigned to one person. On the basis of this information, positions are defined, salaries determined, and suitable people found and assigned for the work.[1]

But this does not mean that administration is a function of personnel; it should be emphasized that the influence of administration is perhaps the most significant of all influences upon the organization:

[1] International City Managers Association, *Municipal Personnel Administration* (Ann Arbor, Mich.: Cushing-Malloy, Inc., 1960), p. 32.

Administration is sometimes equated with the rank-and-file personnel; that is, it is said that the effectiveness of a program depends on little more than the quality of the people functioning in the court, correctional institution, or department. There is considerable truth in this viewpoint. But it is important to realize that the leadership of an organization puts its unmistakable stamp on the character of the organization, and vitally affects the performance of all personnel.[2]

However, without detracting from the organizational significance of the administration, its responsibility for staffing, along with determining staffing requirements, remains critically important:

Manpower planning and the application of manpower economics seem likely to become important in the management of law enforcement and criminal justice activities in the future. The major portion of expenditures to operate police departments and criminal justice facilities is now spent for salaries and other costs directly associated with employment. Because the financial resources of local and state governments are limited, greater interest is being shown in a more rational use of manpower resources to reduce the cost of police protection while improving its efficiency. Any imbalance in the criminal justice system is self-defeating. If a disproportionate amount of the total resources available is allotted to police activities at the expense of other parts of the system, bottlenecks are created in the courts, and correctional institutions are hindered in the performance of their functions.

Manpower utilization planning for law enforcement and rehabilitation activities will have to focus on employing a greater variety of workers and their better distribution. Police departments, especially in large cities, will have to use more civilian workers for many positions now filled by policemen. Correctional institutions will have to employ more workers in rehabilitation services than in security services.[3]

## CORRECTIONAL PERSONNEL

The preceding chapter introduced the third part of this volume by relating correctional treatment to the training of correctional personnel. Regarding the education of personnel—as we noted, not the same as their training—personnel employed in certain institutions may pursue educational goals after receiving correctional training (working for a degree while on the job) but this education occurs in most instances *prior* to employment and training in the correctional field. This then, is the initial

---

[2] Sol Rubin, *Crime and Juvenile Delinquency: A Rational Approach to Penal Problems* (Dobbs Ferry, N.Y.: Oceana Publications, Inc., 1970), p. 6.
[3] Morris Cobern, "Some Manpower Aspects of the Criminal Justice System," *Crime and Delinquency*, Vol. 19, No. 2 (April 1973), 187.

context for discussing personnel requirements—the educational requirement of most correctional positions.

Requirements, sometimes referred to as qualifications, vary from jurisdiction to jurisdiction, but studies tend to indicate certain patterns, as in
the accompanying table. The table, however, shows only the level of educational requirements; in regard to the recruiting implications of these requirements, the administrative picture has brightened somewhat in recent
years.

A significant turnover of correctional personnel plagued the field
prior to 1968. Since that time, however, even during a general slowing
in the American economy, salaries and working conditions have improved. The result appears to be a somewhat improved stability pattern
in the staffing of the correctional field overall.

But while this improvement in correctional staffing has been occurring,
an accompanying trend has been a somewhat militant stance on the part
of employees throughout the public sector—including the correctional
field itself:

> During the past decade, public employees have become increasingly mili-
> tant. With the advent of strikes, slowdowns, and sick-outs, state and
> municipal governments have attempted to find ways of dealing with these
> union weapons without inconveniencing the public or crippling the union
> in its attempts to represent its members. One of these efforts has been the
> movement toward the use of compulsory arbitration. Since 1965, six states
> have enacted legislation that utilizes compulsory arbitration as one possible
> solution to collective bargaining impasses in the public sector.[4]

This trend has caused many correctional administrators to privately
express the view that personnel turnover in the old days was a lot less
trouble than now. Taken in the general context of social change, however, the difficulties appear more than manageable; they will be discussed
later in this chapter.

Recruitment through scholarship, as practiced in the medical or legal
professions, has apparently failed to take hold in corrections:

> In examining scholarship aid in corrections in the United States today, it
> is necessary to be aware that no single resource reports all types of aid
> available and that the total dollar value of scholarship aid in corrections
> cannot be known because of the varied nature of such aid.[5]

[4] Max S. Wortman, Jr., and Craig E. Overton, "Compulsory Arbitration: The End
of the Line in the Police Field?" *Public Personnel Management*, Vol. 2, No. 1
(January–February 1973), 4.
[5] Milton Wittman, "An Assessment of Scholarship Aid in Corrections," in *Manpower
and Training for Corrections* (Lebanon, Pa.: Sowers Printing Company, 1966), p. 66.

## PERCENTAGE OF AGENCIES REQUIRING EDUCATIONAL QUALIFICATIONS FOR STAFF—BY TYPE OF AGENCY, QUALIFICATION, AND POSITION

| *Agency* | *None (Percent)* | *High School (Percent)* | *College Graduate (Percent)* | *Graduate Degree (Percent)* |
|---|---|---|---|---|
| **A. Qualifications Required of Directors and Superintendents** | | | | |
| Juvenile detention | 18.0 | 19.0 | 47.0 | 16.0 |
| Juvenile probation | 10.0 | 12.0 | 63.0 | 15.0 |
| Juvenile institutions | 19.7 | 1.9 | 54.9 | 23.5 |
| Misdemeanant probation | 17.0 | 9.0 | 68.0 | 6.0 |
| Adult probation | 22.6 | 12.8 | 57.3 | 7.3 |
| Local institutions and jails | 52.9 | 39.5 | 7.6 | — |
| Adult institutions | 48.0 | 28.0 | 24.0 | — |
| Adult parole | 34.0 | 8.0 | 52.0 | 6.0 |
| **B. Qualifications Required of Probation and Parole Supervisors** | | | | |
| Aftercare | 2.5 | 10.0 | 60.0 | 27.5 |
| Misdemeanant probation | 7.0 | 4.0 | 85.0 | 4.0 |
| Adult probation | 9.6 | 14.7 | 71.3 | 4.4 |
| Adult parole | 21.6 | 17.6 | 56.9 | 3.9 |
| **C. Qualifications Required of Probation and Parole Officers** | | | | |
| Juvenile probation | 8.0 | 14.0 | 74.0 | 4.0 |
| Aftercare | 5.0 | 10.0 | 82.5 | 2.5 |
| Misdemeanant probation | 11.0 | 13.0 | 74.0 | 2.0 |
| Adult probation | 15.5 | 21.3 | 62.3 | .9 |
| Adult parole | 21.6 | 19.6 | 58.8 | — |
| **D. Qualifications Required of Custodial Staff** | | | | |
| Juvenile detention | 25.0 | 61.0 | 14.0 | — |
| Juvenile institutions | 49.0 | 51.0 | — | — |
| Local institutions and jails | 53.0 | 46.0 | 1.0 | — |
| Adult institutions | 41.1 | 58.9 | — | — |

Source: President's Commission on Law Enforcement and the Administration of Justice, *Task Force Report: Corrections* (Washington, D.C.: U.S. Government Printing Office, 1967), p. 197.

This varied nature of aid relates in turn to the "unlimited definition" of correctional education. That is, correctional education is being taught on some campuses as psychology, on others as sociology, and on still others as criminology or penology. An occasional campus labels it "corrections"; but even there, the content of the curriculum varies from law enforcement to social work, and occasionally psychology or law.

### Professional Education

Unlike the organized body of knowledge that constitutes the educational preparation for medicine, dentistry, law, or engineering, correctional education is often made up of the elective courses in the other professional schools.

This raises the question of how to determine educational requirements. And more basically, and even more painfully for correctional administrators, the question, Is corrections a profession?

One spokesman had this to say:

> . . . Our major problem is our fear of being professional—i.e., of confronting that which needs confronting. We certainly work where the action is. We know the problems. We feel the pain of stagnation. But how do we attack these problems and accomplish the changes that are needed?
>
> We can begin by joining with all those who are so "expert" about our field in the dialogue about the so-called deterrent value of the death penalty, about the children we push out of school and label "dropouts," about bail reform and alcoholic "offenders" and hard-core unemployment. We know about these things! How many hundreds of times have we ventilated our frustrations about them to one another at coffee breaks and at conferences.
>
> We cannot remain mere spectators in this arena. We must concern ourselves less with the internal well-being of our agencies and more with the goals and purposes our agencies were set up to accomplish. . . .[6]

The question of whether or not corrections is a profession gains profound importance in determining educational requirement. How can professional education be defined for corrections if corrections is *not* a profession?

The inability or unwillingness of the correctional field to come to grips with this question may well account for much of the militancy of employee groups that today is characteristic of government staff in general, but with specific correctional implications:

> . . . The findings of this study support the widespread assumption that there will be marked growth of employee organizations among government workers. A majority of all respondents in this survey, while expressing general satisfaction with their jobs, believe that there is need for an organi-

[6] Philip Stein, "Are Probation Officers Really Professionals?" *Crime and Delinquency*, Vol. 17, No. 3 (July 1971), 297.

zation to represent their interests on the job. Unions, while usually not chosen over an employee association as the desired organ for representation, still had considerable support; about 45 percent of city and state respondents who expressed a desire for collective representation stated their preference for a union; among county employees (despite the fact that reported conditions of work were poorer) the support was lower, only about one-third favoring a union. With this level of support even in relatively non-union states, and with changes in legislation that are likely to remove some of the restrictions on organizations among government workers, union growth is highly probable if and when major organizing campaigns are mounted.[7]

It would be unduly optimistic to assume that development of a professional body of knowledge would promptly produce professional education. Equally inappropriate would be the assumption that such professional education would substitute for the government-employee identity apparently related to militancy in all public-employee organizations, including corrections. Indeed, we cannot assume that professional education would necessarily establish corrections as a profession.

But in spite of what isolating professional education for corrections may not immediately produce, there is one thing that would be produced immediately: relevance for the educational requirement.

However, educational requirements, many times combined with experience requirements and similar specifications, are only one of many considerations in contemporary correctional administrations. There are several related personnel considerations, known in some instances as "segments of affirmative action."

### Affirmative Action

A kind of trend in personnel practices has accompanied the growth of the computer era:

Concurrent with the growth of computer-based personnel information systems, emphasis on planning has been growing stronger. The generally accepted concept of management by objectives, originally formulated by Peter Drucker, has brought planning out into all areas of the firm. Given the newly available personnel information, along with the growing emphasis on planning, it is not surprising that personnel departments are now being called upon to perform in areas other than their traditional ones of selection and placement. Manpower planning is increasingly becoming an accepted personnel department function.

Being a relatively new function with not much of a built-up tradition, manpower planning in the personnel department is a task in need of tools. There is available a great body of statistical methods and techniques,

[7] Glenn W. Miller, "Public Employees and Their Attitudes Toward Their Jobs," *Public Personnel Review*, Vol. XXXIII, No. 2 (April 1972), 86.

presently being used in other unrelated fields, many of which could probably be used by manpower planners.[8]

The implications of this trend are already significant enough that most personnel experts forecast a virtual transition to the planning approach for organizational staffing. The concept of manpower planning may also have implications for what appears to be emerging in terms of personnel requirements; such emergence is frequently described by the term *affirmative action*.

Many groups use the term in many ways, but the common factor is the implication that *a positive, aggressive effort will be made to recruit and hire a member of the group involved*. The groups to which federal, state, county, and city governments have addressed such affirmative-action programs include:

Groups by sex
Groups by age
Groups by race
Groups by poverty identity
Groups by educational level

At first glance, the affirmative-action approach appears to reduce personnel requirements. In effect, such a reduction does occur in the typical affirmative-action program, which customarily features the elimination, or at the least the reduction, of educational and experience requirements. Occasionally, physical requirements such as height or weight may also be removed.

However, many affirmative-action programs then insert what amounts to new requirements, which influence toward selection of "newly qualified candidates." In effect, a proportion is determined by various combinations of census and/or demographic considerations, and this in turn translates into a specific number of employees within the organization. In some of the more progressive versions, a goal, or even a quota, is used covertly (in some instances, openly) to gauge the performance of the administrators of the organizations to which the program is geared.

These invariably laudable social movements would deserve the whole-hearted support of every conscientious correctional administrator were it not for the virtual exclusion of *quality* in the process of implementing some of the affirmative-action programs. It is not that the removal of an educational requirement poses any particular administrative problem—at least until professional education becomes professional. But staffing stra-

[8] Gordon L. Nielson and Alan R. Young, "Manpower Planning: A Markov Chain Application," *Public Personnel Management*, Vol. 2, No. 2 (March–April 1973), 133.

tegically significant positions on the basis of sex or race to the exclusion of concern with job-related talent seems an excessive penalty to pay for having prolonged the development of professional standards.

The consistent problem, and the main administrative problem, is that the consequences of such staffing practice are hidden by the clamor for social justice. An administrator raising the question of quality is frequently said to be biased against whatever group is seeking preferential treatment. The real frustration, however, has been the implication that quality is equally distributed among the population, and therefore choices should be made on some other basis.

QUALITY COMBINED WITH AFFIRMATIVE ACTION. Fortunately, there appear to be indications that concern with quality will in fact begin to emerge as a reality in affirmative-action programming. The atmosphere of desperation marking some earlier approaches to affirmative action may now be gradually evolving into sophisticated recognition that quality is the prime requisite of organizational success; that some minority members are extremely qualified and some are not, some women are extremely qualified and some are not, just as some Caucasian men are qualified and some are not.

As the impact of affirmative action (by any name) impinges upon the correctional field, the responsibility of administrators becomes clear: Steps must be taken to unequivocally ensure that no career ladder is unavailable to any qualified applicant, and these steps must include exhaustive effort to insure opportunities for all potential applicants to become qualified.

But in the long run, the real administrative responsibility is to make certain that correctional personnel are qualified—especially during a period in which the correctional field faces the virtual demand for change and improvement. Ensuring that the most qualified personnel from all races, from both sexes, and in any pertinent age range are available to meet the correctional challenge is without doubt the greatest of all correctional administration responsibilities; and it is possible to do this and still ensure the right "proportion," sought by affirmative-action and other related movements.

## CAREERS IN CORRECTIONS

From the great variations in job classification, salaries, and activities of federal, state, county, and municipal correctional personnel, we might assume that little could be said in terms of correctional careers—at least, in a universal context. This, however, is not the case; there is a great deal that is universal. For example, there are common factors impinging upon all those who successfully practice corrections:

The *client* and his capacity to modify attitude and behavior.
The *law* establishes the agency and outlines its function. . . .
*Agency policies* provide operating procedures. . . .
*Community attitudes*, as far as can be determined, provide both opportunities and *limitations* on the type and variety of correctional services.
Resources, to a large extent, determine if and under what program a person can be released. . . .[9]

A correctional career, then, is affected by some form of these five factors, regardless of where or in which jurisdiction. Such universal influence on correctional careers suggests the possibility that certain personal characteristics might prove singularly useful. Although no direct relationship exists between the common factors that might impinge on all correctional careers and personal characteristics, many believe that there are five major personality variables in a successful career in probation, institutions, or parole:

1. The personal ability to form and sustain constructive relationships
2. The personal ability to accept and utilize the authority and the power of one's position without abuse
3. The personal ability to cope with aggression from others
4. The personal ability to work with other agencies and people
5. The personal ability to improve one's performance [10]

### Career Improvement

In terms of the administrative recruitment responsibilities, the fifth characteristic, the ability to improve, is by far the most significant; the others usually develop as a result of it.

In relating correctional careers to this vital characteristic, an appropriate system of personnel evaluation is of major administrative importance:

Certainly one personnel program that has been kicked around for a good number of years is employee performance evaluation. All kinds of criticism has been leveled against it: The supervisor often maintains it's impossible, the employee that it's unfair, and management in general that it's useless.

[9] California Probation, Parole and Corrections Development Committee, "The Practitioner in Corrections," *Journal of the California Probation, Parole and Correctional Association* (February 1969), p. 7.
[10] Walter Hartinger, Edward Eldefonso, and Alan Coffey, *Corrections* (Pacific Palisades, Calif.: Goodyear Publishing Co., Inc., 1973). Chapter 4 elaborates on these five in great depth and context.

There probably has been more rejection of it in most companies and in government than any other program of its nature. And I believe the criticism by and large gives a fair picture of its ineffectiveness. . . .

. . . Perhaps one of the most important considerations in viewing a performance evaluation program is that it exists in an overall system while it is itself a subsystem. It is an integral part of the total management system to be utilized by management in achieving goals and objectives. Moreover, performance itself must be viewed within a system of purpose, goals and objectives. We define *purpose* as an ultimate end result that a system intends to accomplish. *Goals* are intermediate results a system must achieve to fulfill its purpose. *Objectives* are immediate or short-range outcomes to be achieved within a defined (1) period of time, (2) budget, (3) manpower supply, and (4) place. . . .[11]

## Motivation

The value of a system of relating correctional careers to goals and objectives is particularly significant in the context of management systems, as presented in Chapters 2, 3, and 4. Moreover, motivation and the "personal ability to improve" are obviously related, so a clear administrative advantage emerges in terms of these motivational considerations that are key factors in management:

Contemporary writings on human behavior and professional worker motivation lead to the conclusion that while the professional employee may be perceived as somewhat "different," he responds to many of the same motivational factors others do, only placing different degrees of importance on these factors.

Most writers reference, or imply the existence of, a set of needs best expressed by Dr. A. H. Maslow, to wit: 1. Physiological needs, relating to satisfaction of thirst, hunger, sleep, etc., requirements; 2. Safety needs, concerned with security from bodily harm, financial collapse, job tenure; 3. Love needs, associated with affection and belongingness to groups of other people; 4. Esteem needs, being primarily the desire for achievement, recognition, and appreciation; and 5. Self-actualization needs, i.e., an individual must be doing what he is uniquely capable of.

These five needs are typcally seen as interrelated in a hierarchy of prepotency, i.e., the lowest unsatisfied need dominates the individual's direction until reasonably well satisfied, at which time the next higher need emerges.[12]

Thus the administrative perspective of correctional careers includes five "common factors" and five personnel characteristics, and, through a

---

[11] Robert G. Pajer, "A Systems Approach to Results-Oriented Performance Evaluation," *Personnel Administration and Public Personnel Review*, Vol. I, No. 3 (November–December 1972), 42–43.
[12] Bruce D. Evans and Jerry Whitten, "A Critical Reanalysis Regarding the Management of Professionals," *Personnel Administration and Public Personnel Review*, Vol. 1, No. 2 (September–October 1972), 35.

system of personnel evaluation, both factors and characteristics can be related to five "motivational needs." The three sets of five is merely coincidental, but the significance of the context formed by this coincidence is overwhelming in terms of successfully meeting the challenge of modifying corrections toward an effective system.

*Skills*

Assuming recruitment of personnel with whom the "three fives" can be related, there are certain skills required as part of all successful correctional careers—another common denominator. Among these career skills are the following:

> Interviewing
> Communication
> Work organization
> Observation and perception [13]

Of course, the five personal characteristics cited, combined with the training considered in the preceding chapter, tend to ensure the development of these career skills, thus reducing their apparent significance. Nevertheless, the absence of these skills in correctional careers invariably produces administrative difficulty in one form or another.

*Correctional Careers and The Personnel Function*

In the same sense that training remains a key administrative responsibility even though a training director may be held accountable for staff development, the function of personnel is also a key administrative responsibility, even when delegated to a personnel director in terms of accountability.

Beyond the career considerations presented thus far, the function of personnel incorporates a wide range of administrative matters that are all of crucial significance. Many such matters may well be considered trivial when handled well, but they become monumental problems when mishandled:

> The government concept, reflecting a wide range of significant managerial concerns, usually includes the areas of recruiting, screening, testing, indoctrination–orientation, performance evaluation, discipline, job description, classification, promotion, transfer, up- and downgrading, and in some cases, hiring and firing. Of less concern to criminal justice management, but nevertheless often associated with personnel activities, are the areas that deal

---

[13] Hartinger, Eldefonso, and Coffey, *Corrections*, pp. 131–32.

with health and safety, employee services such as insurance and retirement, records, badges, I.D. cards, and so on. All these activities are, in the ideal, a part of the interface between the operational staffing and the methods used to attain goals.

Perhaps this point is significant enough to justify elaboration before moving on to further consideration of personnel services.

Perhaps the reason the *who* function in criminal justice organizations rarely influences personnel activities is the virtual absence of a *functional* definition of personnel in relation to the *functions* of management.

Take, for example, a departmental personnel officer who is respected as a "trouble shooter"—a "guy that solves problems." While this *role* may be played well, it may also obscure the *function* of *preventing* the personnel problems in the first place. By *prevention* is meant the function of determining such things as good typists who fear meeting the public and making this personnel information available to the *who* function *before* the typist is assigned to a task force that requires public contact.

Recalling that a role is evaluated and a function measured, the functional use of personnel activities is established when the presence of personnel problems proves the absence of personnel functions. And in addition to bringing accountability to personnel activities, connecting the personnel function to the *who* function, accountability also increases in middle management.[14]

These remarks are, of course, in the context of the management systems presented in Chapters 2, 3, and 4. Even greater significance can be attached to the "stabilization" of correctional careers. This stabilization, when functioning, seems to minimize the significance of personnel in such a manner that "the presence of personnel problems proves the absence of personnel functions."

The implication of career stability goes far beyond personnel troubleshooting and problem solving. Everything an agency does, without exception, is a potential personnel problem. Administrative inability or unwillingness to acknowledge this reality may well account for much of the employee militancy discussed earlier in this chapter.

While the number of areas that carry the potential of personnel problems is unlimited, there are a few key areas of common concern:

Absence of challenge

Absence of security

Inadequate salary

No promotional opportunities

Absence of career pride

Excessive job pressures [15]

---

[14] Alan R. Coffey, *Criminal Justice Administration: A Management Systems Approach* (Englewood Cliffs, N.J.: Prentice-Hall, Inc., 1974), p. 132.
[15] Hartinger, Eldefonso, and Coffey, *Corrections*, pp. 143–48.

Of course, correctional administrators cannot totally control these potential sources of personnel difficulties. But they can operate a system of personnel in such a manner that it is clear to all that everything is being done that can be done, and this may be more than enough to avert personnel problems.

In the final analysis, there is no set procedure for establishing a system of personnel functions that ensures that awareness, or, for that matter, one establishing a clear relationship between correctional careers and administrative goals. Of necessity, this varies with each correctional organization. But in spite of the lack of formulation in personnel systems, a generalized model can be obtained by examining the personnel approaches of large government organizations. Here is the approach of the federal government:

### The Personnel Officer

(1) Executive Order 9830 requires the head of each agency to designate a director of personnel, or other similarly responsible official, to provide advice and assistance to him in carrying out his personnel management responsibilities. This director or other official represents the agency head in personnel matters; consults with him on personnel policy matters; develops, implements, and reviews the agency's personnel programs; and participates in all personnel management activities. As a part of the management team, the appropriate personnel officer at each agency level has the basic responsibility of helping both managers and firstline supervisors carry out their personnel management responsibilities. The personnel officer generally has such specific responsibilities as:

(a) Representing and advising agency management in relating substantive program requirements to manpower requirements and program decisions to manpower decisions.

(b) Establishing and maintaining an up-to-date manpower information system to provide timely and appropriate information on the agency's human resources, as needed for basic management decision-making purposes as well as for planning and administering an effective personnel program.

(c) Initiating and actively participating in all elements of personnel management essential to the achievement of the objectives listed previously.

(d) Developing technically competent personnel staffs to advise, assist, and train agency managers and supervisors at all levels to carry out their personnel management responsibilities, to meet the needs of managers and supervisors arising from daily agency operations, and to help employees resolve work-related and other problems which may affect employee job performance.

(e) Advising or representing management on labor relations matters.

(f) Facilitating the full participation of managers, supervisors, employees, and recognized employee unions in appropriate personnel management activities, including the formulation and implementation of personnel management objectives, policies, guides, and standards.

(g) Insuring that government-wide and agency personnel management goals, policies, and practices are communicated to and understood by managers, supervisors, employees, and employee groups and that, to the extent possible, the support necessary to make them effective is achieved.

(h) Taking timely personnel actions, promptly processing the necessary paperwork, and efficiently establishing and maintaining required personnel records.

(i) Evaluating the effectiveness of agency personnel programs at each level of organization and management, and providing top agency management with the information needed to evaluate the success with which subordinate managers and supervisors are carrying out top management's objectives and decisions.

(j) Initiating appropriate planning and research to support personnel management programs; informing top management of promising new personnel management concepts; and recommending appropriate changes in agency policies and practices.

(2) The personnel officer must advise agency managers on how the many features and flexibilities provided in the Federal personnel system may be best used to accomplish agency program and manpower decisions. He must make sure that the manager fully understands how personnel management is carried out in his agency. When problems arise in personnel management, whether they come under the primary jurisdiction of the agency itself, of the Civil Service Commission, or some other central government agency, the personnel officer has an obligation to determine the underlying cause and practical effect of such problems, and to propose appropriate action to resolve them, including the revision of statutory law, policies, regulations, or administrative procedures.[16]

Although these personnel concepts may not precisely fit the career concepts and the administrative methods of every correctional organization, they nonetheless afford a kind of conceptual framework within which any correctional administration can approach career personnel constructively. Once this is done, the staffing of the correctional field is bound to improve.

The significance of improved personnel practices flows from the considerations reflected in this chapter. But the administrative approach to

[16] *Federal Personnel Manual*, Chapter 250, "Personnel Management in Agencies," Inst. 121, November 29, 1968, pp. 250–56.

career personnel has a great deal to do with programming not immediately involved in the sphere of correctional careers as such.

In short, personnel requirements are significant beyond the administrative responsibility to improve the staffing of the correctional field.

## SUMMARY

This chapter introduced the concept of personnel requirements in the context of manpower needs for the correctional field. Emphasis was placed upon the distinction between line-work personnel concepts and administrative concern with personnel requirements.

The general educational requirements of the field were discussed, with great emphasis placed upon the lack of and need for professional education, as distinguished from training.

A trend toward more militant orientation within public service was discussed, along with the administrative implication of a related trend known as "affirmative action." An administrative goal of combining quality and fairness was discussed.

Correctional careers were presented in terms of common influences, personal characteristics, and career motivation through a system of personnel functions.

### Discussion Topics

1. Relate the significance of personnel to the significance of administration in the context in which these two considerations were contrasted early in this chapter.

2. Elaborate on the overall administrative significance of personnel qualifications.

3. Discuss educational requirements.

4. Relate professional education to such requirements as an administrative problem.

5. Discuss the potential impact of affirmative action on the correctional field.

6. Discuss approaches to solving problems associated with affirmative action.

7. Discuss methods of achieving the goals of affirmative action without sacrificing quality.

8. Elaborate on factors related to correctional careers.

9. Discuss the need for a system of personnel functions.

## Annotated References

BARUCH, ISMAR, *Position Classification in Public Service.* Civil Services Assembly, 1941. This volume is considered by many personnel specialists to be a classic on the title subject, which relates to what this chapter presented as a system of personnel function.

BUCHLER, R. E., "Our Professional Responsibilities in the Field of Corrections," *Federal Probation,* Vol. 24, No. 3 (September 1960). Good elaboration of the context in which this chapter discussed personal characteristics.

COFFEY, ALAN R., *Criminal Justice Administration: A Management Systems Approach.* Englewood Cliffs, N.J.: Prentice-Hall, Inc., 1974. Chapter 7 elaborates on the personnel function in the specific application of systems management.

GLASER, D., "The New Correctional Era—Implications for Manpower and Training," *Crime and Delinquency,* Vol. 12, No. 3 (July 1966). Good transitional reading to connect this chapter with the preceding chapter.

# The Role of
# Volunteers in
# Corrections

# Chapter 11

## A NATIONAL TREND

The concept of staffing corrections programs with volunteers is not unique:

> We are also reminded by current literature and the prevailing trends in the country that this renewed thrust of volunteer manpower is not unique to corrections. Conversely, it is part of a national movement and community expression of concern for the whole range of social problems experienced in the country today. It further demonstrates the choice of citizens to take personal responsibilities in helping to resolve social problems.[1]

In fact, the concept of citizens participating in the correction of offenders is the very basis of probation:

[1] From a General Membership Paper presented by the California Probation, Parole and Correctional Association Board of Directors, "Corrections Needs Citizen Volunteers," May 23, 1972, p. 1.

Probation began with volunteers; some believe it will end with them, with volunteer probation counselors, tutors, foster parents, office workers, and the like. However that is taken, the early volunteers were honorably discharged as soon as we could pay people, and the pendulum swung hard toward paid professionals in the first five decades of this century. Today the pendulum swings back toward volunteers—but with a difference. Where first probation was all volunteer and later virtually all paid professional, today it is both, and both are here to stay.

Probation will never again be all volunteer. But neither will it ever again be all paid professional. Therefore, the problem of *modern* volunteerism differs crucially from the problem of early volunteerism in corrections, for it becomes an issue of *relationship* between volunteer and paid professional, a problem of defining optimum roles for each in a productive probation partnership. John Augustus, as probation's founding father, incorporated "volunteer" and "probation officer" in one body; just so, we must learn to incorporate in the body of probation both volunteer and paid professional. As in any new marriage, we will have to work at it, and we may still have to be satisfied with something less than perfect integration; but we cannot afford to be content with as little as coexistence. Divorce is impossible. Whatever the secret hopes of some, the modern court volunteer is not going to go away.[2]

Volunteer participation in the correctional field clearly has a history as well as a current status. It should not then be surprising that, even on a relatively limited basis, volunteer programs are being used in the correctional field, and an explicit identity is beginning to emerge, even evolving a specific literature.[3]

In other words, there is a kind of "national identity" of citizen volunteers who are beginning to take active part in efforts to alleviate many social problems. But there is also a gradual trend toward volunteer programs that are identified specifically with certain correctional areas.

There is administrative advantage to both these "identities"—correctional and national. The correctional identity is a valuable recruiting asset, attracting those specifically concerned with the societal problems specifically related to corrections. But the national trend toward volunteer assistance in social problems in general has an advantage in the matter of funding; funds are generally more available for program concepts that have national recognition, while correctional administrators are often dealt with as though volunteer-program proposals are (or should be) free. Of course, while volunteer services cost considerably less, the coordination, supervision, and training involved are anything but free:

[2] Ivan H. Scheier, "The Professional and the Volunteer in Probation: An Emerging Relationship," *Federal Probation*, Vol. XXXIV, No. 2 (June 1970), 12.
[3] See, as one example of an excellent and expanding literature on volunteer correctional programs, James Jorgensen and Ivan Scheier, *Volunteer Training for Courts and Corrections* (Metuchen, N.J.: Scarecrow Press, Inc., 1973).

There is a balance sheet in volunteer programs, too. First, this is because volunteer programs do cost money, and second, the kind of balance we always have to seek is between utter indifference and overconcern to management issues. Funding issues should be raised realistically, but on the other side of a thin line, we should not get obsessed with money. One of the beauties of volunteer programming is that we can do good things without being utterly restricted by financial considerations. We can be positively opportunistic without strangling on our purse strings. On the other hand, without some sort of continued financing guarantee, too many programs get started, raise hopes, and then disappear. While it is possible to begin a program, especially a small one, without having money secured, efforts for ongoing financing should commence right at the start, so as not to lose a good program through indifference of funding sources.[4]

Funding preparations for the department budget are essentially, then, the same for volunteer programming as for any other segment of operations, particularly when administration recognizes the need to expand volunteer services, requiring greater operation costs. And expansion of volunteer correctional programs has been called for for some time:

> One major reason why voluntary efforts should be expanded is that corrections has too long been isolated from the mainstream of community activity. The direct contact of the volunteer with the correctional system provides a means of countering this situation. It is not enough simply to increase public understanding of corrections through programs of public education. Rather, intimate personal experience with the offender has the capacity to make the volunteer an important participant in correctional work and a supporter of correctional effort.[5]

## THE NATURE OF CORRECTIONAL VOLUNTEER PROGRAMS

To ensure that consideration of the nature of volunteer programs is cast in the administrative framework, consider the following job description:

### COORDINATOR OF VOLUNTEERS

*Definition*

Under direction, to plan, supervise and coordinate a program of volunteer services in a County Department.

[4] Ivan Scheier, "Funding and Finance: Volunteer Programs Are Not Free," *Guidelines and Standards for the Use of Volunteers in Correctional Programs*, August 1972, p. 135, as cited by California Probation, Parole, and Correctional Association in Part II of *Task Force Report* on "New Careers and Volunteers in Corrections."
[5] The President's Commission on Law Enforcement and Administration of Justice, *Task Force Report: Corrections* (Washington, D.C.: U.S. Government Printing Office, 1967), p. 104.

*Typical Tasks*

Guides and cooperates with officers of auxiliary associations, community groups, and departmental staff in the development of programs, activities, and services for the clientele of a County department; serves as a liaison between the department and volunteer groups and workers; interviews applicants to determine their aptitudes, abilities and qualifications; orients, trains volunteer workers and supervises their activities; receives requests from departmental staff for services of volunteers, recommends services to be performed and assigns volunteers to these activities; arranges for special events and programs; evaluates the effectiveness of the volunteer program and makes appropriate recommendations; confers with departmental staff and administrators; develops and maintains active interest of community organizations in volunteer programs; speaks to community organizations and prepares news releases; supervises assigned clerical staff; maintains records and prepares periodic reports of activities and performance of volunteers; and performs related work as required.

*Employment Standards*

Training and experience equivalent to graduation from college and one year of experience in welfare, probation, recreation, nursing or service organization work in hospitals, institutions, homes for the aged or community recreation centers.

Knowledge of: Social service organizations and policies; principles of organization, administration and supervision; public relations work as applicable to the organization and direction of community agencies and civic groups; community resources.

Ability to: Supervise and coordinate the activities of volunteer workers; arouse and sustain the interest of others in community service work; speak and write effectively.[6]

The administrative implications of having a staff member with such a broad base of responsibility are considerable. In effect, the coordinator of volunteers becomes a public relations specialist, an interagency liaison specialist, a correctional services specialist, an intradepartment program specialist, and a training specialist—and each specialty is administratively significant.

## Coordinative Function

To explore these administrative implications further in terms of the nature of volunteer correctional programs to be administered, here are excerpts from a brief but outstanding article on the coordinative function involved. Although it is geared to juvenile programming, the administrative considerations in virtually all volunteer programs are reflected in this article:

[6] County of Santa Clara (California) Probation Department, Personnel.

The coordinator of volunteers has the supervisory function over the volunteer program, himself being under the supervision of the judge and the chief probation officer. Since volunteers have no tangible identification with the court in terms of salary, their function is voluntary and without authority. Consequently, they have to be coordinated, rather than supervised.

A coordinator of volunteers is necessary to make a volunteer program function effectively. In many places, this coordinator of volunteers is a full-time worker paid by the juvenile court. In other places, he may be a full-time volunteer without pay. Experience has indicated, however, that better services can be expected from a full-time, paid coordinator of volunteers.

The coordinator of volunteers has the function of recruiting, selecting, training, and supervising the work of the volunteers. Depending on the size of the court, he may have one or more assistants. He must keep the judge and the probation officers informed in order to coordinate efforts and reduce suspicion and apprehension. The volunteer augments and supports work of the probation officer, so this communication is necessary.

Liaison with schools and law enforcement is an important phase of coordination. Liaison with the community, particularly part-time employment resources and other agencies interested in children, is also important for the effective functioning of a volunteer program. The juvenile aid bureau of the police department is an important group with which to establish and maintain contact. . . .

Financing is an important part of any program—including a volunteer program. As previously mentioned, a volunteer program does cost money or its equivalent in staff time because of training programs and the supervision needed that must be done by court staff. In addition, there are other incidental expenses in working with children. . . . The coordinator of volunteers frequently handles the funding problems by private donations, grant requests from governmental agencies and private foundations, getting the volunteer program adopted as a project by a civic club, and other means. The judge includes the salary of the coordinator of volunteers in his budget request to the county commission, but the coordinator, himself, frequently has to "scratch" for other funds.

The coordinator of volunteers must maintain close liaison with the judge and the chief probation officer. He must also maintain close liaison with all his volunteers, over whom he has no real authority. Consequently, it takes a competent person who relates well with people to serve as a coordinator of volunteers. He must provide almost inspirational leadership to coordinate the motivations of the people who volunteered with the needs of the children in trouble within the guidelines of the juvenile court.

Supervision of volunteers is the most important part of coordinating volunteers, even though it is called "coordination" rather than "supervision," because of the unpaid and nonauthoritative nature of volunteers and volunteer programs. Frequent consultation about cases and their progress is essential. Supervision is incorporated in all phases of relationships with the volunteers, including the training procedure. . . . Direction of the volunteer program must be worked out between the judge, the chief probation officer or court staff, and the coordinator of volunteers. Together, they must identify (1) the primary problems in the community and in the court, (2) the interested persons in the community and in the court, (3) the target people, whether only juveniles who have come to the court or children in trouble in school or elsewhere, (4) the goals of the court and the volunteer program, and (5) the delivery agencies or resources available in the community.

. . . Decisions mutually agreed upon and transmitted with supporting reasons and prognostication as to the effects of actions taken appears to be the most effective way of providing direction to the volunteer program. In this manner, everyone will be going in the same general direction with full knowledge of the rationale supporting the policies. . . .

Evaluation is the "bookkeeping" of any social program. Any program, including the volunteer program, should not be learned on a "faith, hope, and charity" basis. Adequate records should be kept as to what was done, when, why, and the results.

Nearby colleges and universities can provide assistance in evaluation. In many cases, graduate students are available in sociology, psychology, and other disciplines who will provide evaluation services as part of their supervised study. Anyway, ongoing evaluation is essential.

The court volunteer program should be rewarding to the court, the probationer, the volunteer, and the community. To do this, any program must involve (1) training and orientation so the people involved will know the objectives, techniques by which they are achieved, and what to expect, (2) finding out needs, desires, and fears for the court, the probationer, the volunteer, and the community, (3) specifying goals as operationally as possible and mutually determined, and (4) developing a system of constant feedback to determine whether the program is affecting everyone involved as favorably as possible. This feedback is essential to ongoing evaluation of the volunteer program.[7]

## VOLUNTEER PROGRAM OPERATIONS

The active operation of volunteer programming is based upon careful planning, as is all effective correctional programming. The significance of such planning is generally recognized, but remains worthy of further consideration.

. . . When starting a new program or reworking an existing one, *we recommend you spend at least three or four months planning before the first volunteer arrives on the scene.* Possibly, you should even spend as long as four or five months planning.

There is a right time for moving from planning to action, usually sometime within the recommended three to five month think period. It is a part of good planning to be able to identify that propitious moment and then *move.* Remember that planning cannot iron out all program problems— some aspects will have to be tested out through actual experience. Moreover,

[7] Vernon Fox, "Coordination of Volunteer Programs," *Juvenile Justice*, Vol. 23, No. 4 (February 1973), 22–30.

some staff may unconsciously prolong the planning period because they fear the program is not ready to be implemented. Planning thus becomes an excuse for inaction, or at least a delaying action.

Planning should not be more sophisticated than the scope and nature of the program. For example, in a rural municipal court, extensive planning may be unnecessary. The best plan here may be to begin with only one or two volunteers who already have much of the background required; for example, a retired insurance agent is already somewhat qualified to conduct pre-sentence investigations. Then, once the program has been implemented, continuing planning can eventually expand it, while sophisticated initial planning would only have delayed it. . . .

Whoever the planner happens to be, however, the following people should be involved in the initial planning: the client, line staff, agency director, and community group(s) that will be contacted for assistance. The client will receive the planned-for services of the volunteers; line staff will be supervising volunteers; the agency director is responsible for programs conducted within his agency, and the community will be involved as volunteers—all must work together in order for the program to succeed. . .[8]

Once the planning function has been performed, and with all the measurable accountability involved in planning other correctional operations, specific operational applications can be considered:

The Royal Oak, Michigan, volunteer program has demonstrated what can be done through the use of businessmen and other interested citizens in the community acting in much the same way that John Augustus started out to perform probation services. Some adult probation cases involve business malpractice, fraud, and violation of withholding tax laws which frequently result at least as much from stupidity as from cupidity on the part of the violator. Successful businessmen can frequently offer invaluable training and advice to persons who have run into such trouble in managing their own small business.

Middle class housewives who have become adroit at managing budgets and juggling credit can frequently be of tremendous help to women probationers whose greatest problem is trying to make ends meet. Some N.S.F. check-writers, petty thieves, and welfare fraud perpetrators can be aided greatly by such volunteers. There is also great opportunity for successful mothers and housewives to provide volunteer services in teaching their complicated arts to less organized women through homemaker services.

The Big Brother programs throughout the country have already demonstrated the importance of the average citizen volunteer in serving delinquent youth.

Finally, Project EPIC at California State College at Los Angeles is showing what college students can achieve as tutors and companions for juvenile probationers. . . .

The Poverty Program has provided new horizons through its development

---

[8] Scheier, "General Principles of Program Management," *Volunteers in Correctional Programs*, pp. 36–37.

of such agencies as the Neighborhood Adult Participation Program and the Neighborhood Youth Corps. Volunteers in Service to America (VISTA) and Concentrated Employment Program (CEP) are also examples.

. . . There are many economic and racial minority group members who are tremendously effective and who can establish relationships and provide leadership for probationers. These people, under the guidance of a probation officer, can work as "cultural interpreters" between the probation officer and his clients. Frequently they also know much better how to secure jobs, find realistic living quarters, stretch low budgets, etc. Their experiences from the cradle up have provided them with understanding and abilities which the probation officer can hardly hope to attain.

The probation officer, on the other hand, knows bureaucratic interrelationships and practices and can negotiate the middle class community far better than the indigenous aide. The two working together can provide highly refined and effective service for poor and minority group probationers and can also learn a great deal from each other so that each becomes more effective in his own role. . . .

Reformed offenders are among the most important change agents. Over the years, Alcoholics Anonymous and the Synanon Foundation have established enviable reputations in the treatment of alcoholics and narcotic addicts.

Student workers up to this time have largely been used for clerical and routine task assistance in correctional agencies. Actually, with their enthusiasm, close involvement with current social science theory, and time schedule flexibility they can frequently be used to advantage as junior caseworkers. . . . Students working in part-time Civil Service positions such as that of Student Professional Worker, or students working as volunteers can provide constant two-way avenues between the university and the field. They are perhaps the most flexible of all auxiliary staff workers.

The foregoing remarks have mainly stressed the use of auxiliary staff workers in the fundamental work of corrections (work with clients). It should be remembered that in all of these categories there can also be important sources for clerical work, administrative and organizational analysis, and, perhaps most of all, public relations functions. The community that is personally involved in correctional work cannot help but realize its importance and the legitimacy of its claim for citizen support.[9]

In addition to these volunteer concepts, correctional administrators with any degree of flexibility can find volunteer medical or dental programs relatively easy to undertake. Indeed, many physicians and dentists would donate two scheduled hours a week to a well-equipped clinic as an expression of their professional ethics. And equipping such clinics may well be partially or totally a matter of donations of secondhand but usable equipment, trade-ins from private practices or hospitals. In fact, many firms would be willing to donate such equipment outright when told of the volunteer nature of the clinic and assured adequate public recognition.

[9] *Innovations in Probation Management—Catching up with a Changing World*, unpublished paper of the Field Services Division, Los Angeles County Probation Department, pp. 15–20.

Such clinics need not be conceptually restricted to correctional institutions. Creative programming could (and perhaps should) make such services available to probationers, parolees, and their families. Of course, such a clinic is not intended to compete with existing health services elsewhere, but to bring offender and community together in every facet of life. The community to which an offender tries to adjust is symbolized by those volunteering, on his behalf, services that constitute very tangible support of his efforts.

Regrettably, the rich potential of such volunteer professional services—indeed, even the more fundamental programming use of volunteers—is largely untapped, in spite of the national recognition of volunteer services:

> (1) Existing evidence indicates that city-municipal courts (courts of lower jurisdiction) and juvenile parole are the principal areas in the criminal justice system which have a low frequency of volunteer programs. (2) Exclusive of city courts, the proportion of volunteer programs dealing with adult as distinct from juvenile offenders is higher than previously supposed.
>
> For purposes of practical strategy, one can conclude that a greater emphasis than heretofore is needed in guidelines and implementary assistance for the development of volunteer programs in juvenile parole, in city courts, and in programs dealing with adult offenders.[10]

Still another consideration may account for the relatively retarded growth pattern of volunteer programming in corrections—the way in which career personnel perceive volunteers.

## CORRECTIONAL PERSONNEL AND VOLUNTEERS

All correctional administrators know that job security is a primary incentive for correctional careers. Civil service in *any* governmental field tends to attract personnel with great concern for job security. It should not then be of great surprise that the concept of "help and support" can and does slip with ease into what is perceived as competition.

### Help vs. Competition

During the years when volunteer programs were manned by what many correctional organizations referred to as "student interns," career personnel could scarcely relate job security to nonpaid workers. By the assignment of the clerical activities of correctional work to such volunteers, a totally unthreatening variety of status quo emerged and survived, in

---

[10] Scheier, "Introduction and Survey Methodology," *Volunteers in Correctional Programs*, p. 11.

spite of considerable resentment by many of the intern volunteers. But with the coming of volunteers who involved themselves in many instances directly with the correctional clientele, something else emerged.

Unfortunately, the concerns of career personnel in this area have rarely been expressed with open candor. Some express through their union and employee groups strong opposing positions, while at the same time professionally supporting the volunteer concept. Needless to say, both sides of this message reach those who would donate their services to the correctional field. In short, volunteers are seen by at least some career personnel as more competition than help, and awareness of this situation may be a deterrent to recruitment of potential volunteers.

A solution to this very real administrative problem is not simple, but it is possible, if volunteers can be seen as help instead of competition. One approach might be to establish clear definitions of volunteer functions in the same way that managerial functions were isolated in Chapters 2, 3, and 4. In much the same manner that one management function helps another, instead of competing, clearly defined volunteer functions could be perceived by career functions as helpful, instead of competitive.

Defining these functions explicitly is by no means easy. Many volunteers are extremely talented in direct-contact services with the clients; many are not. Many volunteers work well with career personnel; others work better alone. Defining the functions is nevertheless possible if correctional administration determines to do it.

The costs of overlooking this problem cannot be measured, because there is no way to measure how rapidly volunteer programs would expand if career personnel gave overwhelming, wholehearted, and enthusiastic support. But it seems reasonable to assume that the costs are high enough to justify taking up the problem immediately. Administrators in corrections are rapidly reaching the point at which no loss of resources can be tolerated. All available help is needed, and the properly recruited and trained volunteer is of great help.

## SUMMARY

This chapter introduced the concept of volunteer programming in correctional administration in terms of both costs and the need to connect corrections to the community.

The nature of volunteer programs was explored as to the coordinative functions involved and some of the typical activities coordinated.

The operation of volunteer programs was examined in the context of examples of applying volunteer concepts in probation operations. Medical and dental possibilities were also considered.

The relationship between volunteers and career personnel was examined in terms of two opposing perceptions of volunteers: help versus competition. A strategy for administrative solutions to this problem was suggested.

### Discussion Topics

1. Contrast "national trend" and "correctional identity" as presented in this chapter.
2. Describe the administrative advantage of having both.
3. Discuss the rationale for considering salary-free volunteers a part of the same budget process as other correctional programs.
4. Describe the nature of volunteer programs.
5. Elaborate on volunteer operations.
6. Elaborate on help versus competition.
7. Discuss the strategy for solving career personnel–volunteer problems.

### Annotated References

COFFEY, ALAN R., *Administration of Criminal Justice: A Management Systems Approach*. Englewood Cliffs, N.J.: Prentice-Hall, Inc., 1974. Chapters 3, 4, 5, and 6 elaborate in depth on what was suggested here as "clearer definitions of functions."

————, *Juvenile Justice as a System: Law Enforcement to Rehabilitation*. Englewood Cliffs, N.J.: Prentice-Hall, Inc., 1974. A comprehensive context for this chapter's discussion of the coordinative function.

————, EDWARD ELDEFONSO, and WALTER HARTINGER, *Human Relations*. Englewood Cliffs, N.J.: Prentice-Hall, Inc., 1971. Elaboration of what this chapter discussed in terms of "community." See also Coffey, Eldefonso, and Hartinger, *Police Community Relations*. Englewood Cliffs, N.J.: Prentice-Hall, Inc., 1971.

————, EDWARD ELDEFONSO, and WALTER HARTINGER, *Introduction to the Criminal Justice System and Process*. Englewood Cliffs, N.J.: Prentice-Hall, Inc., 1974. A broad, all-inclusive context, including adult programs to which the coordinative functions discussed in this chapter might be related.

JORGENSEN, JAMES D., and IVAN H. SCHEIER, *Volunteer Training for Courts and Corrections*. Metuchen, N.J.: Scarecrow Press, Inc., 1973. Good coverage of the title subject and the overall context.

*Note:* The full texts of the quotations in this chapter are highly recommended supplements.

# Special
# Administrative
# Problems

# Chapter 12

In the correctional field, there are many complicating factors that qualify as special problems. Virtually any segment of the correctional process, when isolated in terms of problems, tends to gain the appearance of being unique. Consider the problem implications of any of the following:

The inadequacy of jails
Victimless crime
Wayward youth
Alcoholics
Narcotic and drug abuse
Dangerous drugs
Prostitution
Homosexuality

Compounding these special problems is the fragmentation of the criminal justice system that we have alluded to throughout this volume, including that of the correctional segment of the system:

Corrections has not evolved rationally by devising, evaluating and modifying its programs according to their relationship to explicitly defined criteria. Rather, the field has developed out of efforts of humanitarians and on the basis of public reaction to inhuman treatment and prison riots. But even more important, the lack of systematic information is due to the fact that corrections was developed on the basis of political expediency. Correctional programs have been devised not on the basis of an overall correctional plan, or on the basis of effectiveness, but rather on the basis of "who has the inside track with this or that legislator." [1]

We cannot hope to cover in one chapter the entire subject of the special problems that confront an understandably fragmented correctional system; we will instead focus upon the special administrative problems involved in coping with them.


## CORRECTIONAL PROBLEMS

Conscientious administrators agree that criminal justice is facing major problems, and that corrections is clearly involved:

Few are satisfied with the existing system. The reform movement is powerful, but its direction is uncertain. In the wake of recent events and the realization of corrections' many failures, the traditional functions of corrections (banishment, punishment, deterrence) are being questioned by the press, public, courts, legislatures, and even practicing corrections personnel.

The courts, from local through United States Supreme Court, have abandoned their traditional "hands off" policy toward correctional practices. Attorneys, both prosecution and defense, are taking interest in what happens to the offender after conviction, and are becoming powerful allies in the correctional reform movement.

The public is beginning to demand accountability for the operation of corrections system. It long has been content that "out of sight, out of mind" meant greater community protection. But this trend is ending.

And corrections personnel themselves admit that present systems are not working and that something must change. Although statistics concerning corrections are incredibly poor, it is quite clear that incarceration is a miserable failure, if success is to be measured in terms of returning an offender to the community without further involvement with crime.

Rather than persistently preaching the rehabilitation of others, corrections must rehabilitate itself if it is to do a better job of protecting the community. Corrections must undertake its own overhaul, breaking with the past and regenerating itself in a more realistic and constructive form.

The problems that corrections creates for police and the courts, particularly when corrections fails to accomplish the social reintegration of offenders, is acknowledged. Cooperation and coordination among all elements of the

[1] Peter G. Garabedian, "Challenges for Contemporary Corrections," *Federal Probation*, Vol. 33 (March 1967), 6.

criminal justice system are essential. The movement of corrections toward community-based programs cannot succeed without the support of police and the courts. . . .

. . . It is critically important that all elements of the criminal justice system follow procedures assuring that offenders are, and believe themselves to be, treated fairly if corrections is to release individuals who will not return to crime. . . .

. . . The idea is to prepare the offender to carry on life in the community, not to prepare him only to live in the unnatural lifestyle of an institution. While considerations of incapacitation and punishment are appropriate in some instances, reintegration of the offender should be the primary goal of the correctional system.

Community-based correctional programs are to be given priority. The need to treat problems of crime, as far as possible, in their community contexts rather than with banishment to the remote prison or reformatory is recognized.

The interrelationships of all elements of the criminal justice system is also stressed. Corrections for too long has preferred to isolate itself from the purview of both the public and the other criminal justice system components Corrections can, and needs to, speak from its own standpoint and experience about which offenders it can handle most effectively and how earlier steps in the criminal justice process affect corrections. . . .

It is time that corrections verbalized some of the knowledge it has accumulated about criminal offenders and their treatment, both before and after conviction. Corrections alone cannot solve the problems of crime and delinquency, but it can make a much more significant contribution than it does now.[2]

In making the "more significant contribution" referred to above, correctional administration is not relieved of the many responsibilities discussed throughout this volume. For example, not only does staffing remain an administrative responsibility; making the "more significant contribution" may increase the problems involved in staffing:

At present, correctional work, which deals with the redemption of persons who are usually viewed as "voluntaristically" wayward, possesses few qualities likely to place it among the more preeminent, and therefore the more attractive, vocational endeavors of our society. The definition of most kinds of work tends to take on something of the coloration of the clientele, and correction is concerned with déclassé individuals, persons already removed from the social mainstream.[3]

In other words, if the more significant contribution is in the form of clarifying the nature of corrections, the "coloration of the clientele" is

[2] *Working Papers for the National Conference on Criminal Justice*, Law Enforcement Assistance Administration, Washington, D.C., January 23–26, 1973, pp. c-1-2.
[3] Gilbert Geis and Elvin Cavanagh, "Recruitment and Retention of Correctional Personnel," *Crime and Delinquency*, Vol. 12, No. 3 (July 1966), 233.

likely to become more substantial, and recruitment and other staffing considerations will clearly be affected.

Just as administration is not relieved of staffing the correctional field while making a more significant contribution, neither is there relief from the responsibilities of treatment and training:

> Historically, almost all changes in the mode of dealing with criminals not only have altered the training required for correctional personnel, but also have drastically increased the number of persons employed in correction. This pattern was obvious in the early part of the nineteenth century, when confinement replaced hanging as the standard penalty for felonies, and again in the twentieth century, when probation and parole became widespread. It is even more apparent today, when correctional change is occurring more rapidly than ever.
>
> The changes which now herald a new age in correction involve not so much new tasks as the integration of old ones. Instead of a separation of those who treat from those who confine and supervise prisoners, treatment is becoming the primary concern of all institutional personnel. Instead of a separation of institutional from community services, they are being fused. Even the distinction between research and operations is diminishing. And all of this increasing not just the training needed for correctional work, but also the number of trainees required. . . .[4]

In short, all the administrative responsibilities that have been dealt with throughout this volume remain while correctional administration takes on the additional responsibility to make a more significant contribution. And this contribution must be made if the justice system is to become functional and unfragmented enough to deal with correctional problems in general.

## SPECIAL PROBLEMS OF ADMINISTRATION

All administrative problems, special and otherwise, relate in some way to management–labor. In some instances, this relationship is direct; sometimes it is indirect. But in all cases, a problem for correctional administration is a problem with management–labor implications of some kind, sooner or later.

Notice the similarity between managing craftsmen in private industry, and managing correctional professionals:

> Management can have trouble in supervising craftsmen. Such men feel they know how their job should be done and are therefore reluctant to accept very much direction. They resist being rushed or taking shortcuts that

---

[4] Daniel Glasier, "The New Correctional Era—Implications for Manpower and Training," *Crime and Delinquency*, Vol. 12, No. 3 (July 1966), 210.

violate their conception of correct method. This resistance to close super-vision is often reinforced by strong craft unions that have their own work rules. Well-trained craftsmen who identify with their craft may require less supervision. They are used to accepting responsibility and being held accountable. Note that this arrangement reverses the traditional situation in which management imposes its rules on the worker.

Their independence is furthered by management's recognition that craft skills are scarce and that craftsmen cannot easily be replaced. Knowing and controlling the work, the methods, the pace, and the tools, the employee is not likely to feel dominated by management.

In short, craftsmen generally feel secure. Their only serious fears arise from economic instabilities and the threats of technological change which will render their skills obsolete. . . .[5]

Correctional personnel also feel "the threats of technological change which will render their skills obsolete." With each administrative innova-tion, geared to improve corrections, comes some degree of this threat—with various unfortunate consequences, some of which will be considered shortly.

Thus we must recognize the labor–management implications of even the purely administrative problems in corrections.

### Misaligned Administrative Responsibility

If correctional operations did in fact flow as suggested in the diagram, major problems such as those associated with administrative continuity of programming would be reduced—perhaps by so much that many other special problems would pose far less difficulty, and much more time could be spent on them.

In many jurisdictions, however, what is shown as "Police," the first item on the flow chart, is exactly the same criminal justice administration involved in the very last activity depicted on the chart—"Institutional System." *The implications of this are profound.*

The administration of the correctional system by essentially the same criminal justice segment responsible for safe streets and intake of the system is strange, to say the least. But more than strange, placing under law enforcement the responsibility for operating jail farms and jails that serve as correctional institutions all but eliminates the possibility of cor-rections' making a more significant contribution. A brief review of the functional responsibility of law enforcement may clarify this.

Appropriately enough, police chiefs and sheriffs who are charged with the responsibility of enforcing the law conceive of enforcement as their

---

[5] George Strauss and Leonard R. Sayles, *Personnel—The Human Problems of Man-agement* (Englewood Cliffs, N.J.: Prentice-Hall, Inc., 1972), p. 29.

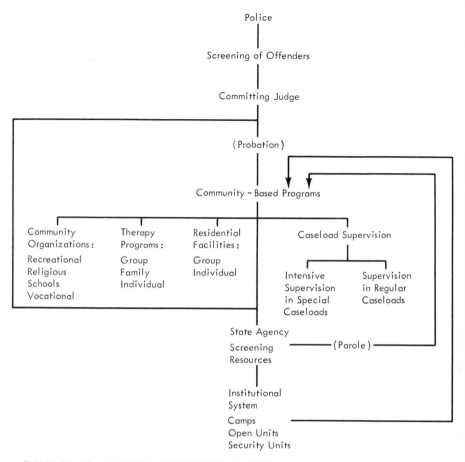

**ELEMENTS OF A MODERN CORRECTIONAL SYSTEM**

Source: President's Commission on Law Enforcement and the Administration of Justice, *The Challenge of Crime in a Free Society* (Washington, D.C.: U.S. Government Printing Office, 1967), p. 182.

primary mission. Corrections, therefore, becomes secondary to them by definition. And despite the conscientious and even gallant efforts of police chiefs and sheriffs, significant contributions are scarcely a likelihood once a secondary status is attached to corrections.

This misaligned administrative responsibility is clearly one of the special administrative problems confronting correctional administrators seeking to resolve other problems while at the same time making a more significant contribution. Solution of the misaligned administrative responsibility requires general and national recognition that the problem exists— recognition removed totally from the influence of tradition or local politics.

## Political Control

In any nation, either the government serves the people or the people serve the government: and to the degree that anything is consistent with more than 200 million people, the government is the servant in America—a government appropriately controlled by elected politicians.

Control, however, is of necessity a matter of degree. For example, a general in the army has far more control over his officers and men than the president of an insurance company has over his salesmen. The warden of a prison has far more control over the inmates than the general has over his men.

Similarly, government agencies are less controlled than the army, but more controlled than most free enterprise. Political control of government agencies is through laws and regulations passed mostly for the purpose of control. In theory, laws and regulations, when properly enforced, exhaust the need for political control of government agencies; an agency meeting its legal obligations in a satisfactory manner should not encounter additional political control or interference.

In discussing the possibility of excessive control, we run the risk of appearing to defend a kind of "agency-sovereignty" doctrine—of appearing to suggest that necessary political control is interference. Perhaps a hypothetical example would minimize this risk.

Imagine a relatively large correctional organization undertaking the administrative effort to improve services. Further imagine that the improvement sought is not by the traditional staff-increase approach, which the administration hopes to avoid. Substantial staff training in sophisticated treatment techniques is planned, in a manner that will not increase the training budget: an innovative use of "in-house" skills, with the already-trained staff training other staff, and so on.

The administrative plan is to rigorously reduce referrals enough for existing staff to receive training and provide improved services, based on the proportional reduction in caseload size. In carrying out this plan, the organization pursues virtually all that was discussed in the chapter on community corrections, and, as a result, does dramatically reduce referrals and caseloads enough to do this.

Now, if political control of the budget of this correctional organization is predicated on improved government services to the electorate, this particular programming effort should look impressive: *more service and more training without more budget or more staff*.

However, suppose that the political position is taken that the ratio between staff and clients is the only measure needed—that increased services, even when measurable, are not relevant. And as a result of this position, suppose that each time the referrals to the agency are reduced by the community programming, the overall organizational staff is reduced proportionately by legislation. Then a political message goes out to a cost-conscious press to the effect that legislators have "alertly cut budget excesses." Finally, imagine this entire process occurring through some system of staff advice that virtually precludes the correctional administration from bringing into perspective the drastic:

1. Reduction in incentive
2. Reduction in morale
3. Reduction in dedication
4. Reduction in effectiveness
5. Reduction in willingness to try again

The drastic reductions, of course, add up to a kind of permanent cynicism, mitigating not only willingness to try again in the near future, but willingness to try again during an entire career. Such political gamesmanship costs far more than the immediate and obvious losses.

This hypothetical situation is a composite of all the worst characteristics of many different political atmospheres impinging upon various correctional organizations. Of course, such a situation would be unfair as a description of most political situations in which correctional administration must operate. But very few correctional administrators would find all of this kind of story totally fictional. In terms of special administrative problems, this same operational difficulty has been presented in a somewhat different, but clarifying, manner:

> . . . To whatever degree criminal justice remains attractive as a political symbol of virtue instead of a desperately needed societal system is the criminal justice administrator faced with a need to cope with politics—that in effect oppose management. . . .[6]

The ability of correctional administrators to cope with all problems facing corrections is determined by the degree to which *this* problem does not exist—to the degree that political control does not prevent administration. In many ways, the political problems of correctional administrations are by far more crippling than even the control problems discussed in earlier chapters in relation to the court.

### Making It Go

The prime ingredient of successful administration is recognition of the truth of the following:

[6] Alan R. Coffey, *Criminal Justice Administration: A Management Systems Approach* (Englewood Cliffs, N.J.: Prentice-Hall, Inc., 1974), p. 311.

In effective management, what is important in dealing with any problem is an approach that focuses on the systematic dysfunction that *produces* the difficulty, rather than on the difficulty itself. This is properly giving attention to management rather than the manager—to measured achievement rather than to any specific person.[7]

However, in addition to this removal of emphasis on the individual manager, it is also essential for the administration to recognize that some managers *are* "the systematic dysfunction that produces the difficulty." This seeming paradox emerges as the core of the special administrative problem associated with "making it go," an expression referring to the overall operation of a successful correctional administration.

The main problem, then, in making it go is with trying to focus upon what causes the problem instead of on the manager involved, while at the same time acknowledging that some managers are part of that cause.

This by no means suggests the need to isolate "fault" as such. Many—perhaps most—correctional managers gained their promotions on the basis of casework skills, not managerial skills. Moreover, many seemingly excellent managers do not manage well when the administrative responsibility to make it go is used as the criterion:

> Another reason for the neglect to provide written standards for managers has been the belief that if managers are chosen by some planned selection process, they will be "natural managers," people who can operate by instinct rather than by technique. In reality, the natural manager is a rarity; in fact, he may be a myth, for if a man is a good manager he will use most of the techniques of good management rather than attempt to operate by ear.
>
> Many of the people in the management ranks who are considered "natural managers" are not really good managers at all. Often their reputation is built on the fact that they possess pleasant personalities and have more than average drive. Quite a few of them are so concerned with acting like managers when the boss's eye is on them that they neglect important parts of the managerial job, or at best handle them poorly. Their personalities enable them to keep things running with apparent smoothness, and they are ready with glib explanations when their practices are questioned.[8]

Like most administrative problems, special and otherwise, this one requires major administrative initiative to resolve. In approaching the format of this initiative, the contradictory nature of the situation can be negotiated in such a manner that the paradox—that of attempting to focus on management instead of the manager while acknowledging the manager as one source of problems—is avoided.

In essence, the method of avoiding such a paradox is to approach the

---

[7] *Ibid.*, p. 326.
[8] Virgil K. Rowland, *Evaluating and Improving Managerial Performance* (New York: McGraw-Hill Book Company, 1970), pp. 137–38.

need for administrative initiative in terms of contributing factors to managerial problems, retaining concern for all causes of the problem even when considering an individual manager. In other words, before the administrative initiative needed to remedy this difficulty is taken, careful assessment of *all* factors is required.

The factors that may be assessed are infinite, but a few are consistent enough to use as examples. Consider, as examples, talent threshold, resistance to change, and incentive/motivation.

TALENT THRESHOLD. By *talent threshold* is meant the ability of an individual manager to perceive, anticipate, and control the wide variety of influences that jeopardize program effectiveness.

Of course, such a general definition of managerial talent intentionally applies to literally every activity of correctional managers. But there is one facet of managerial talent that correctional administrators my find of particular concern in approaching the question of what causes a particular manager to cause problems. This one crucial facet is the ability to perceive and to distinguish between the three main parts of a linear system, as presented in Chapter 5: input, process, and output.

Consider, for example, a prison as a successful linear system:

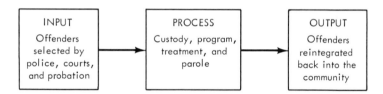

| INPUT | PROCESS | OUTPUT |
|---|---|---|
| Offenders selected by police, courts, and probation | Custody, program, treatment, and parole | Offenders reintegrated back into the community |

Perhaps part of the problem is that career promotions are based primarily upon performance in *process*—that is, they result from the job skills of the job. Managers are promoted not for managerial talent but for job talent, and there is a difference.

In many systems, the transition from job talent to managerial talent could occur at the line-supervisor level, but does not. Regrettably, many supervisors are dealt with by correctional management in a fashion that literally forces a status of "senior caseworker," instead of "supervisory manager."

It should then be of no great surprise that the promotion to managerial position fails to create managerial talent. If talent is defined in part as the ability to distinguish between process and output, and if all a manager's experience has been in process, it does not appear likely that he will be able to make that distinction.

The warning signal that a particular manager may suffer from this perceptual affliction is the great similarity between his managerial decision making and casework decision making; that to him, *everything* is process, to the virtual exclusion of output. This manager is not results-oriented.

Continuing to give attention to management rather than the manager is administratively difficult when evidence is encountered that a particular manager is not output-oriented (or worse yet, not even output-conscious). However, it can be done—indeed, *must* be done if talent thresholds are to be expanded sufficiently to manage the organization toward results. Fortunately, there is a relatively simple concept for achieving the expansion of managerial talent thresholds, although it requires considerable and ongoing administrative initiative.

To the correctional administrator, expenditure of this ongoing initiative is relatively inexpensive when compared to the ongoing problems of narrow talent thresholds—the continuing problems associated with the seeming managerial inability to make appropriate managerial decisions. Of course, the ongoing administrative initiative would ideally be accompanied by at least some initiative on the part of the manager involved:

> . . . It is necessary for the rising young executive to persuade those above him that he has the human relations abilities to be a good member of their "team." But getting along with people is a less significant criterion for advancement than having the analytical ability to diagnose problems, evaluate information, and make sound recommendations.
>
> To put it another way, the successful rising young executive may be the man who can be either conformist or nonconformist as the situation demands. In terms of social behavior and attitudes, he conforms; but in his own area of job competence he takes the initiative *at the proper time*. Perhaps the sense of timing—knowing when is the proper time—is among the necessary requirements of a good executive.[9]

Unfortunately for many correctional administrators, such managerial initiative is not forthcoming; the task of assessing managerial talent falls almost entirely upon the administrator. To compound this problem, both the administrator and the manager may feel that a peak has been reached, thereby reducing incentive to examine talent in terms of threshold:

> Eventually everyone reaches his peak, even the president of the company. For a high proportion of managers, this occurs by age 45. For a high proportion, too, the peak occurs at relatively low levels of management.
>
> In some circumstances, peaking out means merely that a man stays on his present job indefinitely. In others, he moves laterally from positions typically reserved for those who are still upward bound, or he is demoted or fired. But discharge at the managerial level poses such a threat to security that it is rather rare (early retirement is much more common).[10]

9 Strauss and Sayles, *Personnel*, pp. 492–93.
10 *Ibid.*, p. 503.

Nevertheless, managerial talent thresholds *can* be expanded in most cases, with sufficient ongoing administrative initiative extended toward the output segment of the correctional input/process/output system.

If it can be assumed that there are not unsurmountable barriers with regard to native intelligence, virtually any correctional manager can quickly relate to the output nature of assessing his manpower needs. Of course, it is necessary to relate such assessment to the achievement of some particular goal or objective.

The administrative trick, then, is to evolve a management system in which such goals and objectives are routinely set and updated. There are many such systems. If the functional system model discussed in early chapters is used, the correctional administrator can reinforce the output orientation of all his managers by asking that they relate manpower needs to organizational goals through *availability factoring*—a simple, arithmetic operation of immediate pragmatic value to the output-oriented manager:[11]

$$\text{Availability} = \frac{\text{Month} - (A + B + C + D)}{\text{Month}}$$

This equation is translated as follows:

1. Add together:
   a. Regular days off per man per month (averaging weekends plus holidays of staff)
   b. Vacation days per man per month, average
   c. Sick days per man per month, average
   d. Training days per man per month, average
2. Subtract this total from total days in month.
3. Divide remainder by total days in month.

The resulting factor, when multiplied by the number of staff, tells how many man-days staff are actually available.

When programs call for continuous staffing (such as in the case of institutional post-positions), the *relief factor* can be computed with equal simplicity. The availability factor is subtracted from 1.00, then the remainder is divided by the availability factor. This relief factor, when multiplied by the total number of staff, will indicate precisely how many more staff would be required to keep positions filled continuously throughout the month—a precise projection of manpower needs.

The managerial orientation flowing through such a process of concretizing what is otherwise somewhat nebulous frequently generates an instant expansion of talent thresholds.

[11] *Ibid.*, Chap. 5.

RESISTANCE TO CHANGE. Perhaps the most frustrating experience for an administrator is to discover program improvements encountering difficulty after he has carefully developed a participatory and consensually agreed-on approach. Often, but not always, the difficulty begins to occur when managers discover that the improvements require a change of habits.

This problem clearly relates to making it go—but again, in terms of managers rather than management. It is managers, not management, that cause any problems associated with resistance to change. The conspicuous paradox of this administrative frustration is, of course, that corrections as a concept *is* change, by definition. Finding that a manager whose very career is committed to programs designed to bring about this change is himself resisting change, it is not only frustrating; it is excessively expensive, and in philosophical as well as fiscal concerns.

Retaining a results orientation geared to management rather than to managers in meeting this administrative problem requires vigorous effort, but it is possible. The key is to emphasize the participatory management in the continuing process of establishing organizational goals and objectives, since the participation is for the purpose of change. A change-resistant manager in this kind of system soon finds his habits less difficult to change.

This kind of emphasis on change-oriented management, rather than managers, is well worth the effort. Even in the many other forms of resistance to change—whether they are simply a matter of habit or of more deep-seated personality variables—retention of emphasis on the management system rather than the manager in a goal-oriented change context tends to resolve that resistance. The only administrative concern with a particular manager, then, is perhaps some assessment of where the participatory process should be emphasized most.

INCENTIVE/MOTIVATION. Were it possible to administratively create challenging new positions on the basis of need, the question of incentive and motivation would not qualify as a particularly significant administrative problem. But the grim reality is that even the secondary incentives of pay and promotion cannot be easily maneuvered.

One final consideration in special problems associated with making it go is *incentive/motivation*.

One approach to this problem is through systematic variety within an organization—a kind of cross-divisional task-force approach.[12] Simply stated, the task-force approach isolates staff interests and enthusiasm and, through managerial effort, attempts to stimulate them and then to retain

---

[12] The following discussion of the task-force approach is adapted from Strauss and Sayles, *Personnel*, in which the full, comprehensive method of "reflexing synergetics" and the technology of the requisite "taxonomy of ergonesis" are covered in depth in the segments of Chapters 3, 4, 5, 6, and 7 that are related to the Task Force Development Lab.

them. In practice, this can be done creatively by making participation in all new departmental programs open to all department personnel, regardless of their particular job classifications.

This is not necessarily a major management adjustment; some staff will participate minimally, some not at all, depending on their interest. But all personnel can conceive of departmental programming as open to their personal talents or interest. Presumably, participation by highly motivated, interested personnel, even on a part-time basis, affords meaningful and productive effort.

The technology involved is more fiscal than operational, and involves such visionary concepts as these:

Institutional cooks leading a choir
Clerk-typists participating in groups
Office-building custodians co-counseling with PO's
Secretaries leading physical education
Institutional maintenance staff leading nature hikes
Receptionists leading cultural field trips
Transportation officers working with schools

As little as one hour a month is more than enough to spark both incentive and motivation, in the majority of cross-divisional cases. Therefore, for a fraction of the time spent on coffee breaks, incentive and motivation are promoted, where the managerial effort is expended to coordinate task forces.

Whereas the participation of any particular staff member on a task force is part-time and short-lived, the managerial effort is continuous. But in view of this problem's magnitude in many organizations, a TFDL (Task Force Development Lab) is definitely a cost–benefit advantage, no matter how much management time is invested.

And as this time is indeed an *investment*, thought spent on the following is appropriate:

1. The source of potential candidates for government service should be expanded by adopting flexible working schedules.

2. Incentive and job enrichment programs should be instituted to increase the motivation of public service employees for improved performance.

3. The rigidity of the governmental organization structure should be relaxed to permit managers to transfer manpower from areas of declining demand to areas of growing need.

4. Enduring productivity improvement requires internal organizational efforts to streamline and update operational systems, to institute managerial control programs, and to expand the utilization of computer applications.

5. To insure a smooth transition of leadership, manpower planning programs should be developed.

6. The increasing need for interagency communication and cooperation should be met by the establishment of a high-level coordinating function in each agency.

7. Finally, public sector management should confront the task of negotiating needed patterns of change with the two major environmental institutions which are directly concerned, namely, the civil service commission and the public service union.[13]

## CONCLUSION

The intent of this volume was to establish a criminal justice context for the correctional field, and then to distinguish clearly between the *management* of corrections and the *practice* of corrections.

In pursuit of the concept of managing corrections, great emphasis has been placed upon the three functional levels involved: administrative management, executive and middle management, and supervisory management. Against the background of these three levels of management, the operations of probation, institutions, parole, and community-based corrections were isolated within the administrative perspective.

Administrative-level management remained the perspective for examining the qualifications and training of correctional personnel. In this regard, treatment was isolated as only one administrative segment of correctional programs, with emphasis upon the complexity of integrating many other variables with program.

Assistance by volunteers was considered to be of great promise if correctional administration proves capable of resolving functional difficulties between volunteers and career personnel.

The conclusion of this volume reflects what was introduced in the first chapter in regard to the critical problems confronting criminal justice. In this final chapter, however, the focus was on special administrative problems encountered in attempting to resolve other challenges to criminal justice and to corrections.

In the context of separating those problems facing corrections in general from problems that administrators encounter in trying to resolve correctional problems, consideration was given to misaligned administrative responsibility, political control, and problems with "making it go"—that is, making administration correct correctional problems.

In the final analysis, making it go *is* correctional administration.

---

[13] Samuel J. Bernstein and Leon Reinharth, "Management, the Public Organization and Productivity: Some Factors to Consider," *Public Personnel Management*, Vol. 2, No. 4 (July–August 1973), 266.

# Index